S0-BCN-484

WELCOME TO THE JUNGLE

WELCOME
TO THE JUNGLE

A PRACTICAL GUIDE
TO TODAY'S
MUSIC BUSINESS

JOE OWENS

HarperPerennial
A Division of HarperCollinsPublishers

WELCOME TO THE JUNGLE. Copyright © 1992 by Joseph Owens. All rights reserved. Printed in the United States of America. No part of this book may be used or reproduced in any manner whatsoever without written permission except in the case of brief quotations embodied in critical articles and reviews. For information address HarperCollins Publishers, Inc., 10 East 53rd Street, New York, NY 10022.

HarperCollins books may be purchased for educational, business, or sales promotional use. For information, please write: Special Markets Department, HarperCollins Publishers, Inc., 10 East 53rd Street, New York, NY 10022.

FIRST EDITION

Designed by Jessica Shatan

Library of Congress Cataloging-in-Publication Data
Owens, Joe, 1950–
    Welcome to the jungle: a practical guide to today's music business/Joe Owens.
      p.   cm.
    Includes bibliographical references and index.
    ISBN 0-06-055332-4
    ISBN 0-06-096930-X (pbk.)
    1. Music trade—Vocational guidance. 2. Popular music—Writing and publishing—Vocational guidance. I. Title.
ML3790.095 1992
780'.23'73—dc20   92-52631

92 93 94 95 96 ❖/RRD 10 9 8 7 6 5 4 3 2 1
92 93 94 95 96 ❖/RRD 10 9 8 7 6 5 4 3 2 1 (pbk.)

This book is dedicated to Betty Owens-Coakley

—"My, how that girl can dance"—

and to

Shelly Siegel,

who started it all

CONTENTS

THREE: THE NEXT LEVEL

FOUR: LIFE AFTER DEATH

FIVE: THE TEN COMMANDMENTS

FOREWORD

If you are serious about making music your career, you've got to read this book.

Knowing how to play or write or perform just isn't enough anymore. You need to know how the business side works and this is the book that will tell you. To paraphrase a well-known TV commercial, "Joe knows music."

Whether you intend to play music, promote it, or just enjoy listening, you're sure to find something in this book to interest you.

It's a jungle out there, and *Welcome to the Jungle* is the best guide you'll find.

Jeff ("Skunk") Baxter

Guitarist, Steely Dan,
Doobie Brothers, and
Baxter, Entwistle, Thomas

ACKNOWLEDGMENTS

This book owes its existence to a long list of musicians, business associates, and friends who were too stubborn to give up and who serve as an inspiration to me and to today's generation of singers, players, and marketers.

In my twenty years in the business I've been fortunate to have been associated with people who are considered to be among the best in their field, and the knowledge and experience they willingly shared with me has allowed me to enjoy a long career in a business that I truly love.

The list is far too long for me to include everyone, but I would be remiss if I didn't include by name a few of the brilliant minds who took precious time out of their days (and often kept me up all night) to share with me their vision of the business:

Mike Levine, Gil Moore and Rik Emmett, Michael Cohl, Arthur Fogel, Norman Perry, Brad Parsons, Riley O'Connor, Blue, John Meglen, Steve Howard, John Perkins, Ronald Andrew, and all my friends at BCL/CPI. Steve Smith, Jeff Gelb, Lee Abrams, John Parikhal, Dave Charles, Don Lorusso, Gary Slaight, Vinnie Cinquemani, Allen Grubman, The Billionaire Boys Club, Jack Boyle, Brian Murphy, Barry Leff, Jules Belkin, Larry Magid, Ron Delsener, Mitch Slater, Budgie, Tom Cochrane, Francis Davies, Donald Tarlton, Sylvie and Celine Brunetta, Mark Norman, Keith Kevan, Debra Rathwell, Tom Errath, Barry Fey, Wayne Forte, Susie Rosenberg, Mary Ann Farrell, Troy Blakely, Tim Schoen, Bob Franceschelli, Joe Corcoran, Carol Kelleher, Pat Kelleher, Dan Fraser, Paul Farberman, Mike Shallett, Ann Lewis, Len Gill, Steve Pulver, Rick Krim, Tom Freston, Abbey Konowich, Paul Simon, Debbi Lockie and Susan Schultz, Hal Lazareff, Peter Lubin, Irving Azoff, Larry Solters, Richard Palmese, Glen Lajeski, Jock McLean, Bill Graham, Jim Norris, Walt Grealis, David Farrell, Tommy Nast, Fred Rosen, Jane Rose, Bo Overlock, Al Peterson and Cindy Tollin, Nancy Peske, Joseph Rascoff and Bill Zysblat, Erin Riley,

Joel Denver, Bill Hard, Fred Deane, David Knight, Jerry Sharrell, Bob Meyrowitz, Tony Smith, Jeff Shock, Linn Tanzman, Ted Utz, Bill Young, the lovely Valerie Adamson—and a very special thanks to Victorya Michaels, without whom this project might not have happened.

INTRODUCTION

You have to strive for perfection, but in rock and roll
you have to settle for excellence.

—DON HENLEY

Welcome to the Jungle. I'm glad that you've chosen me to be your guide through the jungle that is known as the music business. This is the book the music industry doesn't want you to read. Why not? Simple. After reading it, you're going to know that there is no secret formula, no voodoo, no magic connected with getting signed to a label, finding an agent, making a record, or going on tour. After reading it, you're going to know the inside deal, how it really works. You'll know who is connected to whom, how you can motivate almost everybody that you encounter, and when to push forward or pull back. Drawn from all my twenty years of experience, this book is aimed at helping you find your way around today's music business. I'll show you how to do it by showing you how others have done it successfully and by explaining where the not so successful went wrong.

The good news is that this is a good time to get signed to your first recording deal. Not too long ago the music industry was controlled by a handful of major labels, and if you couldn't make a deal with one of them, you were out of luck. Musically things were pretty dull. But the music business goes in cycles (it always has), and while the megabands were releasing records on the megalabels, new bands were beginning to experiment with new kinds of music. Hip hop, rap, house, thrash-metal and "back-to-basics" rock-and-roll sounds were attracting a new audience that had become bored with the sameness of corporate rock.

At first the major labels weren't interested in the new types of acts, unsure if they were just a fad or if these new ideas would last. Unable to get signed by the big boys, bands and entrepreneurs started independent labels, released records, and built their success from the street up, in clubs, bars, and independent record stores. One by one these new acts cracked the pop charts, and the big labels began to take notice. Throughout the eighties the face of music changed dramatically and with it, the face of the music industry. Indie labels, with two or three hit artists, were able to make deals with the major labels to distribute their records, while retaining the creative control that made them successful and unique. Soon the major labels were looking for acts like the ones they distributed for the indies. Occasionally they were successful, but mostly they failed. The reason? While the majors were signing acts "like" the indie labels, other artists were moving on to new and more daring forms of music, a step ahead of the labels. Thus the major labels were left with little choice. If they were to be able to compete in this new arena of music, they would have to capitalize on the "indie world" in earnest. Some labels hired new A&R directors from among the indie ranks to specialize in finding fresh new talent. Other companies started "boutique" labels, actually a company within a company, which allowed a small staff to operate as an indie label but with all the financial resources of a major. The 1980s was a time of change for the music industry—a change that will be even more pronounced in the coming decade.

Exactly what does all this have to do with you? Easy. More than ever, today is an excellent time to make and market your music. Artist signings at major and independent labels are on the rise. New musical forms are not only accepted, but welcomed by the music industry, the media, and the consumer. And breakthroughs in technology have made it simpler than ever to produce, distribute, and promote your own release independently. The only potential obstacle to success is you. Because you are the one who will have to put all you read in this book into practice for your own career. It takes focus and determination and a lot of hard work, probably the last two words that anyone would associate with stardom.

When most people think of a star, they think of gold records, limousines, private jets, and fabulous parties. Few would consider stardom to be hard work. But being an entertainer, particularly a recording artist, is probably one of the toughest jobs around. Hours, days, months, and sometimes even years must be spent writing songs and perfecting and rehearsing them, to make them ready to be recorded—and that's just the beginning. Only after dozens of hours in a studio are the songs on tape the way you want them. Then there are mixes, changes, more mixes, dance mixes, mastering, and finally manufacturing the product before the public has a chance to hear your songs. Once the album is finished, you have to get to work on the video and then rehearse for your tour. Weeks of practice come before your first concert appearance, which coincides with the release of a new record. And while you're rehearsing, others around you are working on bookings, costumes, lights, sound, and hundreds of other details that have to be finalized before you start your tour. Then comes months of hotels, airports, taxicabs, and, of course, concerts. Every song, every album, every show, is a new roll of the dice and the pressure is intense.

And while the musicians are undergoing their trials, business executives are fighting their own dragons. Contracts, marketing plans, accountants, budgets, and a million other details can cause a music industry executive's ulcers to get ulcers. It's a high-pressure business in which the tension can take its toll if you aren't careful.

Hard work and being careful are what this book is all about. In my years in the music business, I've learned that no amount of talent will achieve anything without the initiative to go out and market that talent. The things that I talk about in this book aren't that difficult to do. Recording a demo tape, creating an image, and negotiating a contract aren't impossible; they just take practice. What is tough is maintaining the perseverance necessary to continue, for what may seem like eternity, to perfect your act and to market, promote, and publicize it until someone notices.

If you want to be a star, this book can help. It will give you the information you need to approach the business like a professional, so you will be taken seriously by those with whom you are dealing. A lot of what you will find here are the inside tricks of the trade that the pros have been using for years to achieve and maintain success. This information, or more correctly, experience, has been gained over a considerable number of years, and I've tried to put as much of it as possible into the book to make your life a little easier.

You'll need inexhaustible energy, confidence and, of course, talent. And you'll need help. This book will give you that help and will direct you to others who can help you, each in their own area and in their own way. They'll help get you recorded, publicized, merchandised, and organized. They'll also help you out of trouble, something that's easy to get into in this business. The book discusses that trouble in some detail, not to frighten you, but to give you some graphic examples of the situations in which you may find yourself if you're not careful. If you learn how to spot trouble before it happens, you won't have to worry about getting out of it.

So let's get started. You've honed your talent, whether in making music or in marketing it, and you're ready to go. The first step on your road to success is the easiest; just turn the page.

ONE

Getting Signed Today

FINE-TUNING

We started so young that half the time was spent
growing up. We've had good times and we've seen
each other go through hell. Ten years is a long time.
Hell, people don't even stay married for ten years,
let alone six people.

—MICHAEL HUTCHENCE,
INXS

If you've gotten far enough along in your career that you've bought this book, you've probably already discovered that the life of a musician is a peculiar one.

You've no doubt had to make some decisions about things that you first thought were pretty obvious but became pretty complex when you thought about them. The decision to be a solo artist or to work within a band was probably one of the first choices that you had to make. As a solo artist, it's easier to pursue your own singular musical vision, but as a member of a band, it's easier to grow and develop musically when you're exposed to the musical ideas of other creative people.

If you chose a group, you probably had to learn early that, in a band, each individual is contributing and working to create a unique sound. If any one member decides that he or she is the star and that the rest of the band is there to back them up, then there may be trouble. You have to be a special person to become a performer, and with this desire often comes an oversized ego. Nothing has done more to destroy a lot of good bands than ego conflicts among members. So choose group or solo carefully and

7

then work to be your best whichever you choose.

Once you get the personal aspects out of the way, it's time to move on to the most important thing—the music. Too many bands skip the music part and go right on to costumes, lighting, and special effects. In fact, it seems that a lot of young bands today think they must first have an "image" or a spectacular stage show. But can they play? Image is important, but no amount of image or production is going to compensate for bad music. Remember, no one would go to see Bon Jovi, Phil Collins, or Bryan Adams if they weren't good musicians as well as showmen.

Once you've reached the point where you feel pretty good about your band, your business, and your chances of moving on to bigger and better things, you'll find that rather than getting easier, the decisions get tougher. On the surface that statement must seem like a contradiction; after all, once you've found the right people and the right chemistry, started rehearsing, decided on a name and an image, and begun to get some momentum going, you'd think that the fine-tuning part would be easy. But that's not the case, and for a pretty obvious reason if you stop to think about it. Putting the finishing touches on anything is usually the most time consuming and always the most important. When you build a house, the foundation and framing go up relatively quickly. The plumbing and electrics take a little longer. But it's the finishing touches like woodwork and trim and decorating that take the most time because they have to be right—everybody sees them, and they are what gives people their impression of the value of the house. The same goes for you and your band. When you think you've got it, that's the point where the real work begins because if you're paying enough attention to believe that you're getting somewhere, that means you're serious and, if so, you'll have to start making serious decisions.

The first hurdle to get over is the toughest one: choosing the band members themselves. To make it, really make it, you have to be as good as you can possibly be. To be that good, you need to understand that if anything in your band can hold you back, you'll have to make some hard choices. The toughest part about analyzing your band members and their contribution is that it isn't just hard business. Chances are that after all you've been through, the people in your band are probably your best friends, but if one of them isn't up to the rest of the group, you may have to decide to replace him or her. It's at that point that your commitment to the music will face its acid test because you may have to choose between friendship and success—a difficult but critical choice.

What fine-tuning really comes down to is this: You and your band members have to decide if you're ready to do what it's going to take to get to the next phase of your career, on your way to the top. You'll need to be ready for just about anything, especially emotional roller-coaster ride that will take you from the highest high to the lowest low, all in the space of a couple of phone calls. It takes mental toughness, patience, and professionalism to handle it, and a commitment to the music and to yourself as well.

I hope I haven't put you out on the ledge of your apartment building with my little speech, but business, any business, is tough. The exciting part is that if you have a plan that you work to, you'll constantly make gains, and from those gains will come the encouragement that will keep you going. The most important thing is to maintain your focus. If you think of your music career as a mountain-climbing expedition, you'll get my idea. No mountain climber stops to applaud himself while he is climbing the face of a mountain because that would require letting go, with both hands, not a good plan when climbing a mountain.

The hard choices that I mentioned are all designed to refine and polish the diamond that you call your act. To make the next step, you'll have to lose some of the rough edges. It's like ball playing. When ball players go from the minor leagues to the majors, they suddenly have hit the big time, and the big time has rules that are different from the rules of the minors. The big leagues are classy and are much in the public eye, as are big-league ball players, so they have to adjust if they're going to remain in the big leagues and to prosper from being there. Make your act as good as it can be and then keep refining it. You'll never know when or how your break will come, but you have to be ready. It's an old cliché, but opportunity does knock only once, and you don't want to be in the shower when it does.

The other element of your career that will pay off as long as you are in the business is your attitude. If you are positive, people around you will be positive; if you aren't, they won't be either. Now I'm not suggesting that you become a blissed-out Hare Krishna. Things will happen that will make you mad or sad or annoyed; that's only natural. And your response should be natural, too, but keep a few things in mind: First, it's business; don't take it personally and don't personally attack anybody with whom you are doing business. Tend to your own business and keep cool.

Second, let it go. Once you've dealt with the problem, it's over. Don't carry it around with you, sharing your misfortune with anyone who will listen. And no matter what, don't talk about your problems to the press. Nothing is dumber than telling an interviewer how terrible things are going after you've just gotten a disturbing call or had a fight with your label, bass player, or manager. Be a pro; keep a good thought and keep moving forward. A friend of mine calls it "pushing the peanut." He says that he once saw a circus act in which a huge elephant pushed a tiny little peanut around the circus ring. He was amazed that this enormously powerful wild animal could keep focused enough to push this little peanut around the ring. Then he found out why. At the end of the act, the elephant got to eat the peanut. So keep at it, and maybe you'll get to eat the peanut, too.

But enough pep talk. This book is not about philosophy; it's about practicality, the steps that you have to take to get from where you are now to where you want to be. I've arranged the book in the order in which things will happen to you or that you will make them happen. Now that you're finished fine-tuning, let's start the show.

BUILDING A TEAM

*We were once asked if we wanted to put Dire Straits
on the stock exchange. I said, "Why would I want to
do that?" They said, "It could make you even richer
than you already are." I said, "But I'd have to write
songs on time." They said, "Yup, the shareholders
would want to know why you don't have a record
out." I said, "I couldn't do that."*

—**MARK KNOPFLER,
DIRE STRAITS**

Racing-car drivers call them pit crews, boxers call them corner
men. Whatever you call them, you will need your own team to support you in the music business. The dictionary calls a team "a
group of individuals working together toward a common goal." For
your purposes that's a pretty good definition. Like a sports team,
your team should be made up of specialists. A baseball team with
nothing but second basemen wouldn't be much of a team; you need
every position to make it work. The same goes for your team: You
need specialists to look after each aspect of your career. But don't
restrict your idea of a "team" only to those who are directly connected with you. You will have to get others on your team as well,
strangers who work for radio stations and record companies, concert promoters, and more. All these people have to be part of your
team—the team that's going to take you to the Super Bowl of rock
and roll.

You don't need all the players right away. In fact, you don't really want all of them right away. First, you want to design your plan

and then fit your players into that plan. Your business plan, will include what you want to accomplish and by what date. Most bands have this kind of plan, sort of, but they never bother to write it down, and that's too bad. Having a plan in writing, with goals, dates, and other plans and objectives is an easy way to maintain your focus and momentum on a continuous basis, even when things get scattered. When you design your plan, you'll want to keep a few things in mind:

1. Your plan should be divided into two categories: time and objectives. For example, if you want to find a booking agent, that's the objective; finding him by December is the time. Generally, it doesn't do a lot of good to have an objective if you don't have some kind of time line attached to it. If you are anything like me, you'll keep putting it off in favor of other things that appear to be more important. At the time the other things may be important, but if you have a long-term objective, it means that you've identified something that you need for the big plan, and you'll be well advised to put aside some of the small stuff in favor of the big plan. Remember David Lee Roth's two rules of life: "Don't sweat the small stuff" and "It's all small stuff."

2. Make your plan realistic. For example, "Headline Shea Stadium in six months" is a bit ambitious, unless you know something the rest of us don't. That's an extreme example, but by way of illustration it makes the point that you should be realistic in setting your goals. "Find an agent in three months and sign with a manager before the end of the year" is a realistic plan because it gives you both realistic goals that you are clearly capable of achieving and a reasonable time frame in which to achieve them. If you're not realistic, you'll end up trying to achieve a long list of things that no one could achieve and, instead of being encouraged and motivated by your small victories, you'll constantly be depressed because you can't seem to finish everything on your list. The point of the plan is to move you ahead, not set you back, so be sure that you design your plan for that purpose.

3. Go over your plan with your mentor. You say you don't have a mentor? Well, then, that should be the first thing in your plan. A

mentor is somebody who has been around for a while in your business, or in any business, who has achieved some level of success,
who you respect, and who is willing to help you along. Generally a
mentor is older than you and has that elusive quality we call wisdom. Your mentor doesn't necessarily have to be in or have been in
the music business. If she was a salesman, executive, lawyer, or
whatever, she has obviously been in situations where she has needed to focus her energies on getting results. That's exactly what
you're trying to do, and your mentor should be able to help you
refine your plan. If she is objective, she will tell you right away
where she thinks you are going wrong, being unrealistic, or wasting
time. You may have to explain certain things to her to put your
plan in context, but once you do, she should be able to fine-tune
your plan so you can make it workable. Find yourself someone you
can talk to; if you don't, you may end up talking to yourself.

4. Learn all you can about the local music scene to help you
with your short-term planning and learn the national scene for your
long-term goals. But don't confuse the two, that is, don't get things
out of sequence. There's no point putting a lot of energy into getting record companies to see you if you don't have a demo tape or
you aren't yet playing your own material. Your short-term plan will
prepare you for the bigger picture, and the work that you get in
clubs and the like will finance your long-term plan. The key is to
be both specific and realistic in what you set out to accomplish.

Making Business Contacts

Protect your ass at all times.

—*Dick Clark*

I'll assume that your plan includes finding the support team we just talked about. Eventually, you'll need a manager, an agent, an accountant, and a road manager. As you find each one, it will become easier to find the others because one will know or recommend the other, and so on. Meanwhile you have to get started making those business contacts. That's where your plan comes in. If you've done it right, you've listed not only who you have to find, but how you're going to find them and where and when. There are a lot of different approaches to making business contacts.

These days, most people will tell you to *network*, but I'm not sure that networking is the best solution. The problem with networking is that you usually do it in clubs or at parties or barbecues, locations that are not exactly renowned for their reputation as business centers. Sure you can do a lot of business at social functions, but *after* you've made the contacts. Now don't get me wrong, I'm not saying that you shouldn't work the party circuit, especially if you're in New York or Los Angeles or if you can hook into parties that include radio and record types in your home town. I'm just saying that it isn't the *only* way.

One-on-one contacts with people who are doing something relevant to your career are the best way to get started. A local booking agency, a local radio station that you believe would play your records, and promotion reps at the local record company are a good place to start. Call them up or write them a letter asking if they would have some time (about an hour or less) to meet with you to discuss the business. Tell them that you aren't selling, but that you're looking for some suggestions. Appeal to their egos; tell them you've heard that they are among the best in the business and that they are willing to help new talent. When you get to the meeting, remember the golden rule, "Keep your eyes and ears open and your mouth shut." Let them do the talking. Choose your comments carefully and keep them brief. At the end of the meeting, ask them if they would recommend anyone you could talk to, specifically those team members whom you are looking for. With a recommendation, it's going to be a lot easier to get the next meeting.

Back to the party circuit for a minute. If you do meet an important contact a party, here's how to handle it. First, don't try to do your business right there. You may be working, but chances are they are not. Nothing is more annoying than having someone tell you the story of his or her professional life or try to sell you something when you're at a party, trying to relax. Tell them you're trying to build your team to get things going and ask if they would be willing to meet with you at another time to talk. Offer to buy them lunch if you can afford it or at least a coffee or a beer. Don't try to get too much done because however nice they seem to be, they just aren't paying attention. And, of course, getting drunk and hitting on their mate or throwing up on their shoes isn't the way to impress anybody. If you are there to party, then party, but if you are there to work, then work. Remember, word travels fast, and if you get loaded and make a fool of yourself, you won't have meetings with anybody.

If you live in New York or Los Angeles or have occasion to go there on a regular basis, you'll need a somewhat different approach. Although both cities are music capitals, the people who work there are *pretty high up the ladder* and *pretty busy.*

Unless you're dealing with an A & R person your chances of sitting down for a chat with the vice president of promotion or the program director of the local station are slim. This is where the social scene comes into play in a big way. Although the music business looks big, it really isn't. Allen Grubman, the megadeal-making attorney in New York, once told me that "there are fourteen people who run the music business, me and thirteen others." The scary thing is that it is true.

For your purposes there are more than fourteen people, but it is still a pretty small club. In New York or Los Angeles it's relatively easy to find people who know someone who works for a label, a radio station, or an agency. The key is not in finding them, or even in getting the meeting, but in knowing what to do once you get the meeting. Again, remember that these people are being sold all the time, and if you walk in wanting something from them, you're going to have to break down a lot of walls to get it. If you try a softer approach, you may do better. Let's take an example of a record company product manager. Until you get signed to the label, there is little a product manager can do for you. (Another point: Be sure you understand the job of the person who you are going to see. Not everybody at a record label can sign you.)

So you meet them at a party and ask if they would meet with you later. They agree, and you finally get them out after work one day for a beer. Here's what to do. First, be friendly. Thank them for meeting with you. Tell them you know they are busy. Show them some respect. Second, tell them why you wanted to see them. Tell them that you are beginning to build your team toward getting a record deal and you'd like some recommendations about how to get started. Third, have a brief synopsis of your career handy. In Hollywood they say that if you can't tell the plot of a movie in one sentence, it's too complicated. The same thing for your career. Don't sit for an hour outlining your entire history, just sketch who you are and where you are now. And fourth, tell them exactly what you want from them. In this case, since a product manager has a lot of contact with artist managers, you may ask for some recommendations on good managers and perhaps even some help in getting a meeting with a few of them. And, of course, give them a copy of your demo, ask them to listen to it, and, if they like it, to consider passing it along to their A & R department.

Be specific. If you meet with a radio guy, ask for help with the A & R people they talk to regularly. If you hook up with an artist relations person, ask for help in finding an agent. If you meet an agent you think you can work with and you make a deal to be represented, ask the agent about managers and so forth. That's how to make the contact meetings work for you.

Attend seminars and clinics. In most cities there are music publications or music stores that, on occasion, host seminars that feature guest speakers from a variety of areas in the music industry. A & R people, managers, agents, publishers, and others regularly participate in these events, which are targeted at the novice musician who is trying to make the next step. I have participated in a lot of these seminars as both a panelist and a moderator. In general, these seminars are pretty good. Sometimes they tend to be a little over the head of some of the people who attend, but, in general, they are good places to pick up a few pointers.

On the other hand, if the panelists are of the type that I just mentioned, it is an excellent chance to make new contacts. Generally, after the panel is over, the panelists are swarmed by people from the audience who want to talk, give them tapes, or otherwise make a connection. Some will ask for business cards so they can call you later. As friendly as the panelists may be, they are in a business and they are busy, so you have to be specific if you are going to be successful in making contact with them.

First, don't try to engage the panelists in conversation after the panel, since they will surely be talking to a group of people and you'll have a tough time standing out; just ask them if you can have one of their business cards. Second, don't give them a tape; since it probably won't even get out of the room with them. Third, don't try to whisk them off for a private chat unless you've set it up in advance, and that's the trick. Get the brochure for the event beforehand and choose the people with whom you would like to meet. Then do three things: First send them letters and tell them that you would like to have thirty minutes with them before or after their presentation to discuss your business plan. Second, contact the organizers of the seminar, meet with them if possible, and explain to them that you would like them to help you set up such a meeting. Third, follow up your letters with phone calls to the potential contacts to try to confirm the meeting. In this way you can attend the event knowing that you have made at least one solid contact.

Remember, you are making these contacts to spread them into

more contacts. So ensure that everyone whom you meet opens a door for you to at least one other person, and in no time you will have established your own network.

CHOOSING THE PLAYERS

Once you've made your contacts, you'll have to move to the next phase: choosing from among these contacts to begin building your team. On the surface this probably seems pretty easy, and in fact it is, as long as you keep a few things in mind.

First, remember to check out each of the people with whom you intend to do business. You can do so in a number of ways. The easiest is to try to find people who have done business with them in the past and ask them. If they are agents or other musicians, try the musician's union. Ask around at some of the local clubs; talk to other musicians and maybe other agents or managers. If you do so, two things will happen: First, you'll probably get a bit more information on which to base your decision and second, these people will definitely hear that you are asking about them and their reactions will speak volumes about them. Don't hurry; take all the time you need to make sure that those with whom you may become involved are the right ones for you.

Second, watch out for long-term agreements. They can be very dangerous at an early stage of your career. Here's how:

Let's say that you find yourself an agent or a manager and you decide that they could do your career some good. You reach an agreement on all the points of your deal and are presented with a contract. If the contract has a long initial term and a lot of renewal options, it could spell trouble. Certain unscrupulous individuals look for new talent, sign up as many rights as they can for as long as they can, and then wait for something to happen. They usually do so with many artists, assuming that the law of averages will increase their chance of finding a winner. They will do little or nothing for your career, and often you'll part company unpleasantly. In general, they will sign you up and then leave you alone until you sign a lucrative deal or have a hit. Then, they will come out of the woodwork, waving their old contracts and claiming that they own the rights that you just sold. As slimy as this practice sounds, the bad guys usually win, unless you and your new label or manager have enough money to fight them off. Therefore, the best course of action is to ensure that, early in your career, you sign contracts that have *definite* terms, preferably one or two years at the most. In this way you are only hooked up to somebody for a short time, and if the deal doesn't work out, you'll be free to move on.

In addition, pay close attention to rights that you assign to anyone, anytime. For example, there is no reason for your agent to have any percentage of your publishing; only a manager, record label, or another publisher should get it. Be sure that you understand all the options and other things in the deal that can extend the contract beyond its original term. And never sign anything without going over it with an attorney. Choose your team members and sign your deals carefully bceause both will have a great impact on your music and your future.

MANAGERS AND MANAGEMENT

A good manager is arguably the most important member of an artist's team. He or she must understand the record business—sales and promotion, contracts, booking, the logistics of touring, lights, sound, press and publicity, banking, bookkeeping, and psychology.

It's easy to become a manager. You just find yourself artists or groups, tell them that you want to manage them, and if they agree, then voilà! you're a manager! But to become a good manager is very hard. You can't go to school for it, and the only real teacher is experience. And just as in any other business, getting the opportunity to acquire experience is tough. Just as a musician has to start somewhere, usually at the bottom, so does a manager, and often that somewhere is as an agent, record rep, or even in an entry-level job like an intern or assistant at a label or agency.

One of your first concerns will be where to find your manager. For most people, finding a good manager is difficult, especially if you are a new act and cannot yet attract the attention of the big guys. And if you live outside New York, Los Angeles, Nashville, or London, where do you look? Among people in the music business, of course. Booking agents, record-company people, and radio-station employees are good people to start with. These folks are in touch with most of the managers in an area because of their day-to-day business activities. Your job is to get the word out about who you are and what you do and that you are looking for a manager. Just like all your other activities, this attack has to be a planned. Each time you play a date, do a promotion for your band, or talk to someone, you have to remember to include your search for a manager in the conversation. And if you get a recommendation from someone, *follow it up!* You do so for two important reasons: First, this person may be the manager you are looking for and second, if the person who made the recommendation finds out that you didn't even bother to make a phone call, you can bet he or she will not be helpful to you in the future. If you make your search public and follow up on any leads, the chances are good that you will be able to find the right manager for you.

If artists were to conduct all their business affairs personally for their entire careers, they would have little time left for creativity, and their ability to achieve and maintain their success would suffer severely. Musicians should most certainly be aware of their business, but at a certain point in their careers they must turn the day-to-day aspects over to others. As soon as most musicians decide to turn professional, however, they think they need a manager right away. In too many cases, managers, at this early stage of their careers, do nothing but boost their egos and perform no real function. It's better to get your career started yourself and then bring in a manager when you have something to manage.

Once you've achieved a certain level of success, a manager acts as a buffer between you and the record company, concert promoters, agents, the media, and the fans. In the case of a young, developing act that is still playing the bar circuit, a manager's role is quite different. He may be the sound man, light man, booking agent, roadie, accountant, and chauffeur—all for a percentage of what, at that stage, can be little pay. As the group develops, becomes more popular, and begins to earn more money, the manager may begin to relinquish some of his functions to professionals in the various fields. A sound man may be hired, and a few roadies, the team growing as the band grows until the manager's function becomes more one of coordination, ensuring that everyone, from the record company, to the publicist, to the road crew, to the concert promoter, is all working toward the same end.

Later in the artist's career, the artist and manager may decide to take more direct control of concert bookings, syndicated radio broadcasts, video production, merchandise and licensing, and the like, rather than relying on the decisions of the record company or agent as they may have done before. This expanded role is usually based on the artist's and manager's belief that they can better manage and, therefore, profit from these areas. As you can see, management is a many-leveled thing. Its most important aspect is to make the right choices at the right times for the artist, which will ultimately result in a long-term, successful career.

Many groups believe that they cannot make it without a manager, but you have to keep in mind that a manager is a financial responsibility and even though she represents the band, she is not a band member and, in fact, is not tied to you for better or for worse. In fact, a lot of potential pitfalls are associated with getting involved with a manager too early in your career. For example, let's say that a few friends get together, form a band, and start performing, first at high school dances and then at local clubs. They are seen by a local businessman who owns a hardware store but who has always had an interest in the entertainment business. He decides that he has discovered the next Rolling Stones, meets with the group, and tells them that he is willing to put up the money for them to do a demo tape at a local studio. The band members think that since he is willing to put up money, his interest must be genuine, and they decide to make a deal with him.

Before investing the money, however, the businessman presents them with a contract that outlines, among other things, their indebtedness to him for the money that he is investing and a management agreement for a term of four or five years. The group signs, thinking they have nothing to lose at this point.

The band goes on to become successful and well known locally. Their manager, however, is preoccupied with his hardware business and treats them only as a hobby. Meanwhile, the band discovers that their manager's show-business contacts don't extend beyond the local bar and grill. The band sends a few demo tapes to record companies and receives favorable replies. Suddenly the prospect of real artistic and financial success enters the picture, and so does Mr. Hardware, who is, once again, very interested in the group. Although the band no longer wishes to be associated with him, he holds a valid contract with them for five years! Since the contract is a legal document, the band is forced to take the manager to court to try to get rid of him. In a case like this, the band is generally forced to continue paying the manager some percentage of its earnings for the duration of the contract, which, if you become successful, can be a great deal of money. All in exchange for a few hundred bucks for a demo tape.

Before deciding on a manager, think hard about how necessary that person is to your career right now and how much he or she can add to your business. To retain someone so you don't have to be bothered with business is just laziness, and by removing yourself from negotiations with club owners, promoters, and booking agents early in your career, you are giving up valuable experience that will be vital to you in the coming years. When you can no longer pay attention to business details and make good music, then it's time to get a manager.

If you are approached by anyone for a management deal, check the person out, and if he has no experience in the music business, forget him. When it comes time to find a manager, talk to other groups and, if they are satisfied with their managers, meet with these people and discuss a possible representation agreement. If you have a booking agent, talk to him. He is constantly in touch with many artist managers and will know the ones who will best suit your needs.

One question I am often asked is, "How much should I pay a manager?" The answer is: Whatever is fair. Managers become part of your team to make you money, not to cost you money. Therefore, if a manager becomes a financial burden, something is wrong.

In the early stages of your career, you'll want to make some careful decisions about management based on your needs and ability to pay. There are essentially two ways to be managed. The first is the one with which most of us is familiar: Someone represents your interests for a percentage of your income. The second is a somewhat new phenomenon: the consultant manager.

The traditional deal that a manager receives is a percentage of the artist's income. In other parts of this section, I've talked about having to make a decision about when, how, and by whom to be managed. I'll assume that you have made those decisions and that now it's time to get down to making the deal. Here are a few things to keep in mind:

How High Should the Percentage Be?

> *Too many guys go into the business and the only cash they make is from managing the group. This leaves the group at a terrible disadvantage. There are so many young managers charging established manager rates and I find that really offensive. When I started out with BTO [Bachman Turner Overdrive] I was making seven and a half percent and gradually it worked its way up to a reasonable percentage.*
>
> —*BRUCE ALLEN,*
> *MANAGER OF BRYAN ADAMS*

If the manager is making more money than the band, it's a hint that the percentage is too high. Most management deals call for a percentage of 10 to 25 percent of the artist's income. Anything higher is extreme. Early in your career your manager may want to take 25 percent because the overall revenues will be lower. But one-quarter of your income is a lot of money. Offer the manager a smaller percentage. The manager should have another source of income anyway, and you should not be responsible for 100 percent of his expenses as well as your own.

As you become more popular and your income increases, your manager can then take a slightly higher percentage, but the percentage does not have to be very high, for if you are doing well, she will make a lot of money.

Get some information from other musicians, the union, lawyers, and anyone else you can about management percentages and compare it to your deal. In the end you will have to come up with what you both agree is fair; otherwise there won't be any deal.

WHAT SHOULD THE PERCENTAGE BE BASED ON?

In your first conversation with the manager, you must define what he or she will be taking a percentage of: Will it be gross revenues, net income, publishing, performance money, record advances, or your paper route or pizza-delivery job? I have seen some deals in which the band had to get regular jobs between gigs and some idiot manager tried to take a percentage of their salary. Be specific! Remember, if the manager gets a percentage of your gross income, you are paying him a commission on the expenses that you have to pay. Don't sign a contract with a manager figuring that you're not making that much anyway and therefore have little to lose. Contracts have a way of hanging around and then turning up at the most inconvenient times. Figure out what the manager will be doing for you and then work out what is fair compensation. Sometimes, if the manager is well financed, she may take no actual cash and may even put the band on a salary until it gets into an earning position. This arrangement sounds great, but be sure that you know what the terms are. Is what the manager is paying you accruing interest? How does it get paid back? From royalties or fees for live performances? And what if you don't earn it back through business, are you on the hook for the debt personally? Find out before you sign anything. It's good for you and for the manager if both of you know exactly where you stand.

Post-termination compensation (PTC) allows a manager to collect for certain deals made for the artist even after his contract with the artist is up. It applies particularly to publishing, and some artists see it as unfair. Prince sued his former managers to overturn the PTC clause on royalties from publishing his songs. "To an artist," Prince said, "songs are like children, they're our creation." The idea of PTC is to allow a manager to profit from deals made for an act after she has gone to another manager. Some managers think they have no protection against an artist who will use them and then move on to a new manager. The PTC clause, they believe, gives them some insurance against this situation. Since the post-termination clause has not yet been definitively ruled on by the courts, it is something you should be on the alert for in any contract you may be asked to sign with management.

WHAT IS A FAIR DEAL?

Sign a short-term agreement with options to renew. If somebody wants to tie you up for a long time early in your career, forget it. Work together for a year and, if you are satisfied, renew the option for another year or two. This way, you won't be stuck if your manager turns out to be a lemon. Keep in mind that if the manager invests any money in this first year and you don't renew, he is sure to want to be paid back. Be sure to work out how that payback takes place before you sign the agreement. If you don't the consequences could be messy.

THE CONSULTANT MANAGER

In recent years a new phenomenon has emerged in the management business, the *consultant manager*. As artists become more sophisticated and aware of their business, the management of their careers becomes more of a partnership, with decisions made jointly by them and their managers.

Some artists have opted for an arrangement whereby they hire professionals from among the ranks of booking agents, record executives, publicists, or promoters and pay them a consulting fee to handle their business. The artists retain final approval over all deals, contracts, and the like, but don't have to do all the work themselves. This arrangement has a lot of benefits and only a few drawbacks.

On the positive side:
1. You know exactly how much you are paying each year to be managed.
2. You have someone acting as your representative, rather than having to do your own business.
3. You have someone to take away all the day-to-day details that can drive you crazy.
4. You maintain total control of your career and artistic direction.
5. You have someone to blame if things go wrong (just kidding).

On the negative side:
1. A salary-only deal may take away some motivation, so you should build some bonuses or incentives into the compensation package.
2. You become an employer, which brings with it certain obligations, like making sure you always have enough money in the bank to pay your manager.
3. You do have to trust the decisions that this person makes.
4. It takes time to find the right kind of person for the job.

In addition, this is a good way to find someone in whom you feel you could place sufficient trust ultimately to become your manager, for a percentage of your income. After all, if the consultant does do your business for several years and everything works out and your career prospers, there's no reason not to continue with the person who is, in large part, responsible for your success. I still maintain that early in your career you should do as much of the management work yourself as possible. Once the work becomes too much, then you can take the next step and get involved with a manager.

WHAT A MANAGER DOES

> *We had reached a brick wall in 1983 ... and our*
> *record company and management weren't thinking*
> *big enough. The first step was to find new,*
> *powerful management.*

> —*ANN WILSON,*
> *HEART*

A manager's job is to coordinate the business aspects of an artist's career. The manager is responsible to his or her client in these areas, and this responsibility motivates a good manager to make what he or she believes are good and profitable decisions.

After signing an agreement with the artist, the manager begins to guarantee that all the forces that act on an artist do so with a profitable outcome. It is the manager's job to make sure that the recording company to which the act is signed properly markets the records at the radio, video, and retail levels and that sufficient quantities of records are available in the stores. With the aid of an attorney, she ensures that the record company lives up to the contract. In a dispute between the artist and the record company, the manager smoothes things out or negotiates a release from the deal. In financial matters, the manager operates the artist's bank accounts and handles tax returns, audits, and other related matters. He keeps an eye on the royalty statements from the record company and publisher to make certain that the artist is receiving all the money that is due and that nothing is being improperly withheld. This work with the record company is probably the most important aspect of the manager's services. Regardless of anything else an artist may be able to do, it all starts with a successful record. Whether the artist is a hit on contemporary hit radio (CHR) radio with top-selling singles, on album-oriented rock (AOR) with hot album tracks, or in the clubs with the next new dance sensation, it is the manager's task to ensure that the record label maximizes not only the sales that result from the airplay or club play, but the publicity that it can generate. Radio play creates a demand for the group to play live in the market. A live date boosts merchandise sales. A live tour may also attract money from corporate sponsors, and so on. It's all connected, but it all starts with a hit record.

Therefore, it is up to the manager to establish relationships with the label's head office and field staff that allow him to work hand in hand with them to get and keep the act's product on the air and on the store shelves.

A manager needs to know how radio works, who the key programmers and consultants are, how the trade magazines create their charts, and the activities of the label in relation to all these areas. When a new act is signed to a label, one of the first meetings that takes place is between the manager and the promotion and sales staff. If, in that meeting, the manager demonstrates knowledge of how the radio and retail business works or if a manager already has a reputation for success in those areas with another act, the label's staff will react differently to the new signing, and the band's chances of getting a good shot from the label, and thus their chances for success, improve dramatically.

A manager's relationship with the label is a crucial element of success for any artist. Each manager has his or her own style. Some are brash and argumentative, others are manipulative, and still others are just straight-ahead good business people. Whatever the case, it is the managers who must keep the label staffs motivated and involved in the artists' recordings for the benefit of their entire career.

THE MANAGER AND THE BOOKING AGENT

Your booking agent must be constantly debriefed, providing you and your manager with information about who has been contacted on your behalf, upcoming engagements, and the like.

A good manager will motivate the agent while maintaining control over the quantity and quality of shows booked for the artist. As the group or the artist grows in stature and popularity, the manager may take a much stronger hand in directing the agent and actually control the booking of engagements, retaining the agent only to produce contracts and to confirm concert details with the concert promoters. For example, for acts that have multi-platinum-album sales like the Rolling Stones or Van Halen, the managers are instrumental in all aspects of their booking, fees, routing, and security for tours. Your booking agent's responsibility to the manager is the same as it is to the group, and the manager's job is to make sure that the agent continues to operate in your best interests.

MANAGERS AND RECORD COMPANIES

As I said before, the manager's work with the record company is among the most important functions that he or she performs for the act. Here the manager performs much in the same role as he does with the booking agent, but in an expanded sense. The manager will deal with the promotion department to ensure exposure of the act on radio and will work with the marketing department to coordinate radio, television, and print advertising, as well as the design and production of posters, radio and television spots, and other promotional materials.

The manager will also work with the artist-relations department to cover tours and live appearances and with the publicity department to ensure adequate press coverage. She will deal with the accounting, royalty, and business-affairs departments in matters that involve the contract or financial arrangements with the company. The manager also performs a public relations function between the act and the record company by getting to know the executives in each department so the relationship runs smoothly. He works with the artist and repertoire (A & R) department in choosing producers, studios, budgets, and other areas of recording and with the graphics department on designing and producing artwork for the album. Finally, the manager attempts to get to know the president of the label either directly or through the artist's attorney, a valuable relationship when things are not going well or it is time to renegotiate the contract.

MANAGERS AND THE MEDIA

In most situations, other than interviews, the manager is the spokesperson for the artist and, in the case of superstars, is quoted by the press as the "spokesperson for ..." A manager's role with the media is to be sure that the artist's image remains consistent and that whatever appears in print or on the electronic media is true, or at least based on fact.

Occasionally managers and the media will clash. Often these clashes get pretty violent, not in the sense of actual physical confrontation (although it has happened), but in threats of lawsuits, countersuits, and other legal actions. In the past ten years, journalistic sensationalism has reached an all-time high, and managers wage a constant war to ensure that their artists are accurately portrayed to the public. To deal better with the media, managers usually arrange for recording companies to retain independent publicity firms to handle the press on the artists' behalf or will hire the firms themselves. Interviews, feature stories, and the like are handled by these firms, which, like booking agents, also have rosters of artists whom they represent. The manager's role in this case is to coordinate the activities of the publicist with tour dates, radio airplay, and other such press-worthy events.

OTHER AREAS OF MANAGEMENT

A manager also oversees the artist's merchandising and licensing. Merchandising is the sale of T-shirts, buttons, posters, jackets, programs, and other such items at concerts and other personal appearances and in retail stores. Merchandising has become a multimillion-dollar industry in the past few years, and it now rivals even the sale of records or concert tickets as a source of potential revenue for an artist. The manager negotiates a contract with an merchandising firm that gives the merchandising company the rights to use the artist's photograph or logo on merchandise in return for a fee or a percentage of the proceeds from the sale of these items.

Through the merchandising company, the manager also polices the illicit sale of counterfeit merchandise, which is called *bootlegging* (after the old term used for the illegal making of whiskey during Prohibition). As with counterfeit or bootleg tapes, the artist receives no royalties from illicit merchandise that, in the case of a major act, may amount to millions of dollars. If a manager uncovers a bootlegging operation, he will pursue it, with the merchandiser, through local law enforcement officials or the courts to try to recover the money due the artist and to insist that the offenders are punished.

Managers also negotiate syndicated radio, cable and pay-TV broadcasts, and home-video deals, all relatively new fields of musical reproduction and promotion. As well, they may be active in their artists' music publishing businesses. Publishing may be an extremely lucrative aspect of an artist's career that can earn money for the artist far beyond his or her years as a performer. In all areas the manager acts to protect his or her client and helps maximize financial situations while simultaneously developing their career and talent.

How to Be Managed

I always say, "I can only work with what you give
me." You might be the greatest act in the world,
but if you only sit in your garret making tapes
and cutting your ear off,
what am I going to do with it?

—*ED BICKNELL,*
MANAGER OF DIRE STRAITS

This statement is not as silly as it sounds. Everything that we do that is new to us has its pros and cons, and we regulate our behavior in each situation by what we have learned about it. Now that you know some of the things that a manager does, you can consider how much control you want your manager to have over your career.

In the initial stages of your involvement with a new manager, you may want to sit in with the manager in meetings. This is not to say that you have to watch your manager's every move, only that if you and the manager are new to one another, the manager may not know everything about the act or may not be aware of some past situations, both of which could put him at a disadvantage in a meeting or negotiation.

These choices are up to you, but understand that in making a management deal with an individual or company, you are not required to hand over your entire life and career. If a manager requires this kind of control as part of the agreement with you, you have to make a decision. The best advice I can give you is that if a manager respects you as a person as well as an artist, then she will treat you with understanding and will honor your requests to be involved and informed. If you aren't treated this way in your initial meetings with the manager, steer clear. Remember you are the bottom line. Without you, a manager has nothing to manage.

By the time you've signed the management agreement and are beginning to work together, you've probably laid down the ground rules, you and your manager understand the relationship, and you have confidence in his or her ability to represent you. *Listen to your manager!* Occasionally you will disagree; that is to be expected, but if you continually second-guess your manager or contradict his or her suggestions, then something is wrong, and one of you did not understand the original deal. This is something that you had better straighten out—and fast!

If you trusted your manager enough to sign the contract, then trust him to do your business. As I've said before, there's nothing wrong with sitting in on business meetings with your manager and, in fact, it's probably a good idea because it will give you the confidence in him that you will need to have peace of mind later, when you are on the road or in the studio and he is handling all your business. But once you've made the commitment to him and the deal between you is done both, on a business and a philosophical level, don't struggle. Let your manager do the business in the best way he or she knows how. If the arrrangement works, continue and if not, you can move on.

WHEN TO CONSIDER A NEW MANAGER

There are basically two situations in which you should consider a new manager. The first is a disagreement about the direction of your project. If, for example, your manager wants you to add a female singer to your group and start playing lounges, but you want to stop playing bars altogether and do only concerts, then you have some talking to do. If you can't resolve the differences, you should split up. The tension in a situation like this will increase and will get in the way not only of your business but of your music.

The second situation is when you find that you are outgrowing your manager. That is, when your reputation grows quickly because of your talent and you are teetering on the brink of stardom and have to start dealing in the big leagues, you may find that your fledgling manager just isn't equipped; then you may want to say good-bye. This may sound unfair, and you may want to consider some kind of arrangement to compensate the manager, perhaps with an ongoing percentage for a time. But remember, you get only one chance, and it has to be your best, so consider your management moves carefully.

For the third situation, you will probably need no advice about what to do, but here it is anyway: If you find that your manager is stealing from you and you have proof, then fire him—immediately! If you can afford it, sue him, not only to recover the stolen money, but for damages as well. Also check with your lawyer and see if you can file criminal charges, and if you can, do so. Theft from an artist by a manager is the lowest blow, and too often a petty theft by some mindless, small-time hustler can ruin an artist's career. Show no mercy if you catch him.

MANAGING THE SUPERSTARS

One of the biggest responsibilities that any human being can assume is the management of a superstar act. As soon as your act becomes of megastatus, a lot of the rules change, not the least of which is "how much are you worth to do X." It's a difficult position to be put in, and yet many of the most unflappable managers are the ones who manage the biggest talents. One of the most colorful characters in the management business is Prince Rupert Loewenstein, the manager of the Rolling Stones, and he is a real prince. Even though the Stones are surrounded by a battery of business managers, accountants, advisers, and attorneys, it is Prince Rupert who helps the band make all their most important decisions and negotiates all their most important deals. Prince Rupert is exactly the way you would picture him: a round, gray-haired, charming and delightful gentleman whose personality is so disarming that you could initially overlook that he is a shrewd and hard-nosed businessman. He has been with the band for many years and has guided them through their most important dealings, including their gargantuan 1989 and 1990 world tours, which grossed over $250 million for the group. Like any good manager, Prince Rupert negotiated the group's record deals and acts as a buffer between them and rest of the industry.

Another superstar manager is the irrepressible Doc McGhee. Doc has what is often referred to as a "checkered" past. He has run afoul of the law on a few occasions and got into the business by offering agents and record and radio people trips to his home in the Cayman Islands and other perks. Flamboyant style aside, Doc is one of rock's premier managers whose business sense is uncanny and whose creative concepts are dazzling. In addition to management, Doc also pursues a variety of interests, not the least of which is a joint venture with the Home Shopping Club to start a rock and roll version of the shopping channel to sell rock merchandise, records, and other souvenirs. On the surface it may seem that his motive is simply to make money on the sales. However, he has stated that his main interest in the venture is to establish a data base of rock fans' names, addresses, and phone numbers, so he can communicate with them one on one. This is the kind of marketing that AT&T, Ford, IBM, and other corporate giants are moving toward in the nineties, and Doc is on the cutting edge of it in the music business.

The management of a superstar act requires a comprehensive knowledge of practically every detail of the music industry. Recording agreements, royalties, publishing, live engagements, all must be a part of the manager's repertoire. He must also be a shrewd businessman. Superstar acts make enormous amounts of money, and since they have to be residents of some country or another, governments are just itching to get their hands on some of those huge incomes through taxes. It is the superstar manager's job to protect as much of that income as possible, through tax shelters, corporations, and other legal and accounting maneuvers, to ensure that the artist retains the maximum amount of the fruits of his or her labors. Finally, the superstar manager must be a superstar psychologist. Superstars are not, shall we say, the easiest people to manage. They have achieved a level of success beyond mere mortals, and many consider themselves to be above it all. It is the manager's job to convince the group to make those moves that are important to the continuance of their career even when they may have no interest in doing so. Superstar managers are superstars in their own right, are usually hard negotiators, and have created their own substrata in the hierarchy of the music industry.

Managers form the link between artists and the music business. An artist creates, but it is the successful marketing of those creations that results in the artist's ultimate fame and fortune.

THE MANAGEMENT CONTRACT

The American Federation of Musicians makes available a standard personal manager's agreement. Of the dozen or so managers whom I spoke with in connection with the writing of this book, only three had heard of it, and only one of the three had seen it. Most managers rely on contracts created by their attorneys, rather than on anything from the union. They do so, no doubt, because the union does not license managers and, other than in California, does not really have anything to say about management. In California, it says that you cannot be both an agent and a manager. Outside California, the union says that if you are an agent and a manager, you cannot take more than an aggregate 25 percent in commissions from the act for a live engagement. But otherwise the union has stayed out of the artist management business.

When I spoke to them about their agreements with their artists, most managers outlined pretty much the same type of agreement, and the following sections describe some of the key points that you should look for in any management contract.

Term

A manager will try to sign an act to as long a contract as possible. You should try to make the initial period as short as possible, but bear in mind that you will need to make it long enough for the manager to make a difference in your career. One to two years is about right, with options. The manager will probably want these options to be his, but that's too one-sided for my liking. Try to make the option either mutual, you must both agree to renew the contract, or make it the manager's option, but exercisable only if the manager has attained some specific, measurable objective for you like a certain amount of gross revenue per year.

Also, don't let the manager make contracts for you with third parties if these agreements go beyond the term of her contract. For example, if you have a two-year deal with a manager, don't let her sign you to a three-year deal with an agent. Contracts should be coterminous, that is, running for the same term. The only exceptions are publishing deals, which run for the length of the copyright and record deals, which may run longer than your management deal.

Duties

The contract will outline the duties that each of you is expected to perform. For example, the manager may be expected to negotiate your deals, arrange your live engagements, and handle the finances. You, on the other hand, may be required to show up to perform as scheduled, live up to your contracts, and pay commissions to the manager. Whatever these duties are, they should be clearly outlined because they will form the basis of the deal upon which the breach-cure and termination clauses will be built.

Power of Attorney

Most management contracts give the manager limited power of attorney for the act, ranging from the right to sign live-engagement contracts to checks and other documents. You should base this privilege on two things: your level of confidence and trust in the manager and what the manager will need to do the job effectively. Rely on your lawyer for advice on how far to go with the power of attorney.

Expenses
This area is handled differently by each manager. Some managers charge back everything to the artist—faxes, photocopies, messengers services, and so forth—just like a lawyer. I even know of one well-known manager who has separate phone lines for each artist that are billed directly to the artist's account. In this way, the manager not only charges back direct expenses like airfare, hotels, and the like that are incurred in doing your business, but is writing off his overhead, thereby making the cost of running his business zero.

Other managers believe that only direct expenses should be charged back and that they should absorb their own overhead, as a cost of being in business. I'm not making a value judgment on either method, although charging back only direct expenses seems fairer. But if your manager is doing a great job and is making you money, then he is worth both his commission and whatever reasonable expenses he may charge back. One manager put it this way: "A manager should increase and decrease based on his percentage. He should increase your gross equal to the percentage he is taking and should decrease your workload in business matters." That's a good way to look at a manager's role.

Commission Percentages
Like the earlier quote from Bruce Allen said, a manager should charge a commission based on the band's ability to pay. Most good managers use a sliding scale for their acts in which they take a small percentage when the band is making a little money and will miss it most and a larger percentage when the band is better able to afford it. (One manager I know of takes 10 percent of the low-dollar gigs, 15 percent of the larger gigs, and 20 percent of the biggest gigs.) However, most managers have an agreement with their bands that the bands will never pay more than a total of 30 percent to them and to agents and have cut a deal with the agents that whenever a gig is over a certain dollar amount, the agent must reduce his commission to 10 percent from 15 percent. In this way the bands are protected from paying too much at the top end and are not forced to turn over large sums on their lower-paying gigs. This formula, of course, is targeted primarily at developing bands

because the deals that are cut with big-name talent differ considerably.

With big names the percentages may slide the other way, with the large commissions for the managers on the lower-paying gigs and smaller commissions for the higher-paying gigs. Also some of the bigger acts dictate what their managers may and may not take in commissions. These days, many acts are struggling to prevent managers from commissioning publishing money and are especially fighting PTC, which continues to pay the managers even after their contracts with the acts have expired.

Other

The remaining points of the contract will be the standard contract language: termination clauses, breach and cures, indemnifications, warranties, notices, and the like. They are all much like those you have seen or will see in publishing, recording, and other agreements.

As with all other legal documents, I cannot stress enough your need to have an attorney's advice in signing any contract. Even though they may seem expensive and time consuming initially, the services of a good lawyer can save you years and millions of dollars in the event that you attain the level of success that you are reaching for.

BOOKING AGENTS

*We were the group you could actually see. It wasn't
like Zeppelin was out there on the road in America
all the time. We were America's band ... the garage
band that made it real big, the ultimate party band.*

**—JOE PERRY,
AEROSMITH**

To build a following, you'll need someone to do your touring business—someone who knows the circuit in your area, who knows how to sell and how to get the best possible price for you and your act. This person is a *booking agent*.

But not every agent is for you. Here are some ways to ensure that the agent whom you hook up with is what you are looking for. If you are looking for someone to book your hard rock act, and all you see on the walls of an agent's office are pictures of accordion players and magicians, you're in the wrong place. The reverse is also true. Just because a local agent is good at booking rock, it doesn't mean that he or she can book your country band or rap act, and there is nothing more deadly for any performer than ending up in front of the wrong audience. Check around. Ask other performers who do what you do (rock, folk, country) who their agents are, if their agents honest, hard-working, and so on, and get as much information on your prospective representative as you can. Remember, you are making this person a part of your act and are putting your life and talent in his or her hands, so choose wisely.

Let's say you enter an agent's office in Duluth or Grand Rapids, and you see photos of superstars on the walls. If the agent claims to represent Van Halen, Tom Petty, or Aerosmith, keep in mind that there are two types of booking agent—*national* (or international) and *local*. An act like Tom Petty, for instance, would be handled by a national agency or, more properly, an international agency who books him worldwide. The chances of this agency being located in New York or Los Angeles are very good. The chances of this agency being located in Duluth or Boise, however, are not so good, if you get my drift.

A local agent, on the other hand, who may be located in Des Moines or Rochester, may handle entertainment buying for most of the local clubs, schools, and the like, and in the course of his business, may book groups for state or local fairs. Many times these fairs will book a Tom Petty or a Bon Jovi as their one big act of the year and, in this case, the local agent actually works with the big-name artist. We call this working as a subcontractor, a local party who has direct contact with the employer (in this case, the state fair), but still has to buy the superstar artist or group from the national agency. For his part in the transaction, the local agent receives a small percentage or is paid a fee directly by the state fair. In any case, the agent does not represent the big-name act and if he suggests that he does, look out! Sometimes, in an attempt to impress someone new to the business, a local agent will try to dazzle you with the names of artists with whom she has worked. She won't say that she actually represents them, but she'll imply it by using the superstar's name on her brochure or by displaying a photo in her office. Don't be fooled or overly impressed by what an agent may tell you in your first meeting. Who he has partied with is irrelevant; it's what he can do for *your* career that's most important. Music is a business, and if you treat it that way, you'll avoid many of its pitfalls.

CHOOSING YOUR AGENT

Choosing an agent is difficult. Often, you will have no way of really checking agents out and may only have a passing knowledge of their business dealings. How do you find the one who has contacts with big agencies, record labels, managers, and promoters who can really help you? The consensus among most of the agents I talked to seems to be that you should try to find an agent who has worked with acts in your area who have already made the move up the ladder to the next stage of their careers. The other suggestion these managers seemed to agree on was, "Don't believe a lot of what you hear or are told." If an agent tells you he is going to make you a star, pay no attention. Agents can only help you; they can't *make* you anything. If an agent says she knows John Smith from Epic records, for example, pick up the phone and call John Smith. You'd be surprised how easy it is to get a lot of people in the music industry on the phone, especially on the local level. What have you got to lose by calling? You may get your reference and make a business contact at the same time. The best way to find the agent who's for you is to find a band in your area whose career path you'd like to emulate and then find out who is doing their business. Call a club they are playing at, ask who their agent is, call the agent, and see if you can arrange a meeting.

When you find an agent in whom you are interested and have the first meeting, go slowly. Bear in mind that at this point you are not looking for the agent to get you a recording contract, a publisher, or a manager. You're looking for someone to get you work. Make it clear, with a hint that if things go well, possibilities in other areas could develop. If you have talent, a good agent will recognize it, and you will be in a position to carry on business that is based on a relationship of mutual respect.

A prospective agent will want to see your act (be wary of anyone that doesn't). Either you or the agent will have to arrange a showcase, that is, a performance at which the agent can see you do your stuff. Try to make it during one of your regular engagements in a place that is familiar to you, where you are known and you can depend on the reaction of the audience. A rowdy crowd or an empty room, complaints that you are too loud, or a lack of seating for the agent and his or her guests could make your first big chance a nightmare. When you finally get the time and the place for your showcase, plan your attack with the following steps:

1. Put together a set of your best songs. Vary the tempos and include material that goes over well in the place you are playing.

2. Keep the set at a reasonable length. An agent simply will not be impressed by a twenty-minute drum solo in the middle of the second song.

3. Agents want to see energy, enthusiasm, and talent on stage, not posing and self-indulgence, so keep the music hot and the theatrics calculated and interesting.

4. Make sure that the agent's name is on the free-admission guest list and that the agent gets a good seat. There's no point going through all this for an agent who isn't there or can't see you.

5. If you're playing a club, be sure to put at least some of the agent's drinks on your tab. You have to be entertaining in more ways than one to get yourself started.

6. Practice your audition set before the showcase and save it until the agent arrives, even if he or she doesn't get there until the end of the night. Don't play your best stuff early to try it out on the audience. If the agent arrives in the middle of it, some of the effect will be lost and the songs will lose much of their impact on the audience the second time around. If you get to the last set of the evening and the agent hasn't showed up by then, play your audition set. If the agent walks in at that point, at least he or she will hear some of your best material and if not, it will at least make you feel better after you have been stiffed by the agent.

7. Don't get bitter if the agent doesn't show up. Contact him or her the next day and find out why. If you can't get past the secretary, then you know that the agent doesn't care and simply can't be bothered to tell you. In that case, just be glad that you didn't get involved with this weasel. If, on the other hand, the agent is apologetic and has what sounds like a good excuse, forgive this time and set up another showcase. If it happens again, forget the agent and start again. One note: Don't say bad things to other musicians about any agents who you think have wronged you. You never know who you are talking to, and the music industry is a small community. Someday the agent may be in a position to help you or to hurt you, and there's no percentage in burning any bridges. If you get stiffed, just keep quiet, cross the agent off your Christmas-card list, and continue with your career.

One way to get the attention of an agent is to appear on the bill with another act who you know the agent will be coming to see. Faith No More, for example, were seen by their agent on a date with the Red Hot Chili Peppers in New York, but it wasn't until a year later that they were actually signed. Another interesting part of the Faith No More story is that from the time the agent first saw them to the time they were actually signed, they had changed lead singers. Even though the agent wanted to sign the act, he made it clear to the manager that he needed to see the band *with* their new singer before he could make his final decision. One other element made it easier for the agent to become involved. The manager for the band was already doing business with the agent and therefore the agent knew the manager's style and could make a decision on the act based on that additional information.

Much the same thing happened the first time that an agent friend of mine went to see the Red Hot Chili Peppers. It was one of those true music business moments:

One night I was invited out to see a band that I had heard a lot about in LA called the Red Hot Chili Peppers. The manager had invited me out, so I went and brought a friend along with me to watch the band. After I had watched about half the show I looked at my friend and we both agreed that the band just didn't have it. We wanted to leave the club but saw the band's manager standing right by the front door. We didn't want to insult the guy and walk right past him while his band was onstage but we certainly didn't want to listen to them any longer. Then I remembered that there was a window next to the men's room in the back of the club. So we sneaked down the hall, climbed out the window, and left the club. I got up the next morning and while I was in the shower I realized that I was unconsciously humming one of the band's songs from the night before. I thought to myself, "You know, that was really a catchy song they played last night" and began to think that maybe I had been a little hasty in my judgment. So I called the manager, went out and saw them again and eventually signed them. From climbing out through the bathroom window to avoid them, to a deal with our agency—sometimes this can be a very strange business.

Sometimes you'll hit with an agent right away, but other times it will take a trip out the bathroom window to get the deal. Whatever the case, don't get discouraged. If you keep at it, eventually you'll end up making an impression on someone who will offer you a chance to take the next step.

Getting signed by an agent is the most important part of your career, but agents can't sign every act they see. There are definite criteria that agents use in deciding when to sign an act. The most important one is what they hear, even more than what they see. Most agents believe that what they hear has to be something that there is a need for in the business. Maybe it's a new sound, or something else about you that an agent feels is truly unique yet is still commercially acceptable. There has to be something there that the agent believes will make you stand out from the crowd.

But not every band has to be totally unique to get a deal, and not every agent is out trying to discover brand-new bands with brand-new sounds. It's talent that they are looking for, talent that they think can be marketed to a mass audience.

On some rare occasions a band will appear that is so new and on the cutting edge that a major agent will want to get involved even before a record label or a manager. This allows the agent to present the act to labels and managers and to bring it to people's attention for the first time. If the act becomes successful and the agent did, in fact, discover them, it goes a long way toward enhancing the agent's credibility. But the major agents seldom take this kind of chance, preferring to let the labels do the A & R chores (or, more appropriately, take the A & R chances) before they choose to get involved.

You can get signed by a booking agent several different ways. First, the agent has to be brought out to see you. One of the first things the agent will consider is who told him about you. If he is asked to see your band by someone at a record label, for example, he will first be able to get some information about you like whether a manager is involved or how are you to work with. If no manager is involved, then the agent will probably try to sign your act through the person at the record label.

Second, if a manager asks an agent to see a band, then obviously the agent will work with the manager on signing the act if she likes them. Agents are most comfortable with this scenario because the manager of an act is usually the last word. If a band doesn't have a manager and the agent tries to sign them before they do, the band may then pick a manager with whom the agent doesn't have a relationship, and the agent will end up not getting the band after having invested considerable time and energy trying to sign them. So agents usually take the safe route and look for acts who already have managers and, ideally, for acts who are managed by people with whom they already have done business.

Third, big national agents generally won't sign an act that doesn't have a record deal, for obvious reasons. Without a record, there is nothing for radio stations to play, and without airplay or sales of some sort, there is no demand for the band. If there is no demand, there is nothing for the agent to sell, and no fees for her to commission. Therefore, the best time to approach the big agents is after you have a record deal. A lawyer sometimes tells an agent about an act he or she is working on who doesn't have a record deal yet and may send the agent a demo tape. Sometimes the agent may even actually listen to it, but because of the politics involved with record labels, agents prefer to get involved later in the game.

Since you can't get a major or a national agent to sign you before you get a record deal, what do the big guys recommend for acts who do not yet have deals? The consensus of the national agents is that local bands who do not yet have record deals should work with local agents. In fact many big acts and agents started their careers with small, local agencies. The good news is that the small agents are everywhere. My advice is to play every possible date at every possible place you can and be seen by as many people as you can until finally a local promoter, club owner, or someone else in the area with whom you are working brings your name up to someone at an agency. It's just a matter of working your way up the ladder. As a local act in East Lansing, Michigan, for example, your real goal is to make it to Detroit and Chicago, for the bigger the market, the higher the profile of the places you can play. The promoters in those markets are the big ones, and people from the big agencies are always coming through town.

But as I've said before, you don't have to sit around waiting for people at the agencies to come out to see you. Here's how one musician friend of mine puts it: "Get them to get their butt out to see you." One tool you will find invaluable throughout your career is the Album Network's *Yellow Pages of Rock*. The Yellow Pages is a listing of every major record label office, both national and regional; booking agents; concert promoters; independent record promoters; radio stations; and much, much more. It gives you company names, contacts, addresses, and fax and phone numbers. I've seen new acts, superstars, managers, and label presidents lugging this book around all over the world. My own copy is always within reach, and I use it at least a few times every day. It's updated annually and includes just about all the contact information you will need to work the agents in your area. There's no magic here; just find their names and numbers in the Yellow Pages, call them up, and invite them out to see you. Follow up your call with a letter giving all the details of your show and call them again on the day before the date and remind them or their secretaries that you'd like to see them there. Take a look in the back of this book and you'll find all the information on how to get your copy of the Album Network's *Yellow Pages of Rock*.

But the *Yellow Pages of Rock* isn't the only way to ferret out the agents and record types whom you want to get out to see you. The phone company's Yellow Pages lists entertainment agencies, and although it may take you some time to go through them to find the ones that specialize in your kind of music, you'll be able to make some connections. The club owners around town, as well as other musicians, are another source of information about agency contacts. And your local radio station may be willing to give you some information, especially if you have sent someone there a tape or if they've heard you live and liked what you do. The key, of course, is initiative and persistence. You've got to go out and get these people, for although it's their job to discover new talent, there is so much new talent around that it's up to you to ensure that you stand out from all the others. And the way you do so is to get in their face in a friendly and professional way and convince them that an investment in you will pay off for them.

THE EXCLUSIVE AGENT-MUSICIAN AGREEMENT

In the booking business, exclusivity is essential. If you are available only through one agent in your area and you are in demand, your agent is in a good position to make good deals for you, both financially and for the kind of conditions in which you want to perform. Exclusivity may sometimes work against you, however, if you sign with an agent who is not working in your best interest. You will not only be out of work, but because of your exclusive contract, you will not be able to book yourself or be booked by any other agent. To add insult to injury, any work that your agent does allow you or another agent to book is commissionable by your "do-nothing" agent, so be careful when it comes to making an exclusive deal with an agent.

The union issues the *Exclusive Agent-Musician Agreement* for bands and agencies that is the only authorized contract between a union band and a union-licensed agent. (Some agencies have a *side-letter* agreement with the bands they represent, which may outline certain things that have been agreed to by both parties, but a clause in the union contract states that the union contract is the only binding agreement and that no other letters or deals supersede it.) All booking agents who book union acts into union-licensed venues must have the authorization of the American Federation of Musicians.

When you see the agreement, you'll notice a disclaimer at the top that is not to be used in California. When it comes to actors and other performers, the State of California has a considerably different view from that of the rest of the world. In California things like *suspension clauses* (clauses that allow a label or studio to extend a contract beyond its term when the talent fails to perform obligations on time) in actor's and musician's contracts will not stand up as well as they will in courts in other parts of the country. Unlike any other part of the United States, California courts are squarely on the side of the artist; hence most companies are reluctant to have their contracts with acts be under the jurisdiction of the California courts. But for the rest of the United States and Canada, the union's *Exclusive Agent-Musician Agreement* is recognized as the only official, enforceable agreement between musicians and their agents. Here are the agreement's key provisions:

Scope of the Agreement

First, the agreement outlines its *scope*, that is, what the agreement will do. In it, the musician appoints the agent *"exclusively, throughout the world, as agent, manager and representative, for all musical endeavors."* This phrase means that you are relinquishing to the agent, all negotiations and therefore all commissions, for all your engagements, whether the agent gets them for you or not. However, it doesn't make the agent your manager even though the word is used. The agreement is for booking only.

Duties of the Agent

Next, the contract outlines what your agent will do for you. The particular thing to note in this section is that the agent cannot accept any engagements for you that you do not approve. The section does say that the approval will not be unreasonably withheld, but it's difficult for any agent to prove that you are turning down a gig unreasonably. Otherwise, this section simply indicates that the agent will handle all the business of promoting you within the industry, find you work and do all the detail work connected with that work, maintain sufficient office facilities to represent your act, and comply with all union and other laws and regulations.

Rights of the Agent

Here's one that you need to read carefully. This is the section that spells out, in detail, what rights the agent has concerning your career.

First, it says that the agent can render services to others and may engage in other businesses. If you sign with a relatively large agency, it isn't a problem. But if you sign with a small agency, it could present some difficulty. If your agent runs a small operation or if you sign with a large agency, but your act is not a priority for the agency, you can get lost in the shuffle. Under the agreement, you can't hire any other person or company to perform the same services to be performed by your agent so if your agent is too busy or distracted to perform his or her duties, and you try to break your contract based on a claim that the other businesses in which the agent is engaged are taking up too much of his or her time, you will probably not be successful, in that you acknowledged these other activities when you signed the agreement. Worse yet, in the event that the agent doesn't work for you, you're unable to hire anyone else to do the business for you. This provision is tempered in this section by a remedy for the breach that says that if you break your agreement, all the agent has coming to him or her is outstanding commissions for services rendered and nothing more, and you pay only after you've been paid for the engagements booked by the agent. So although it looks ominous, you really aren't that much at risk, as long as you monitor the situation and are prepared to leave an agent if the job isn't getting done.

Compensation of the Agent
This section is divided into several parts:

1. The agent receives 15 percent for gigs of two or more consecutive days in one week and 20 percent for one-night engagements as long as they are for different employers in different locations.

2. The agent must ensure that regardless of any commissions, the amount of money that the musician receives equals or exceeds the minimum union scale for the engagement. Also, this section prohibits the agent from taking any money or consideration that exceeds the commission that he would be due for the gig. So, for example, if a promoter were to offer an agent an extra payment (read bribe) for making sure that he, not his competitor, gets your show, the agent would be prohibited from accepting it.

3. Commission have to be paid to the agent upon receipt of payment by the musician. However, if you get stiffed by a promoter and he doesn't pay you, even if it is your fault, you don't have to pay the commission to the agent. But hold on a minute. This isn't a good way to economize because the agent then has the right to take his case to the International Executive of the union (the governing body that arbitrates disputes), which has the right to force the musician to pay damages amounting to the unpaid commissions and possible interest to the agent.

A few more notes: commissions are paid on gross earnings, which are defined in the contract as gross amounts received by the musician less any costs incurred in collecting the money. If you have any contracts outstanding when you sign the agent's agreement, you can choose to pay or not to pay commissions to the agent on those gigs by initialing this section of the agreement. The agreement also provides for advances on commissions to the agent for engagements, plus information on accounting practices.

Duration and Timing of the Agreement

On the front page of the agreement, there is a line that indicates the amount of time that the contract is to be in force. There are blank lines for the start and end dates, which are written in by the contracting parties. The agent will want to make this period as long as possible, and you, the musician, will probably want to make it as short as possible. The right answer is about one year. One year is enough time for the agent to develop her relationship with you to the point where she can get you serious work, but it is not so long that any real damage will be done if she doesn't perform well.

Besides, there are clauses in this section of the agreement that allow you to get rid of the agent if he isn't doing a good job. The contract states that if you are unemployed for four consecutive weeks or don't work for at least twenty cumulative weeks in each of the first and second six months of the contract (that is, you don't get at least forty consecutive weeks of work in a year), you're out of your deal. There are legal definitions of what a *week* means in the agreement (a *week-long* engagement in a club, for example, may consist of four days, rather than seven), but the bottom line is this: If the agent doesn't perform, you can get rid of him, although you will have to wait at least four weeks to prove that he has breached the agreement.

Other Stuff

Two more important items: First, the contract is not assignable. That is, if there is new ownership of the agency, a merger, or a takeover, you can get out of your deal and cannot be stuck with the agency if you don't want to be. This provision is particularly helpful if, for example, you are with one agent who does a poor job for you, you leave and go with another agent, and then your new and old agents become partners and your old agent tries to get even. Finally, the agreement itself is not in effect until a copy is filed with the union, within thirty days of signing. In this way, the union knows the details of the deal and can help you out if you have a dispute with the agent.

Side Letters

Most agents will attach a *side letter* to the contract that outlines the specific details of their arrangement with you. And although nothing in this side letter can supersede the union contract, it will be seen as a legal document in the courts, and you can be bound by a side letter beyond the officially sanctioned union deal, according to the law.

In the side letter the artist gives the agent the right to represent her for live engagements. The commission agreement between the two parties is spelled out (the union contract provides guidelines for the percentages, but remember there is a cap, according to the union, on what the agent can take). Now this may seem a bit confusing. If a side letter can't supersede the contract, why have one? The answer is simple, and to explain it I'll use an example outside the music business.

At some time in your life you may have signed a lease to rent a house or apartment. As you know, a lease is a legal form that outlines the terms of your agreement with the landlord. Well, let's say that you and the landlord make a deal that allows you to buy the house after a certain period of time and that a part of your rent goes toward the purchase price. Rather than putting it into the lease, you would probably have a side-letter agreement. It would still be legally binding but is not really a part of a rental deal. The same goes for a side letter with an agency. It's a legally binding document, but the terms fall outside those controlled by the union contract. The same holds true for the musicians' union. The *Exclusive Agent-Musician Agreement* sets out the rules by which all union members, musicians and agents, have agreed to act. The union provides guidelines, not civil law. A side letter may specify a certain commission structure that is higher than the union allows. In theory, it is a legal document and a court may enforce it against you, but if you take it to the union, the union can suspend the agent's license and forbid any union musician or other union member or club to do business with the agent until he or she abides by the union rules. The agent may legally bind you with a side letter, but the union can step in and seriously affect the agent's ability to do business in the music community.

In some side letters you will find a few "extras" that you will have to negotiate. Some agents include the right to deduct amounts from your commissions for promotion and publicity. You need to advise the agent, and write it into the agreement, that the costs must be approved by you and that receipts must be presented to back up the deductions.

Some agents will also include the right to negotiate corporate sponsorships or merchandise deals on your behalf. Be careful here. If you agree to this clause, you are doing two things: First, you are giving the agent the right to act for you in areas beyond live engagements and second, if your manager gets you a corporate sponsorship or merchandise deal, you will have to pay the agent a commission. My advice is to strike out these clauses from the side letter. Unless you need the agent to act in these areas, the agent should stick to getting you live-engagement work. Leave the merchandise and sponsorships to your manager or other professionals in those areas.

Finally, the side letter will stipulate that the artist warrants that he is free and clear to enter into the agreement, that is, that he isn't under contract to any other agent, which would expose the new agent to a lawsuit. Also it includes a clause that obligates all band members to be bound by the agreement.

As contracts go, the *Exclusive Agents-Musician Agreement* is a good one. It is heavily weighted in favor of the musician and allows sufficient opportunity for the musician to terminate it if things are unsatisfactory. It's one of the few contracts that you will see in your career that is a "win-win" for you.

WORKING YOUR AGENCY

One of the necessary ingredients in success is the ability to always maintain your sightline on the goal.

—DWIGHT YOAKAM

Just having an agent is no guarantee of work. Most agencies have what is called a *roster* of talent, that is, a list of all the attractions they represent, and you'll find that it is usually pretty long. Therefore, you are going to have to figure out some way of ensuring that you have the agent's and the agency's attention, so they will work hard to get you work. One way to do so is to maintain a high profile within the agency. Your manager should make a schedule of calls, letters, and visits to the agency and should insist that the agent who is responsible for your act is in contact with him at least once a week, either in person or by phone, to discuss what is being done for you.

When you deal directly with the agent, don't let her treat you like an idiot! Make it clear that, as well as a musician, you are a businessperson and that you are aware that you are in a competitive industry and therefore wish to be kept abreast of all developments.

When you sign with an agency you will usually work with one particular agent. If he or she is not the boss or one of the owners, insist that he or she introduce you to the president and vice president; it is important that you maintain a relationship with them.

In your manager's meetings with the agent, he should go over upcoming bookings and find out who the agent has spoken to about you that week and what the reaction was. If you or your manager have any suggestions or information about new places to play, make them known to the agent and follow them up in subsequent meetings. The agent and the whole agency need to be aware of you as both an entertainer and as a businessperson. If you don't have a manager, you'll have to handle these things yourself, and you must be sure that people take you seriously. Later in your career, you can, and should, turn this stuff over to a manager, but for now only half your work is done on the stage. The number of well-known artists who take an active part in their business affairs is growing steadily. Mick Jagger, Alex Van Halen, and Madonna are all very involved in the day-to-day management of their careers. But it's important that you be able to separate your artistic temperament from your business. Many artists have felt they could be their own managers, and then have proceeded to throw endless tantrums, which, instead of advancing their careers, alienated everyone with whom they tried to do business. If you handle it like a pro, however, the lessons that you learn will be invaluable to your future success. Be a pro onstage and in business, and the respect that you need will come by itself.

How an Agent Works

All agents maintain a list of clients—a list that is their life blood. Clubs, high schools, colleges, concert promoters, fairs, festivals, trade shows, conventions, lounges—all these make up the list upon which agents rely to obtain engagements for their artists.

In some cases the agent arranges an exclusive contract with these clients, which means that her agency is the only one that sells talent to them. In other cases, the agent books with major concert promoters that buy from all agencies. It follows that an exclusive agreement with a client allows an agent to obtain more work for her groups because each week she has to provide each client with a new act for his venue. With enough exclusive clients, an agent can essentially route her own mini concert-tour circuit, starting an act in club A and winding up in club Z twenty-six weeks later.

Generally, an agent contacts his clients each week by telephone to discuss their entertainment needs. If your act is new, he will talk to club owners, promoters, or campus entertainment coordinators about you, extolling your virtues and talent. He may, just on the strength of his reputation or relationship with the client, be able to get you work without an audition. In a situation like this, it is important that you make a good showing. An agent takes a long time building a relationship and if you damage that relationship, your chances of working again for that agent are slim.

There are times when, through misunderstanding, you may have problems at an engagement. If the agent has presented you as something other than what you are (a rock band in a country bar, for instance) just to get you work, you can either make the best of it and try to accommodate the client or contact the agent and tell him to send a replacement. You can see why I stress the point that you should never allow an agent who hasn't seen your act to book it. Nobody wants to end up being the right band in the wrong place.

Your agent will negotiate a price for your act with the client. Be sure that he understands your needs, or to put it bluntly, don't let him give your act away just to make a commission. If you need travel money, accommodations, or the like over and above the fee, be sure that the agent knows about it and makes it part of the deal. Also, the agent should not collect a commission on any kind of travel money or other allowances over the fee. He gets a commission only on the actual money that you are being paid to play.

But be responsible! Don't go traveling off to the middle of nowhere unaware of the terms of the deal and then call the agent in the middle of the night complaining that you have nowhere to stay. Likewise don't play for a week and after expenses for hotels, food, gas, and promotion, end up making nothing. Work this out with your agent in advance. Things will go much more smoothly if you do.

Whether you book yourself or employ the services of an agent, the key to securing live engagements is persistence and profile. If you don't get work right away, don't get discouraged; keep at it.

And when you do land a gig, promote it. Make sure that people know that you're going to be there and that you're going to do a great job onstage. If you do both these things, you'll draw crowds and you'll turn them into fans. After doing so a few times, the work will come to you.

Agents and Superstars

An agent's role for a superstar act is considerably different than it is for breaking a new band. When an act starts out, the goal is "subsistence" and "existence." An agent has to make sure that the new band plays enough gigs so they have enough money to subsist and then has to make sure that they are playing enough dates and the right type of dates to exist in the business. Once an act breaks big, the agent still has to worry about their existence, but obviously not as much about their subsistence because that part of their career, the money, is already coming in. When an act gets big, the agent's job is to make sure that they are playing in the right places for the right promoters with the right packages and that they are marketed in such a way that they will have a long career. An agent's job is as much to sustain an already developed career as it is to break a new act. In fact, sustaining a big act is the most important thing the agent does.

Many agents get lucky with short-term hits. These agents will generally sign a lot of acts and turn them over quickly, dropping them if they don't produce. But the best agents have ten or more years with acts, and that is the important thing—the management of successful, credible, and productive careers over a decade or more. That is how unknowns become stars and stars become superstars. They have the time to develop, grow, and prosper to attain superstar status.

LAWYERS

If I'd gone through school, I'd probably be a lawyer.
Then I could take the people that screw me to court.

—AXL ROSE,
GUNS N' ROSES

Lawyers are the bane and boon of the music industry. They are the deal makers, the litigators in lawsuits, the advisers, the writers of contracts, the good guys and the bad guys, all rolled into one. There are times when their attention to detail makes the business run like a Swiss watch, and other times when their lack of action makes it falter like a cracked hourglass. If you keep a few things in mind, though, you can make your attorney a valuable cog in your music machine.

If you already have a lawyer who has handled business matters for you, he or she can probably help you work out any contractual situations. But keep one thing in mind: The music business is unique, and some clauses or wording in music contracts that are peculiar only to the entertainment industry may be considered out of the ordinary by an attorney who is not familiar with the business. You must be sure that your lawyer doesn't argue points that he or she simply doesn't understand. In such a case, you need expert advice.

There are attorneys that specialize in the music business. Call various law offices in your city and inquire about their lawyers' expertise and experience in the music business. If your lawyer doesn't have the correct experience for your needs, he or she probably will be able to recommend lawyers who do, and can consult with them in music matters or can refer you to their firm.

In the music business an attorney's function is to advise on important matters of contracts or law, so it is imperative that you find someone in whom you have a high degree of confidence. Usually when it comes to attorneys, physicians, or other professionals, people have a peculiar attitude that the expensive ones are the best and that professionals who charge less are less effective. This just isn't the case. Many young lawyers, who are uncomfortable in the corporate large-firm environment, are opening private practices and are specializing in entertainment law. Check around with other musicians in your area, and you should be able to get a recommendation.

How to Use Your Lawyer

What do you want your lawyer to do? One of the things that you don't want him or her to do at this stage of your career is to negotiate all your deals for you because most lawyers charge by the hour, and you can be stuck with sizable legal fees. For a live engagement, for example, you should be able to negotiate the basic stuff yourself. "How much will I be paid?" and "Where do I have to play and for how long" simply aren't things for which you need an attorney. The trick in the music business, as in any business, is to keep the costs to a minimum. However, if you are presented with a contract for something other than a live performance (for example, a recording or publishing deal), then you must find a competent attorney. Use your lawyer as an adviser, not as a manager or a guru. You want his or her legal opinion about whether the terms and conditions of a particular agreement that you are being asked to sign are in your best interest. The lawyer's comments are not law, nor are they necessarily the whole truth. Read the contract yourself and make notes. All the sections of a contract are usually numbered or otherwise identified for easy referral. Include these numbers in your notes, so your lawyer will know exactly what part of the contract you are talking about.

Write down your specific questions: "What do they mean by default?" "What is a waiver?" Even if you think you know the meaning of a word in English, like *default*, for example, be aware that it can have a different, specific meaning in certain kinds of contracts. Don't take anything for granted.

Try to zero in on what you don't understand, rather than ask a lot of general questions like, "Is it a good contract?" or "Will I get a lot of money?" Also, make a list of the things that you think should be in the contract. You may not be a lawyer, but you'll find that your instincts are pretty good. If you think that anything is missing from the contract, tell your lawyer what it is and why you think it should be in the contract. You will be surprised to discover that, in many cases, the items on your list will already be in the contract, couched in such tangled legal language that you would never recognize them. No contract is perfect, and there are probably clauses in it that you will want to take out. Your lawyer will let you know the benefits and the drawbacks of each item in the contract.

Don't get too complicated. The person with whom you are doing the deal has to understand what you are talking about, and crazy convoluted clauses can drive a negotiation into a black hole. Be straightforward, work with your lawyer, and try to come out with a document that is simple, fair, and concise.

You should always have a few days to examine a contract. If you're ever in a situation in which someone produces a contract from a desk drawer and insists that you sign it on the spot—*run!* At this point you are no longer doing business, you are fighting for your life. No self-respecting, honest company or individual will ever demand that you sign a deal in this manner. And don't let anyone intimidate you by using the old, "You're blowing your big chance, kid" routine. You are probably just saving yourself an expensive legal battle later in your career. A contract, like a marriage or a fight, is very easy to get into, but very difficult to get out of. Only after your lawyer has seen the contract and given you advice, should you consider putting your name on the dotted line.

You wouldn't pick an attorney out of the telephone book any more than you would a doctor or a dentist. Try to find others who have been involved in music-business contracts and negotiations and find out about their lawyers, that is, whether they have been satisfied with their lawyers' service, fee, attitude, and results. Don't panic and go with the first attorney you run across. If possible, take some time. Talk to a couple of lawyers through introductions from friends or family members until you find one who you like. Don't get pressured into using someone with whom you aren't comfortable. You must trust this person because he or she will be representing not only your career, but your life. If you already have an attorney for your personal affairs, ask directly if he or she has any music business experience and gauge your involvement with him or her accordingly. As I've said before, the music business is different from other businesses, and if your lawyer has no experience in dealing with it, he or she could actually do you more harm than good.

Lawyers are generally expensive. Their cost, naturally, is relative to their effectiveness in securing the deal that you are after. A three- to five-year deal with a major label for big bucks that costs you ten thousand dollars in legal fees is really a bargain considering what you may earn from the contract. But a bad deal that costs you only five hundred dollars in fees can kill you.

Make sure that the lawyer you are using is the right one for the job and be conscious of your wallet. You don't necessarily need an attorney to shop your deal to publishers or record companies. Your or your manager can make the initial contacts and turn it over to the lawyer when you get some real interest.

You'll no doubt be told that without a lawyer you can't even get into a record company, but that simply isn't true. Color Me Badd got their deal by sending a demo tape to the label, and their debut single rose to number one on the charts. Once you get some interest from a label or publisher, then it's time for an attorney. If your dealings include conversations about large budgets, long-term agreements, and the like (and they will), the record company will probably suggest that you hire a lawyer if you don't have one.

A little paranoia here: If the label recommends a particular lawyer, he or she may not necessarily be the one to use. That lawyer may be too close to the record company, and you don't want any confusion as to whose interests your lawyer is representing. This isn't to say that you would be knowingly cheated, but if it comes down to something in the contract that isn't harmful to you but isn't beneficial either and the lawyer does a lot of business with the record label, he or she may leave it in the contract instead of fighting for every detail to be in your favor.

THE BIG GUNS

If a contract contains items that are a problem for you and your attorney, you may want to bring in one of the music industry's heavy hitters to have a look at it. These lawyers are expensive, so you'll want to minimize their involvement. Use them on a hourly basis for consultation. If they suggest that they can get you a much better deal if they do the direct negotiating with the record company, consider the offer carefully. These big guys work well for already-established acts when it comes time for renegotiation, since they have some leverage at that point. With a new act, like you, the record company is taking a gamble, and whether it's your lawyer or one of the high-priced big guns, the deal won't differ substantially. If, however, you listen to the heavy hitter's pitch and think that the deal you are currently being offered isn't a good one, you may want to consider involving the record-biz professional. Recall your conversations with the label. If you think you are being treated fairly and the deal is beneficial to you and your long-term career, don't let the attorney convince you that you are getting screwed and don't get greedy. If you become successful, you can always renegotiate your contract later (although some don't agree with this, my business philosophy has always been of the bird-in-the-hand type). If you would like to get more out of the company and decide to use the big gun to do it, work out your deal with the lawyer before he or she even goes near the record company on your behalf. It's hard to refuse to pay what the lawyer asks once he or she has made the deal.

Lawyers' fees aren't carved in stone, so find out how much money the lawyer wants to represent you and negotiate. Negotiating will do a couple of things for you: It may get you a better deal with the lawyer, and it lets you see how good a negotiator the lawyer is. Remember, negotiation isn't bullying; it's more like stern diplomacy. Also, don't let a deal drag on for too long. Make the point to your lawyer early that you want to close your deal within a reasonable amount of time. Sometimes deals drag on for so long that the record company simply loses interest. Don't waste time, and be sure your lawyer doesn't either; it's the most valuable commodity you have. Remember that you are the client and that you are entitled to information and action. It's hard work, but if you make the deal you want, it's worth it.

If you go to a large firm and the attorney with whom you first meet turns your project over to a student working at the office, make sure that your top man—the one you are paying the big money for—is making the decisions and that the student is just doing the legwork.

Don't let the firm shove you off to underlings because the big lawyers are too busy to deal with you personally. You are not paying for students, and their lack of experience could get you into trouble. You wouldn't let a medical student take out your appendix, would you? Well, a contract is even more serious. If the medical student blows it, you won't have anything to worry about—at all—ever. If a law student flubs it, you could be stuck in a horrendous contractual relationship, a fate much worse than death.

SEND LAWYERS, GUNS, AND MONEY

The "excitable boy" Warren Zevon made this request of the folks back home in what I consider to be one of his most entertaining songs. We've all felt like this at some point in our lives when we found ourselves in trouble that looked serious, at least to us.

No matter how careful you are, trouble may find you at some time in your career. A large part of your lawyer's job is to get you out of it. The most obvious trouble you have to get out of is being sued. A lawsuit, however, calls for a different kind of attorney than the deal makers about whom I've been talking. In a lawsuit you will need what is called a *litigation attorney*—one who is experienced in matters pertaining to the law and its relationships to contracts.

It's easy to be sued. In the music business somebody is always suing somebody for something. Generally, that something is some kind of breach of contract, and one thing is always the same: They are suing for *money*.

The plaintiff (injured party) always claims a loss of revenue arising from some situation or other and seeks payment for damages. If you change your booking agent or manager, miss a concert, fire your drummer, assign a song to a publisher for which you may not own all the rights, or refuse to deliver a finished recording to your label, you can be sued. Here's what to do:

1. Don't panic. Most people take one look at a lawsuit and go into shock. Usually you have thirty days to respond to the charges, and when you think about it, your reply will often clarify the matter, if only in your own mind.

2. Don't get angry. I know that sounds silly, but anger usually leads to some sort of foolish gesture that can only make the situation worse. When you receive the papers about the suit, call your lawyer and set up a meeting to discuss the problem. When you meet, tell your lawyer the facts as you remember them and bring any documents, letters, telegrams, or the like to support your case.

3. Don't alter the facts. You may be called on to testify in court, under oath. A lawsuit seeks financial damages; perjury—lying under oath—is a criminal offense that could put you in jail.

4. Let the lawyer handle it. The lawyer may suggest a counter-suit, that is, a suit filed by you against the party that is suing you. In this instance, you are saying that *you* are the party that has been wronged and are entitled to damages. Or, the lawyer may suggest a *settlement,* an offer from you to pay or in some way make good for the other individual's claims.

5. If you don't think you are in the wrong and your lawyer insists that you are, get a second opinion. It may cost a bit more, but the second lawyer may find something that the first attorney missed.

But let the lawyers do it. Don't go off and try to make war or peace with the party that is suing you. It doesn't work, and most times you just get yourself in deeper.

6. Stay in it; after all it's your case. Remember the story of the criminal lawyer whose client, after losing a Supreme Court appeal, said, "Well, counselor, where do we go from here?" and the lawyer replied, "You go to jail; I go to lunch."

Remember also that you can sue others if you feel the need to protect your rights. Do so carefully, however, because lawsuits take a lot of time, cost a lot of money, and should be undertaken only when all other actions fail. The toll that a court battle can take creatively and emotionally, not to mention financially, is seldom worth the outcome.

WHY USE A LAWYER AT ALL?

Why use lawyers at all? They're expensive and besides, the companies with whom you will be dealing—publishing, recording, booking, and management—know what they want from you and you know what you want from them, so why not just shake hands and get on with business together? Well, as we've already agreed, the world isn't perfect and because of that there are laws to protect both parties. Since these laws must be reflected in any business arrangements, the terms of the agreement must be written down.

It would be too complicated if each group of people decided to use their own form of agreement. Therefore, attorneys have adopted a set of standard practices in drafting of a contracts. In this way they save wear and tear on artists and executives by handling all the business details that go into an agreement between two parties.

In many instances, lawyers can also maintain an objective view of the situation, thus avoiding some of the ego or personality conflicts that could arise between an executive and an artist in a face-to-face confrontation over a contractual point.

As I said at the beginning of this section, lawyers provide a key service in the entertainment industry when they're employed wisely by their clients. There are, of course, disreputable individuals in all areas of business, and you must always be sure that all the details of your understanding are clear and within the law. If you try to maintain a good working knowledge of the business and combine it with the assistance of a conscientious attorney, the contractual aspects of your career should be as melodic as your music.

So that's the team: your manager, your agent, and your lawyer. Now you're ready to tackle the next steps of your career: the writing, publishing, and recording of your hit music.

WRITING HIT MUSIC

A song expresses emotion most if the person in the song is speaking. Then, as you write about the common ground you've been experiencing, you begin writing from the heart. You slowly realize it's not "them" you're writing about anymore. It's you.

—LITTLE STEVEN

No book can teach you how to write a song. Songwriting is something that you feel, not something that can be taught by books. But I can give you some inside tips on what makes a hit song that will get listened to by record companies and get played on the radio. To keep the marketplace supplied with hits, the music industry relies on hooks in songs. A *hook* is a repeated catchy melody, lyric, tempo, or rhythm that makes a song unique.

It isn't always easy to create a hook. You can write a melodic ballad or an up-tempo song that sounds great, and it may be great. But a hit song has that something extra that will keep it on the radio and in people's minds for years to come. If you are one of those lucky individuals like Paul McCartney, Phil Collins, or Bryan Adams whose musical minds are overflowing with hooks, then you are destined for a long and successful career as a songwriter. If you're like most people, however, you'll have to work hard to come up with the hook for each of your songs, and that means practice. Listen to music—on records, on the radio, live, or anywhere else that you can hear it—and try to pick out the hooks. Think back to your favorite songs and hum the part that you remember—that's the hook. Coming up with a commercial hook is often frustrating even for the best songwriters.

This leads to the second component of songs: lyrics. Lyrics must tell a story, relate an emotion, or exhort the listener to do something like sing or dance, while eliciting an emotional response from the listener as he or she relates to the song. Over the years I've received hundreds of tapes at record companies, and the bad songs all had one thing in common: meandering, almost meaningless lyrics that were usually cosmic or spacey. Phrases like "drifting through the cosmos of your mind" can only be comprehended after heavy sedation.

Keep your lyrics simple. The best lyrics are the ones that talk about universal themes to which everyone can relate: Falling in love, breaking up with a lover, jobs, how hard it is to get up in the morning, and how much fun it is to party all night. Look for an interesting hook and make your lyrics work for you. After you write them, either with or without music, read them out loud. Do they flow? Lyrics should roll off the tongue and should be melodic and musical themselves when read aloud. Try to put together phrases that will stick with people. Tell a story.

A lot of first-time songwriter's compositions are filled with clichés and trite phrases. Both weaken your songs. Be creative. If you're going to use a cliché, turn it around. If you are a country singer, for example, and are writing a song about hard times, you may want to say something like, "There's a light at the end of the tunnel, but it's probably an oncoming train." Bad rhymes also can weaken your lyrics. Buy a rhyming dictionary. The only word in the English language that doesn't have a rhyme is *orange* so there's no excuse. Don't neglect the words. They must be honed and crafted to fit perfectly with the music.

It's important to remember that a song, music and lyrics, is a single creation, a unit. It is important to keep this thought in mind when matching the two. Combining a lyric like "the warm glow in your eyes when I touch you" with a blistering guitar riff or putting "Baby let's rock and roll tonight" with a classical piano part, not only weakens the song but, in most cases, sounds downright ridiculous. Balance, rhythm, emotion, personality, and a hook are all the elements of a hit song.

EXPERIMENT

> *Sometimes the things I want are so out of synch with fashion. ... I've been in this business long enough to have bucked these things before. The difficulty is in holding your ground and maintaining confidence in your own ideas against unanimous expertise.*
>
> *—JONI MITCHELL*

Don't be afraid to experiment; just because a song starts out as a ballad doesn't mean that it has to stay a ballad. Try new tempos and rhythms that may better suit the instrumental riff with which you began.

Don't worry if you can't complete a song in one sitting. Paul McCartney tells a story about the song "Yesterday," in which he says that he had the melody line for weeks but just couldn't come up with a lyric. To practice and refine the song and keep the rhythm consistent, he found he had to sing some kind of lyric, so he chose the phrase "scrambled eggs," which he sang over and over again with the melody. The final lyric to "Yesterday" is a long way from "scrambled eggs," but if it wasn't for those eggs, one of the most successful Beatles' compositions might never have been created.

Write as much of the song as is comfortable in one session. Don't get angry or frustrated if all the ideas don't come to you right away. Make a rough cassette recording of it, jot down a few notes on paper, and then put it away. When you play the tape a few days later, chances are that you'll hear it differently and be able to make some progress.

There are many stories about songwriters who claim that they "just sat down and wrote the song." These stories are great in the press or in radio interviews, but instant songwriting doesn't happen often. Most songs are the product of many hours, days, and sometimes weeks of hard work.

REWRITE, REWRITE, REWRITE

One of my favorite fiction writers, Stephen King, once said, "Only God gets it right the first time." If you've written a good song, why not write a great one? Rewrites are the best way to ensure that you are comfortable with the final product and that it says what you want to say, in the particular way that you want to say it. When you finish a new song, put it on tape and then put the tape away for a while—a day, a week, a month, as long as you like—and then take it out and play it. I'm willing to bet that there will be at least one thing that you'll want to change.

Songs are like wine; they get better with age. Rewrite as many times as you like, always striving to turn the phrase a little better or to make a little more impact with a chord change or riff. Songwriting is an art and a craft, and you won't see a cabinetmaker tossing off a couple of pieces of furniture in an afternoon. Get it right. Your songs will be around for a long time, and there's nothing worse than hearing a song that you wrote and wishing that you had made just one little change that would have made it great. Once it's out there, it's hard to take it back.

Well, that's it. Pretty simple. No, not really, but if you pay attention, take your time, and craft your creations well, even if they never become hits, you'll still be proud that they're yours. (Although I will admit that if they become hits, it's a lot more fun.)

PUBLISHING YOUR MUSIC

The world of publishing can be incredibly complicated for the novice, and publishers often sound like they're speaking another language with phrases like *cover versions* and *compulsory licenses*.

More than in any other area of the business, you have to know the rules of publishing before you can even think about playing the game. Publishing is a delicate machine that must be approached carefully, with more than just passing familiarity.

At the turn of the century, publishing meant actually printing the notes on paper, creating sheet music of popular songs for people to play at home on their pianos or other instruments. The writer was paid for each piece of sheet music sold, and that's how the songwriter made money. Then modern science began to alter this relationship. Edison's gramophones and Victrolas made recorded music available to people who could not play an instrument themselves, by electronically reproducing music on wax cylinders or discs—the first records. Suddenly, a composer's music was selling in much larger quantities than before and some system had to be devised to pay the writer for these sales. I won't go into all the legal actions of the first fifty years of the 1900s, for even now, new laws are being drafted to protect songwriters.

Publishing was then expanded to include payment not only for sales of sheet music, but for sales of that song on cylinder or disc as well. Live performances, jukebox play, and radio airplay introduced many other areas of financial compensation for songwriters.

Today, "publishing" is taken to mean any money that is due a company or an individual for the sale, airplay, or performance use of a particular copyrighted song either, in part or in its entirety. In this section we'll look at what you can expect from a business relationship with a publisher and concentrate on what to do with your music once it's written, with publishing as a final goal.

COPYRIGHTS

One of the first things you'll have to think about is protecting the ownership of your song. Unless you register the song in some way, there's nothing to stop some crook from ripping you off by stealing your song and putting his own name on it, depriving you of the benefits of your talent and hard work. In publishing, as in any other business, there is a chance that you will be swindled, so you have to protect yourself, and the good news is that it's relatively easy to do so.

The United States government has made it simple and cheap to protect your songs from theft. It's called a *copyright*, which means that your words and music, as you wrote them, are registered in your name, and no one else can claim to have created that song either on purpose or by accident.

Copyright *infringement*, or the unauthorized use of your song, is punishable by law and carries with it a stiff fine. The U.S. courts enforce these laws, and you have a civil right under the law to sue an offender for damages. The U.S. copyright law is the strictest in the world, and there are serious penalties for violations. Among the most common copyright infringements of the past twenty years is *piracy*, the unauthorized manufacturing of records and cassettes. Pirates rob the music industry of millions of dollars of revenue each year. In many cases, the counterfeits are of such high quality that it is almost impossible to tell them from those that are legitimately produced. As the costs of producing a product and operating a record company increase, the lost profits from these counterfeit sales force the recording companies to raise the price of their products, in which way you, the consumer and the artist, are cheated by the counterfeiter.

Federal authorities in the United States have made a number of arrests and handled numerous prosecutions, but regrettably, in other countries where the copyright laws are not as strict, pirates cheat labels and artists out of millions of dollars each year. It stands to reason, then, that you want your copyrights registered in the United States, where your music will be afforded the greatest protection. To register a copyright for a song, you simply send an application form, which you can get by writing to the Copyright Office at the Library of Congress, and a copy of the song, that is, lyrics and music. The Copyright Office also accepts audiotapes, but you'll have to file a different form ("SR" for sound recording). Send two copies of the audiotape along with a sheet of paper on which you've written the chords and song lyrics. Since these tapes are put on file, make sure you send a copy, not your original.

A copyright is registered to protect a musical composition. This term includes original compositions consisting of music alone or of words and music combined. It also includes arrangements and other new versions of earlier compositions. *Musical compositions*, as defined by the Library of Congress Copyright Office, however, refer only to combinations of music and lyrics. Song poems or lyrics only cannot obtain a copyright as a musical compositions.

After you've obtained a copyright on a particular song, that song is yours to do with as you please. The copyright office allows you to publish copies, make new arrangements or versions of the song (which in some cases can also be copyrighted), perform it in public for profit, and make sound recordings of it, all of which are protected by your copyright. And if the song is recorded or performed for profit by anyone else, you are entitled to compensation.

Duration of a Copyright

A copyright begins on the date that a song is first published, but if the song is registered in an unpublished form, the copyright protection begins on the date that the song is registered. Look at it this way: If you write a song and don't intend to perform it in public or play it for anyone, then you need not register it right away. A copyright is good only for a certain period and has to be renewed. There's no need burning up time unnecessarily. A copyright lasts for the life of the author plus fifty years from the exact date that it is registered. After that the song becomes part of the *public domain*, that is, it can be recorded by anyone without royalty payment to you, the composer. In that case, the arrangement of the song can be copyrighted, and the arranger obtains payment for use.

How to Register Your Song

The first thing that you should do is to contact the Copyright Office in Washington, D.C., and obtain the proper form to register your piece or "musical composition." If you live outside the United States, be sure to tell the Copyright Office where you live and of what country you are a citizen, because there are different forms for different countries. For example, if you are an American citizen living in a foreign country, the form you use is different from the one used by a U.S. citizen living in the United States.

Once you've obtained the form by return mail and filled it out, you send it with a twenty-dollar fee and a lead sheet or two tapes to the Copyright Office (use a check or money order for two reasons: first, you can cancel it if it gets lost in the mail and second, if your song makes any money, you can write off the registration fee as a business expense on your taxes, so the check or money-order stub will serve as your receipt).

There are certain steps that you have to follow in submitting the song. If you send a lead sheet only, you have to write it out in some form of legible notation. Lyrics and chords are not enough; you need a melody line. If you don't read music, find a friend who can help you. Write the notes on music manuscript paper and put the words beneath the notes to which they are sung. This manuscript is called a *lead sheet,* and it is good for the registration of whatever material it contains. Remember, however, that you will file the lead sheet for an unpublished work and if there is a more complete version of the song after it has been published or recorded, you should send another lead sheet of the completed version to the Copyright Office to ensure that the new version is protected.

Second, the Copyright office does not consider a cassette or other tape or any other recording of the song to be a *copy,* and unless you send a Sound Recording form, two tapes, and a lyric-chord sheet with your submission, your application will be returned to you.

Finally, after you've sent your copy of the song, the application application form, and the fee to the Copyright Office, you will receive a certificate that is your proof that the song has been registered. After you obtain this certificate, no further action is necessary, and your song is protected from the rip-off artists.

Copyright Notice

Another way to protect your music is to use of the copyright notice. Understand that the Copyright Office in Washington does not grant or issue copyrights. Copyright protection is the protection of your musical compositions that the U.S. federal law provides, and all you have to do to obtain this protection is to announce publicly and prove that the musical composition that you claim is yours was created and made available by you at a certain time. As I just described, one way to do so is to register the copyright with the Copyright Office. If your material is published or if you release it in some form yourself, another way to do so is to print a copyright notice on your material.

A copyright notice is the small "c" in a circle with a name and a date after it that you see on the back of a cassette or compact disc or at the end of a television show or movie. Generally it looks like this:

© John Smith 1991

To secure copyright protection for your published work, you must make sure that this notice appears on your lead sheet and on the label and box of your tape. This is called a *statutory copyright notice*, which means that your work is protected by the statutes of the law governing copyrights. Remember, though, that this notice works only for published material, that is, reasonably large quantities manufactured and sold or distributed publicly. The idea here is that widespread distribution of your notice sufficiently advises the world of your claim. It doesn't really apply to demo tapes sent to publishers or record companies or to lead sheets that you may distribute to local bands or singers to try to get them to record your song because you haven't made enough of them to circulate them widely and to establish your claim of ownership, although it is advisable to use the notice nonetheless.

If you do publish the material, that is, if your song is recorded, manufactured and distributed, printed, or otherwise made available for sale and forget to include the statutory copyright notice, copyright protection is lost, and you can't add it later. For example, if you published copies of a particular song in July 1991 and forgot the notice and then reprinted it a year later in 1992 adding the notice © *John Smith 1991,* the Copyright Office would not view your copyright as having been in effect for that one-year period, and any claims that you might have against someone for unauthorized use during that time will not be considered.

Once a publishing company agrees to handle your material, it will take care of all the legalities to ensure your protection. In the meantime, while you are trying to make deals for your material, there's another form of protection that you may find useful if you don't want to spend the time and money to register the copyrights. Put a copy of your songs in "lead sheet" form and a tape and letter signed by you, dated and witnessed, into an envelope; seal the envelope, address it to yourself, and mail it by registered mail. When you get the envelope back in the mail, *don't open it!* Put it, and the receipt of registration, in a safe place. This interim form of protection for your music while you are showing it around is seen by the court as evidence of your ownership in a dispute with another songwriter. In fact, when you are addressing the envelope to yourself, the best way is to handwrite the address across the sealed flap of the envelope, rather than on the front as you normally would. In this way you can show a judge your uninterrupted pen strokes across the sealed flap, demonstrating that the signed and dated material inside is genuine and that your claim to the song predates that of the person with whom you are having the dispute. This method is not as good as a copyright, but it is a basic form of protection for you in the meantime.

MAKING A PUBLISHING DEAL

So now your music is on tape and protected. What next? Send your music to publishers, of course. But where do you find them? Well, the first place to look is in one of those handy music-industry sourcebooks, such as Album Network's *Yellow Pages of Rock* or the *Music Industry Sourcebook*. Another source is the local offices of ASCAP, BMI, or SOCAN, which publish newsletters containing lists of their member publishers.

Every major record company has a publishing division that is always looking for good songs. The record-company approach is a good one, particularly if you are interested in a recording contract; it is another way to have an audition.

Here are a few tips about the presentation of material to a publisher: If you are lucky enough to live in New York, Los Angeles, Toronto, Nashville, or London, where publishers have their headquarters, you've got a bit of a head start. You can contact the publishers' offices by telephone and try to arrange appointments.

If you are unfamiliar to the publishers, however, you probably will be told to send a tape of the material that you want them to consider. In most cases these tapes are reviewed by the publisher's staff whose job is to sort through the thousands of tapes (yes, thousands!) that are received each year and present the best ones to their superiors for consideration. Your job is to make the first cut. This is where your presentation is of utmost importance. As I said, thousands of tapes are reviewed each year, and it takes something special to make a tape stand out. That something special can be anything from a spectacular song to simply a good-quality tape.

Just bear in mind that listening to as much music as these staff members do each day is a tough job. They've heard just about everything that can be imagined, so you must be creative. Don't send a poorly recorded tape, with no song titles, lyrics, or letter to accompany it. This sounds obvious, but you'd be amazed at the number of tapes that are received this way. You don't need a twenty-four- or forty-eight-track digital recording, but just because you are selling your songs, not your band, doesn't mean you can get away with demos recorded on your boom box. A good-quality tape will enhance your chances of selling the song and, if this is your route to a recording deal, you want to make as good an impression as possible.

A brief letter with the song titles, containing your name, address, and telephone number, and a printed sheet of the lyrics is enough. You can send some additional information about yourself if you are a performer, but go easy. Publishers and record companies get hundreds of tapes each year that contain everything but the kitchen sink.

Put your best material on the tape and send it off to a few publishers. It's usually a good idea to start with something up-tempo. Put the songs on the label in the same order as they appear on the tape (it makes it easier for the listener). Be patient. The publisher isn't going to rush to the tape machine as soon as your tape arrives in the mail as if it were a new work by Madonna. Contact the publisher on a regular basis and politely check to see how things are going. Publishing is a business, and you have to treat it as such. Perseverance is the key. Even if you don't make it on the first tape, you are building relationships that will be of use to you for the rest of your musical career.

On the day when you finally capture the attention of a publisher, you will be asked to sign a publishing agreement for your material. That's the next step in your musical career.

PUBLISHING CONTRACTS

A publishing contract is an agreement between the songwriter and the publisher that outlines the rights, obligations, and benefits for each party with respect to the deal. It contains such things as *songwriter's warranties* (which has nothing to do with repairing a songwriter for free if he or she breaks down before twelve months or twelve thousand songs), *royalties, power of attorney,* and a lot of other great stuff. Of all the contracts that you will come across in your career, publishing agreements are among the most complicated. They are so partly because the publishing business itself is complicated and partly because the publishers and lawyers have made up a secret code to confuse the rest of us.

To explain publishing contracts and not take two hundred pages to do it, I'm going to have to oversimplify a little. But I think I'll be able to give you enough information so you'll be able to get the drift of what's going on.

There are two basic kinds of publishing agreements: a *song contract,* in which the publisher licenses the rights for one of your compositions from you, and a *writer's contract,* in which a publisher hires you to write songs for the company.

The contracts themselves are basically the same. They both include provisions for royalties, exclusivity, copyrights, and the like. They differ in the term of the agreement and the nature of the services rendered. Before I get into the actual contacts, however, I'll need to explain two things: the types of deals that exist and how a publisher looks at the percentages of ownership of a song.

Types of Deals

Within the two agreements I just mentioned (the song contract and the writer's contract), there are three subtypes of deals that cover how the ownership of the songs in your deal will be divided between you and the publisher:

1. A *writer's* deal, in which you will be paid 100 percent of the writer's share of the publishing royalties. Most new writers start with this one.

2. A *copublishing* deal, in which you will receive 100 percent of the writer's share and 50 percent (more or less) of the publisher's share of the publishing royalties. This deal is for more established writers.

3. An *administration* deal, in which the publisher acts as your collection agency and you agree to pay it a percentage of the publisher's share of the royalties (15, 20, or 25 percent is average). In this deal the publisher acts as a bank, advancing you money before it has collected it. (The reality of its percentage is this: If the publisher gets 20 percent, only 3 or 4 percent is its profit, and the rest represents interest charges on the money that has been advanced to you.) This type of deal is usually reserved for writers with an active catalogue of songs or records.

How a Publisher Looks at Percentages

In publishing, the percentage of ownership rights of a song adds up to 200 percent: 100 percent for the writer's share and 100 percent for the publisher's share. For example, if you are a songwriter and you co-write a song with a friend, you could share the writing credit in one of the following ways: (1) If you write the music and your friend writes the lyrics, you each get 50 percent of the writer's share; (2) if you write the music and part of the lyrics, you get 75 percent of the writer's share and your friend gets 25 percent; or (3) if you write all the music and most of the lyrics and your friend contributes only a line or two, you get 90 percent and your friend gets 10 percent. As you can see, there are many ways to split up the writer's share.

On the publisher's side, the examples are the same. Let's say that you make a copublishing deal in which your own company shares the publisher's share with the publisher. Your split could be 50 percent–50 percent or any other combination that would add up to 100 percent of the publisher's share between the two of you. These splits, between writers and publishers, are the ones that will affect how you will be paid, no matter what kind of contract you have with the publishing company—a writer's deal or song contract.

The Song Contract

The basis for the single-song contract is that the writer is licensing the song to the publisher, and the publisher is going to try to get the song recorded or performed, collect the royalties, and pay a share of those royalties to the writer. In this agreement, the publisher is acquiring rights from the writer, which it will exploit for their mutual profit.

Assignment of Copyright

The contract will contain a clause in which the writer assigns all copyrights for the song and any extensions or renewals of the copyrights to the publisher throughout the world, in exchange for the royalties that the publisher has agreed to pay. This means that the publisher will do all the paperwork required to register the copyrights for the writer with the Library of Congress.

Also in this clause, the writer allows the publisher to renew the copyright on the writer's behalf and assigns the renewed copyright to the publishing company, along with the rights to make money from the copyrighted song throughout the world. This agreement guarantees that the publisher will have control of the song for the duration of the original contract period and throughout all renewals.

The copyright question is a hard one. After watching all his early material, which is published by Northern Songs, go to Michael Jackson, who promptly sold off the Beatles' classics for TV commercials, Paul McCartney warned, "Never give up your copyrights." The bottom line is that Paul is right. If you can hang on to the copyrights of your songs, it is definitely the best way to go. But it is also the hardest way. Any publisher who offers you a contract will insist on owning the copyrights, so if you want to do the deal, you'll have to compromise, at least early in your career.

One thing to remember is that copyright ownership is not about money; it's about control. Even though you may transfer copyright ownership, you must be compensated and you never give up the right to make money from your songs. But it's the control issue that is paramount in some songwriters' minds. If you don't want your songs in commercials, for example, you lose that control when you assign the ownership of the copyright to a publisher. But your lawyer can, and should, insert language in the contract that stipulates certain uses that must be approved by you, even though the publisher controls the copyrights. The music business has changed a lot in the past ten years or so, and such language in agreements is not uncommon.

Songwriter's Warranties

In the third paragraph of the sample contract that I am using, the writer warrants to the publisher that he or she is the original writer of the song, either in whole or with a partner; that the song is original and not a copy or derivation of anyone else's work; and that the writer has not assigned the rights to the song to any other third party or sold or tied up the rights in any other way. What the publisher is looking for here is protection against some of the abuses of years gone by. One of the old blues legends in New Orleans made the rounds of the publishers selling his songs. Several of them liked one particular song, so he sold it to them. To all of them. Exclusively. Each publisher gave him a contract that he signed, and each gave him an advance. The publishers finally found out that they had been swindled, but the blues singer was long gone. And the best part of the story is that it wasn't even his song. He had stolen it from another bluesman. Publishers now make you warrant that it is your song and that you haven't licensed or sold it or even pledged it as collateral for a loan to anyone, so they can be sure that it comes to them free and clear.

Royalties

This is my favorite part of all contracts, the money part. In the royalties paragraph and its subsections, the royalty structure for the song is outlined. It usually goes something like this:

1. The songwriter receives an amount for the sale of sheet music, usually about 5 to 10 percent of the wholesale price of the sheet music. The contract stipulates that the publisher does not have to pay the royalty on any copies given away for promotion or for which the publisher does not receive payment.

2. The songwriter receives a royalty amount for payments for any mechanical reproduction of the song. Thus, any time the song is recorded and manufactured on tapes or compact discs or in any other way, the writer receives a royalty payment for each unit manufactured. This is called a *mechanical royalty.*

3. The royalty clause also stipulates that the writer will receive performing-rights royalties directly from the performing-rights society (ASCAP or BMI) of which he or she is a member, with no percentages deducted by the publisher.

It is usually in the royalty section that the percentages due each writer in a co-writer situation are spelled out. Each writer agrees that the song is composed of parts that are dependent on one another and cannot be split up, and all the writers agree to be bound by the terms of the contract. This agreement avoids the problem of one writer in a co-writing situation turning up at a later date claiming more money or trying to prove that an instrumental version of the song, if he or she is the writer of the music, isn't covered by the contract.

The accounting periods for the payment of royalties are usually twice a year. The publisher sends out a royalty statement for all the uses of the song, along with a check for royalties. Generally, if you have a problem with the accounting, you have one year to challenge the publisher. If you wait more than a year, you lose your right to audit or file any claim against the publisher. So royalty statements must be reviewed as soon as you get them if you believe that there may be a discrepancy.

Name and Likeness
Somewhere in the agreement, the publisher receives the right to use your name and likeness in the promotion of the song. What this means is that you grant to the publisher the right to promote the particular song or the fact that you are signed to that company. It's all targeted at getting your material recorded. There is little harm in this clause until you become relatively well known, at which time you may want to exert a certain amount of control over this

use so as not to be overexposed. In any event, it's a good idea to ensure that the contract specifies what uses the publisher wants and to grant only those in the agreement.

Use of the Song
In this clause the publisher's right to exploit the copyright in any manner is detailed. If you have a specific way in which you don't want the song used, you have to deal with it here. If your song is about flying, for example, and your publisher decides to let the U.S. Air Force use it in an enlistment commercial and you have strong antimilitary feelings, there is nothing you can do to stop the publisher if you have left this clause in the agreement. So deal with this one carefully if you think there is any manner in which you may not want the song used and specify it.

Expenses
The clause that deals with expenses defines "net sums" paid to you as being "gross income" received less any costs incurred by the publisher in the collection of royalties, costs for subpublishing agreements, or any other charges which the publisher can deduct according to the contract. What the publisher is not allowed to deduct, however, is overhead, that is, his phones, fax, rent, staff, and the like. So take a look at your statements and if you see any deductions for those or similar costs, take it up with your manager, who should then take it up with your publisher right away.

Indemnities
In every contract that you will sign, you'll find a section on indemnities. An indemnity is your promise that you will protect the other party from any damage it may suffer because of your actions or lack of action. In this clause, the writer indemnifies the publisher against any legal actions that may arise out of any breaches of the warranties made by the writer in the contract. For example, if you say that you are the sole writer of the song and it gets published and recorded and becomes a hit and someone suddenly sues the publisher for royalties claiming to be the co-writer, you as the writer have to reimburse the publisher for all costs if it turns out that

the suit is justified and you did collaborate on the song. On the other hand, if the publisher decides to sue a third party for infringing on the rights granted to it of your material, the publisher agrees to indemnify you by paying the costs of the actions and to pay you (customarily) 50 percent of any money recovered in the lawsuit. This clause goes on to state that if others sue you and the publisher for infringing on their copyright, the publisher has the sole right to settle the claim and can withhold royalties from you during the suit, pending the outcome. If you are proved guilty of wrongdoing, the publisher will pay any settlement and court costs out of your royalties and deduct them from payments to you. The George Harrison case for the song "My Sweet Lord" was settled out of court by Harrison and his publisher with the publishers of the sixties hit "He's So Fine," which a judge ruled was close enough to Harrison's song to constitute infringement. Indemnities exist to protect the contracting parties in the event that their partner in the contract has misrepresented any of their rights or promises.

Assignment of Contract

Most contracts also give the person or company with whom you are signing the deal the right to transfer the contract to some other person or company. In the case of a songwriting or publishing contract, the publisher will want the right to assign the agreement. It does so not only to be able to assign it to another publisher in the case of a merger or buyout, but so that it can assign the copyrights to the bank as collateral on a line of credit to run the company. This is standard language and unless your lawyer comes up with a good reason to advise you otherwise, assignment of the contract is generally acceptable.

Breach

Almost everyone enters into a contract intending to do what he or she is expected to do. Then, reality rears its ugly head, and sometimes people either can't or won't honor the terms of the agreement. This is called a *breach* of the agreement. Most contracts contain a clause called the "breach-cure" clause. Every publishing contract has one, and it basically says that if the writer says that the publisher did not fulfill some part of the agreement, the publisher has a period of time to correct the problem, if it can be done, from the date of written notice of the breach. If the publisher doesn't cure the breach (fix what's wrong), the contract should be terminated. However, most publishing agreements contain a line in which the writer acknowledges that no breach of the agreement by the company is incurable. That is true; no breach is incurable, but be sure that by acknowledging this fact you do not prejudice yourself in the event that the publisher does not correct the problem in the allotted time. Also, make sure that you get the same amount of time to fix any claim of breach against you by the publisher. Sometimes companies give themselves sixty days to do so but give you only ten days. Be sure that you get the same deal that you are expected to give the publisher.

Advances

In this section of the agreement the advance schedule is outlined for the writer. On signing, the writer usually receives a nonrefundable advance that is recoupable against royalties, which means that when the song begins to earn money the publisher retains the royalties you would normally be paid until the advance is paid back. The amount of this advance will depend on the writer's track record in the marketplace. If you are a new writer, it may only be a few hundred dollars. If you have a track record of hits, it could be several thousand dollars. A second advance should be paid when the first commercial recording of the song is released. This advance is usually a little larger than the first one. And, finally, there is a bonus schedule based on the *Billboard* singles chart. When the record gets on the Hot 100 Singles Chart, for example, you may receive another advance. And you may receive further advances when it hits the top fifty, the top ten, and number one.

Other Stuff

The rest of the contract is what is called *boilerplate*, that is, the legalese of the contract. This is basic legal language, and your attorney will deal with it. In some cases your attorney may want the contract to be subject to the laws of a different state if he or she believes that you can get a better deal in court if you have a dispute. These issues are important, but are not as much a part of the business of songwriting as they are the business of lawyers.

So you see, a publishing agreement is a pretty straightforward contract, not too tricky. However, it does contain a lot of concepts and language specific to the publishing industry, and your lawyer should review it closely to ensure that you are getting what you and the publisher agreed on when you made the deal in the first place.

The Writer's Agreement

The writer's agreement is designed for those musicians who are not interested in performing or recording, but have decided to make their living from creating songs for others to record and perform. Bernie Taupin, Elton John's co-writer, is just this kind of musician. Although he released an album in the seventies, he prefers to remain in the background as a writer, rather than as a performer.

Most of the terms of the writer's agreement are the same as those of the song agreement, with a few exceptions. First, it is primarily an employment contract in which the writer goes to work for the publisher to write songs.

The writer agrees to write a specified number of songs each week, month, or year. The publisher then automatically owns the copyright to those songs and works to get them recorded. In return, the publisher agrees to pay the writer a salary, which is actually an advance on royalties.

That's it. Nothing to it, right? Well, as I said, don't mess around with publishing. Your songs, as Prince says, are "your creations, your children," and if you want those children to take care of you in your old age, don't go signing the rights to them away now. Protect your music; it is your *most* important asset.

Movie and TV Music

Getting your music into a movie or a hit TV show is easy—a piece of cake. Just like climbing Mount Everest. You know, all you have to do is ... you know ... climb it. Well, doing it can be tricky, and it's usually your publisher that will be doing the doing.

Movies and TV shows used to consider music to be simply background for the action and not really important. Unless it was an Elvis movie or some other obvious teenage film, music didn't really matter much. It wasn't always like that, of course. Throughout the forties and fifties, *musicals,* usually film adaptations of hit Broadway shows, were big box-office draws. In the late fifties and sixties, teen exploitation films became the rage, and Frankie Avalon and Annette Funicello sang and surfed their way up and down the coast of California. Around the end of the sixties, most Hollywood movies (nonmusicals) relied on orchestral music for themes. Meanwhile TV was content to use game show–style music for just about everything.

But in the late seventies several films capitalized on the teen-genre concept, and movie soundtracks began to become big business again. Now, hardly a movie gets made without at least a few big-name hits from which to create a soundtrack. Anyway, as I said before, it's usually your publisher that gets the call for material for a film. If you've been lucky enough to make an album and it got some airplay, your publisher may get a call from a film-production company or TV show asking for a license to use one of your songs in its production. In this case, your publisher will charge a straight fee for the use of your song. This fee is called a *synchronization license,* that is, the right to synchronize your song with the production. This is the same kind of license that must be obtained to make a video of the song. Any time you join the song with pictures, you need a "synch" license. And each time you set it to a different set of pictures, you need to reapply for a synchronization license. This is obviously good for you, the songwriter, in that, whoever wants to set your music to pictures has to pay for the privilege. In some cases, you'll also receive performing-rights money, especially for TV broadcasts, which can amount to a substantial sum for use on a network TV show. All the publishing rights stay the way they are; all the film or TV company gets is the right to use the song.

If the movie studio or production company intends to do a soundtrack album, then your publisher will have to negotiate those rights to ensure that you get paid a prorata (prorated) share of the royalties. For example, if there are ten songs on the soundtrack, you will receive one-tenth of the royalties if your publisher has arranged something called a *favored-nations* clause in your contract. This clause means that no other artist on the soundtrack gets a higher royalty rate or, more correctly, that if another artist is getting a higher rate, you automatically receive an equivalent rate. So, if you and Bruce Springsteen end up on the same soundtrack, you both will get the same royalty rate if you have a favored-nations deal. Sometimes a movie or TV company will want an original song for its film or program. In this case, you will be offered an amount of money to make the recording, as well as an amount equal to a licensing fee.

You should be ready for a few things here. First, the movie or TV company will probably want to have a lot of input into the writing and recording of the tune. Since it has a specific use in mind and is paying for the recording, you should be prepared to cooperate with the company. Second, the company will probably want some kind of split on the publishing percentages. This is the norm for the business, and you should simply make the best deal possible. A third case may or may not affect you directly, but more and more writers are finding that the world of jingles and soundtracks (the instrumental background music that you hear in films) can be lucrative. If you are familiar with a variety of synthesizers, emulators, and drum machines, then you can create the sounds of an orchestra in your own home. This kind of soundtrack work is particularly attractive to film companies, which can save a bundle if they can get the same music from one keyboard player that they used to have to pay an orchestra for.

In all, movie soundtracks and TV work are a good way to bring in some extra money and can be financially rewarding in themselves. Be sure that your publisher is active in these areas in addition to the regular business of trying to have your songs recorded by other artists. There's money to be made, and maybe you'll even get a chance to write the theme song of Rocky XXV.

Performing Rights Organizations

A performing rights organization does just what its name implies. It grants to night clubs, radio and television stations, concert halls, and any other outlet that uses live or recorded music the right to do so. In return for this right, these outlets pay an annual fee to the performing rights organizations, which is then divided among all the composers whose material was reported as being used during one of the annual accounting periods.

As you can imagine, this is a colossal bookkeeping task, so the organizations have devised a system in which music used at specific times in specific places is *logged,* that is, written down on an official reporting form supplied by the organization. The log contains the name of the composition, its composer, and the publisher who published it. With the aid of computers (if you can believe it, this job was previously done by hand) and a complex formula, the organization decides which composers are to be paid, and how much they are to receive, in an equitable fashion.

Performing rights organizations account individually to the publisher and to each person involved in a song's creation. For example, if you wrote the lyrics to a song and your friend wrote the music, then you would receive a check for the *writer's share* of the performing rights royalties of that song for its use in public performance on the radio, on TV, or in a concert, and your friend would receive the other share. This direct accounting is done to eliminate a situation in which one person or company could withhold money from another and to ensure that there is an equitable distribution of funds.

The performing rights organizations in North America are ASCAP (United States), BMI (United States), SESAC (United States), and SOCAN (Canada). If you are a songwriter, you should definitely be a member of one of these organizations, or you run the risk of losing potential income from the public performance of your work. Generally, a performing rights organization will ask you to sign a contract for a five-year period at the end of which the contract is renewed automatically for an additional five years unless you advise the organization otherwise. Also, should you decide to form a music publishing company, you should register it with a performing rights organization, for, as I have already said, publishers also derive income from the public performance of material that has been signed to them.

Songs are registered to a performing rights organization by title only, and each new composition that you write should be registered with the organization just before it is performed live or recorded and released on record. The key words here are *performed live or released.* Some organizations do not register your compositions unless they will definitely be performed or released. As you can imagine, if the performing rights organization were to register every one of the millions of songs that were submitted, the paperwork for all the songs that would never see public performance would be an astronomical waste of time and money—money that rightfully belongs to those artists whose material is being performed. Also, don't be confused here. Registering your song title with a performing rights society is not a copyright and affords you no legal protection against having your composition stolen. Performing rights organizations register the titles of your songs only so the songs can be reported and used as a basis for determining royalty payments.

Here's an example of how these organizations work. ASCAP monitors important radio and television stations at random on a year-round basis. Because the big stations in major cities pay ASCAP more money each year for the use of music, they are monitored more frequently to determine how the fees that they collect will be distributed among ASCAP members. BMI methods are different, but the object is the same—to monitor broadcasters that use music so that the creators of the music can be compensated.

The organization then goes to your file to see how many times you have been listed and to determine what percentage of the money collected should be yours. It uses a point system, which assigns a value to different kinds of performance. Once it has determined how much of the pie is yours, it will check the files again to see if you have taken any advances on these royalties.

That's right, if you have a proven track record of earning money, you may, in some situations, be able to get the money in advance. The organization will then deduct these amounts from money owed to you at an accounting period. The nice part about these advances is that they are interest free. Don't get excited, though, for if the most money that you have ever earned through public performance is fifty bucks, you're not going to get a fifty-thousand-dollar advance. You could, however, get fifty bucks, and that, after all, is a start.

RECORDING YOUR DEMO TAPE

On the best albums we had all the songs down before
we went in and recorded them. If you leave some
space, you can write in the studio, but you have to
have the framework.

—*JOE PERRY,*
AEROSMITH

Ever since Thomas Edison invented the phonograph, people have been trying to get themselves recorded. "Making music" has become "making music that the public can hear, buy and appreciate." Over the years the recording industry has grown by leaps and bounds, and today it is a worldwide multi-billion-dollar business. And it is a business that relies on a combination of art and science to be successful. Making recordings has become an incredibly sophisticated and expensive process, as the recording industry competes to keep up with the high-quality reproduction technology of DAT and compact discs. From the artist's side it is also a business that happens in stages. Artists' first recordings are different from the recordings they make once they become successful, both in technical quality and cost, but every artist has to start somewhere, and that somewhere is usually at the beginning.

In the fifties, sixties, and seventies, demo tapes were usually primitive, made on four- or eight-track machines, and did little more than give listeners a rough idea of what they could expect from a finished master. Today, however, the state of the art is such that demo tapes are, in most cases, better than the quality of the master tapes that were used to manufacture the phonograph records of the fifties and sixties. Now you can have a multitrack tape machine, a computer, and midicontrolled keyboards in your home and can produce master-quality recordings in your own living room. Incredibly, these multitrack machines have the capability far beyond the studio machines that were used for the early recordings of the Beach Boys, Rolling Stones, and Beatles. Now I'm not suggesting that you should expect to go off and record *Rubber Soul* this afternoon. I'm only suggesting that the quality of technology available to you offers you an opportunity to make high-quality demo tapes to get your music heard.

Home recording, however, is just that—a way of working up your material to get it ready for real recording in a studio. Sure, we've all heard stories of artists who made their demos in a garage or basement or the case of Michelle Shocked, who made her album on a Walkman in a field by the highway. But that's the exception, not the rule, and in the real world it works differently.

The best way to record anything, of course, is in a recording studio. The experience of recording demos in the studio is much the same as is it for recording at home, the difference being that the technical aspects are attended to by the professionals, and your job is to produce a good-quality musical product. Here your nerves are your worst enemy, and, if you allow them to control you, your chances of coming out of the session with something of which you'll be proud are somewhere between slim and none. So the first thing you have to do is to relax and enjoy the experience.

But just how long should it take you to record your demo? I'm afraid there is no single answer. But there are some guidelines and some tricks. Your engineer is key. Find one with imagination, who is willing to go against conventional wisdom. I've heard people say that if you are going to use "live" drums, a sixteen-track session is barely enough. This is true only if your engineer won't lay down the drums first, mix them down to two tracks, keep the kick drum and the snare separate, and open up twelve tracks for the rest of your instruments and vocals. Remember, this is a *demo*, not a master, and all you should be aiming for is high-quality sonics that showcase your strengths. If you try to duplicate a $200,000 session with a $10,000 budget, you will fail. But, through ingenuity and high-quality engineering, you can accomplish what you need to do to represent yourself properly to any label.

Following a few basic rules will make your first professional recording go a lot smoother. As an example, let's talk about a demo session that is booked at a local recording facility. Later I'll talk about how to economize to get your demo done for a minimum investment.

• Your first task is to find a good studio at a reasonable rate. Check your local telephone Yellow Pages and call some studios. These calls should provide you with a basic list of studios in your area and a good idea of the price range. Check with other local musicians and discuss their studio experiences, good or bad. Visit the studios you are considering until you find the one with the best deal and where you are most comfortable.

• "Don't panic." To get over your nerves, visit the studio a week before your session and get to know the place. Meet the engineer who you'll be working with and have a brief conversation with him about what you'll try to do in your session. Look over the facilities, decide where you're going to set things up, and talk to the engineer about the setup. Just try to do as much advance work as possible, so the place is familiar to you when you start your session.

• Ask the studio manager if you can listen to some of the other tapes that have been recorded there. He should be glad to play them for you and discuss your project. If not, go elsewhere because the lack of interest in you as a client and a musician will probably carry over to your session and to the way the studio is run.

• Check the studio's maintenance record. You don't need the studio breaking down in the middle of your session. Also check whether the studio is available for an extra day or two after you are scheduled to be finished. Recording sessions usually go over the allotted time, and it's nice to be able to finish the next day instead of having to wait a week until the studio is available again.

Once you've found a studio that's to your liking, you're ready to book your session. Booking is more than simply finding a block of time that is convenient. You're going to be making music and you don't want to do it unless you are at your best. Don't book your session at the end of your workday. Even if you don't feel tired, you may not have the emotional and physical reserves necessary to pull off a stellar performance. Book your session on your day off. Three songs, if rehearsed, will take you about ten to twelve hours to record, including about two hours to set up, six hours to record the tracks, and four hours to mix, although you can always come back on another day to finish your mixes if you run out of time.

Make it clear to the engineer how much time and money you can spend and how much material you want to record. Don't be embarrassed to be on a budget. Even the biggest stars have financial limits on their recordings. In this way, the engineer will have the same goals as you and won't unknowingly waste a lot of time going for a particular kind of guitar sound. Then practice; get everything down so well that you can do it in your sleep. Remember, at fifty bucks or more an hour, the studio is not a place to rehearse. If you need to make a change in the song in the middle of your session, stop the session and work out the change. Bands often fool around endlessly with a minor alteration instead of concentrating on the song and waste hours of valuable studio time on one simple musical revision. Keep focused and keep to your plan. Then you'll be able to maintain a momentum that will carry you through a successful session.

Once you've established your studio plan, the rest is up to you. Again, going into the studio fully rehearsed, with some notes about the songs, and discussing the project with the engineer before the session are the keys to a successful studio experience and to making a high-quality demo tape, one of the most important tools of your career.

DEMO RECORDING ON A BUDGET

I've been in studio situations and I can't understand,
even if you have the money, why on earth anyone
would want to spend $300 an hour to play Pac-Man.

—KRAMER,
PRODUCER, AND OWNER OF
SHIMMY-DISC RECORDS

Well, now you know the basics of getting a demo recording done,
let's talk a little about how to get it done cheap. First, the disclaimer, "You only get what you pay for." But "pay" is a relative
term. Because there's another old saying, "Only an idiot pays
retail." There's always a deal to be made and, like my old daddy
used to tell me, "Son, you're born and you die; everything else is a
negotiation." So here are a few ways to negotiate yourself to an
economical yet high-quality demo session.

•*Downtime.* Every studio has downtime, that is, time between
sessions, late at night, or early in the morning, when no one else
wants to record. During these periods, the studio usually does
maintenance or just sits empty. Studio time is a lot like airline
tickets, once the plane leaves the ground they never again have the
chance to sell the empty seats. Once the downtime hours pass, the
studio can never get them back to sell. So, if you offer to work your
session around the studio's schedule, you may find that you can
make an attractive deal. This kind of deal means that you may
have to pull a few all-nighters or be prepared to change your plans
at a moment's notice to play a session. But the upside of obtaining
a high-quality demo at half the price or less should be worth it to
you.

•*Work at a studio.* In addition to engineers and tape operators
and such, studios also need runners, secretaries, and general help.
These jobs don't pay much, but they give you an opportunity to
hang around the studio, become familiar with the management,
and begin to book some downtime to make your recordings either

in lieu of payment for your work or because the manager thinks your music is good. Whichever, you are in the studio making music. This approach has an added benefit of allowing you to become more familiar with the technical aspects of the studio, which will allow you to approach your project from a different perspective.

•*High schools and colleges.* Many high schools and colleges have recording facilities as part of their communications or recording courses. You can usually arrange to use these facilities at no charge in exchange for allowing students in these courses to experiment with your recordings. It may take a little longer, and you may end up taking your rough tracks to a professional facility to be mixed, but it is worth it if you can save substantial money on laying down your basic tracks.

•*Radio stations.* There are two ways that radio stations can help. The first is for you to participate in some kind of station-sponsored concert activity. If the station has a beach party or a fund-raiser at a club, volunteer to play for free if the station brings recording gear to record your set. Most stations have a mobile facility that can make live recordings; if not, they can probably do a deal with a local studio to get one. Granted this will be a live tape, but like the school route, you can always take the basic tracks to a studio to sweeten and remix them. By the way, a live tape is sometimes preferable to a clean studio tape, especially if you had a large and good crowd, if your band is particularly good live, or if the kind of music you play is conducive to live recording.

Tell the station people that you want to make a demo tape to try to get a record deal, and you'll be surprised at the response you get. Not only will the station most likely do the deal with you, but if the tape turns out well, its staff will probably be willing to help you get it to the labels. In addition, if the tape is of good quality, they may give it a few spins on the radio to get reactions from listeners or disk jockeys. These local radio people can be an enormous asset to your career, and you should get to know them as well as possible, as soon as possible.

Another way that radio stations can help you is through what are called "homegrown" contests. In many markets, local stations hold talent competitions each year to create an album of local talent for sale for charity in their city. The station asks local bands to submit demo tapes and chooses ten from among all those submitted to go on the record. The top two or three acts usually receive a block of time at a local recording studio as a prize. The number of tapes that the stations receive may appear daunting at first, but many of them are from rank amateurs and are discounted immediately. If your band is hot and you can put together a good one-song demo, you have a chance to win the contest and get the studio time. The bonus is that the first prize of studio time is usually accompanied by cash and a possible record release—a pretty big prize for an aspiring artist or band. So the homegrown contest is another opportunity.

•*TV stations*. Another way to get your demo tape is through local TV stations. Each year most stations look for local talent to appear in their annual charity telethons. If you are an unrecorded act with a small following, your slot will probably be in the middle of the night, but it doesn't matter because you are there to make a recording, not a TV appearance. Talk to the organizers and ask if they will run tape while you play. You will need your own sound engineer in the booth with the audio mixer because the recording will probably be in mono or, at best, in two-track stereo, so there will be no chance to repair it later—what goes on the tape is what you get. If the recording is good, you'll get not only audio but video, which can be used in a variety of ways to get your record deal.

•*Grants*. Don't forget about arts grants. Most local and state governments and even the federal government provide grant money for arts projects. Although you (and possibly they) may not look at your three-piece metal band as art, you have as much right to the grant money as does any dance company or painter. Find out about these grants and apply for one. If you get it, congratulations. If you don't, you can contact your local newspaper and make a stink about how the government discriminates against rock and roll, and at least you'll get some press out of it. Either way you win.

These are just some of the ways that you can get recorded on a budget. The key is to keep your eyes and ears open and seize any opportunity to be recorded. Putting together a good library of tapes early in your career allows you to refine your material, as well as have some representation of yourself besides your live show.

WHAT IS A DEMO TAPE?

There are a few things about a demo that should always be kept in mind by anyone who sets out to make one. First, demos are not masters; otherwise they'd be called masters. And if you try to make a master with a demo budget, you will be shooting yourself in the foot, which, in the event that you have never done it, hurts like hell. When you begin your demo session, bear in mind what you're setting out to do: To put down on tape a good representation of the song that you would ultimately like to record. Bryan Adams put it like this: "When you send a demo to somebody you are saying, 'Here's a really good example of how good this song could be.'" Notice what Bryan did not say was: "This is *exactly* what this song will sound like on record." Don't try to make your demos sound too much like records. One complaint that I hear a lot from A & R people at labels is that many bands seem to be auditioning as producers, rather than as musicians.

Because you just don't have the budget, an overproduced demo always sounds like nothing more than an overproduced demo. So here are a few things to focus on when making your demos:

•Keep it simple. Your arrangements should be straightforward, so the listener gets a clear idea of the song structure. If you muck them up with a lot of overdubs, harmonies, and such, the focus can be lost, and the listener with it.

•Get the lead vocal up front. On a demo you normally put the lead vocal more up front than you might on a record. You want the listener to understand the words and to hear the lead vocal clearly. If you want to add some effects to the lead vocal, be sure they make the vocal stand out, rather than muddy it up or allow it to fall back into the mix.

•Feature the hook. Don't have so many parts in the song that the listener has to try to figure out what the hook is. If you want to have an intro, fine, but not a two-minute orchestral piece. The KISS rule is best here: "Keep it simple, stupid!"

•Limit the effects, overdubs, and guitar, bass, or drum solos. It won't hurt to include a short solo, but a demo is not the place to ego out. You're trying to sell the label a well-written, well-performed song with a tight arrangement.

•Have an arrangement. If you do one thing on your demo, find yourself an arranger and have him or her create a simple, straightforward but economical arrangement. The song should have a beginning, a middle, and an end. It should have distinguishable parts and a sense of purpose and direction. All these things will come from a good arrangement.

•Don't be cute. Outtakes, talk-back, messages, and the like have no business on your demo, unless it was recorded at a live gig. Just include the music. Save the other stuff for your album.

•Finally, I don't think I have to say this, but I'll say it anyway. Be accurate and good. You can't fix anything in the mix. If you sing flat, fix it. If you missed a note in a solo, fix it. A sloppy tape is a bad way to start a relationship with anyone, particularly a record label. If you think they won't hear it, you're wrong.

IMAGE

The craziness is in large part a myth which is as much the press's creation as my own. It's easy for a writer to go "Oh yeah, the guy who vomits and breaks pencils and rolls in glass and bites hot dogs, etc., etc." I don't really think that reflects the mood of the real people who actually come to see the show.

—IGGY POP

WHAT IS IMAGE?

Image is an important part of any performer's career, and it's never too soon to begin learning how to make it work to your advantage in the press. It is hard to define image exactly. The easy answer is that it is how your look, music, personality, and attitude come together to communicate something to your audience. The dictionary defines *image* as "a representation, a likeness." But that definition doesn't really capture what an image represents or, more important, how to create one. What is easy to identify and distinguish are those images that are genuine from those that are manufactured. It's pretty obvious that the images of Bruce Springsteen, Sting, Phil Collins, Peter Gabriel, and Bonnie Raitt are genuine. These stars walk the walk and talk the talk. Their images are who they are, and they come from many years of working in the business on their own terms. New Kids on the Block, Tiffany, and even superstar Michael Jackson are, to a large extent, "image creations" (or Teenage Mutant Ninja images, as I like to call them) whose public personalities have been carefully assembled or created to suit a specific approach.

I'm not saying that there is anything wrong with creating an image, especially if it works, as long as the artist is a willing participant. The difference between the two groups of artists I just mentioned is that the image creations sometimes go wrong when the artist's real personality starts to emerge. A case in point is some of the activities in which the New Kids on the Block engaged during their 1991 tour. Allegations of slugging female fans and burning down hotels are clearly not what their managers had in mind when they created the squeaky-clean image of this group. With artists like Bruce Springsteen, Bonnie Raitt, or Sting, you don't have the same risk. They have always been the same people from day one, so nothing changes, and whatever they do is usually consistent with who they are.

The images of another group of artists are contrived, but contrived by them so cleverly that the images are nothing short of brilliant. David Bowie and, of course, the most incredible image creation of them all, Madonna, put on images and take them off about the same way that you and I change our socks. And yet, through all their image transformations, the element of artistry that is unique to them shines through.

Image, then, is the public persona that an artist develops to set himself or herself apart from other artists and, it is hoped, a vehicle for communicating the artist's musical message better. (I'm starting to sound like a textbook here, but you get the idea.)

WHERE DO YOU FIND AN IMAGE, AND WHO DECIDES WHAT IT WILL BE?

The first question is, Where do I get one of them there image things? My best advice is to start with who you and your band really are, both as people and as musicians. If you are crazy, funny, and energetic, then your image should reflect these qualities. If you are more serious, are politically and environmentally concerned, then go with these things. In the long run, who you are will serve you best because it will always be relatively the same, and it's easy to change clothes, haircuts, or whatever if your personalities are intact.

There is only one answer to the second question, Who decides on your image? That is, you do. Others can only make suggestions about how you may best communicate your image with clothes, biographical materials, photos, and such, but you will have to create your own public personality and whatever changes it will go through throughout your career. Some managers like to talk of giving acts a new image when they take them on. They buy different clothes, take a few photos, and show the band how to move around on the stage. To some, this is image. Even the media will buy the new image for a time, but slowly the real artist will emerge, for better or worse, and you, your manager, and the media will have to deal with it. And dealing with change that you are not controlling is tough in the entertainment business.

Madonna's image changes because she wants it to, and she is in control of it every step of the way. And when it comes to image, control is the cornerstone. You should never let anyone else control your image. You should see and approve every piece of publicity material that goes out on you, no matter how big a star you become. In that way you will always know who the hell you are supposed to be. Here's what I mean: You may want to revamp your image every time you release an album. Perhaps you want to get a new haircut or change your style of clothes, the look of the band onstage, or whatever, just to freshen things up a little without really changing the entire thrust of the act. This is a decision that you should make in conjunction with your team—your manager, agent, publicist, and record label—and you should all agree on the changes. Once you have agreed, then changing your image becomes a team effort with you as the quarterback. This approach makes sense because it is you who has to carry it off. If you let some publicist dream up what you should look like in your photos and you feel like a geek, it will never work.

Photos are a particularly sensitive area, and people make two mistakes here. First, they print up thousands of copies of a particular shot, which is usually outdated in a few months when clothing or hairstyles change or a band member quits, and use them for three years. This is silly. You should make up a few hundred copies, and when they run out, change photos. It helps people have a sense that you are not made of cardboard and that you do have at least one change of clothes and expression. Second, people want to see you, not your fantasy of yourself. When I was the general manager of a successful independent label and again at CBS Records (now Sony Music), I constantly received photos of people dressed like pirates or spacemen, standing in fields, on bridges, in airplanes, or on the moon. Save that kind of thing until you put together an outrageous stage show or album cover or until you get a gold record and can dress up any way you want.

Make the photos interesting, but not ridiculous. Your face should be recognizable, and the photo should be in focus and on a neutral background for best print reproduction. A black background will look lousy in a newspaper. Also, keep a few color slides in the event that a glossy magazine decides to do a piece on your band (these magazines generally prefer color shots). Remember, your photograph projects your visual image and many people who see it may never meet you, so consider what kind of impression you want to make as an artist and as a person before you have your photos taken.

Another important element of image is your interviews. Once again, you and your team need to agree on what your public position is going to be on issues, touring, your album, the planet, or whatever. What you don't need is conflicting stories in the media about who you are or what you stand for. Take a page out of the politician's handbook on this one. Politicians decide on their positions on issues, and their entire camp is consistent on those answers and issues. If you do so, it will make for a much smoother road with the media. Nothing sets a reporter sniffing around more than does contradiction.

Your live gigs will also send a clear message about your image. At a certain point in your career, where and when you play and for whom becomes almost as important as if you play at all. For example, when you are just starting out, you will generally play for any promoter who offers you a gig. As you become more famous and in demand, however, your agent will try to ensure that you play for the biggest or the rightest promoter in each market, that is, the one who plays the really big acts. After all, we are all known by the company we keep, and you can't portray yourself as a big star if you are playing for the minor-league promoter in a city.

Your choice of benefits also is important, not only who you play for but with whom. For example, you may be approached to do something for the Brazilian rain forests, for Amnesty International, or for AIDS research. Early in your career, you will probably try to do all three or if you are not able, you will choose the one that makes the most sense logistically or the charity that you personally feel strongest about. As you become a bigger star, however, your manager will start to think about who else will be playing on which benefit show, which one will be on television, where you can get the best billing, and so on. Your manager will then counsel you to choose the benefit that is most consistent with your overall image and beliefs, as well as where you will get the most career profile.

How Important Is Image?

If you heard an ad that referred to a car as "the new really fast sports car from Japan," how would it affect you? The answer is pretty matter of fact, I would guess. But if you heard the same ad and the car was called the "Intruder RX-11," you would get an entirely different feel, a large part of which would be emotional. Giving the car a fancy name is called *packaging*, and in the nineties and beyond, it will be a major element of successful music marketing.

As an artist, you need a package—a consistent combination of record, tour, video, look, and style—that is attractive, consistent, exciting, and unique. Packaging is where far too many artists and bands go wrong. The successful communication of your image is vital to a successful, career and your control of that image is what will make it a success. A good package will accurately communicate your music to the media, industry, and fans and should be a major consideration for you and your management team.

Image Creations, Problems, and Recovery

We're all familiar with the various image creations that have come and gone on the scene today and in years gone by. Kiss, New Kids on the Block, Debbie Gibson, and Tiffany are just a few of the long list that come to mind. These are bands or artists who are packaged in some unique fashion including a lot of high-powered public relations or some kind of stunt to capture the public's attention. Sometimes it works, sometimes it doesn't. Generally, it doesn't make for long-term careers, but every now and then a band like Kiss will make the transition from gimmick to legitimate act. In the mid-seventies the Bay City Rollers and the Knack were two acts who attempted to re-create the phenomenal popularity of the Beatles for themselves and failed.

Today's audiences are bombarded with packaging for everything from cars to food to movies (the combination of the right stars, director, scriptwriter and studio for a film is called "packaging"), so they've become used to it and are far more susceptible and willing to embrace a packaged musical act than were music fans of the past. Andy Warhol once said that the day would come when "everyone will be famous for fifteen minutes." I believe him because we are living in an era of instant communication.

In the fifties, the world heard all about some southern white boy singing black music long before Elvis ever appeared on the "Ed Sullivan Show." When Elvis finally appeared on the show, his movements were so controversial that he was shown only from the waist up. The time that elapsed between the world hearing about Elvis and actually seeing him was forever by today's standards, but it was sufficient to allow word of mouth to create the image among young rock and rollers and their terrified parents. Likewise in the sixties, we heard about four mop-topped kids from Liverpool who were turning England and Europe upside down with their great music and, particularly, long hair. But again it was months, and several chart-topping singles, before the Beatles actually came to America.

Today, we hear about a new act in the morning, see them live on a worldwide satellite hookup at noon, see the gold-record presentation with the president on the White House lawn that evening, and watch a career retrospective about them on MTV that night. Granted it probably doesn't happen quite that fast, but it sure seems that way sometimes. What makes it hard for artists is that this instant communication, which can dangerously overexpose an act in a short time, reduces an artist's already short life span and earning potential. Artists like Madonna, Phil Collins, and Michael Jackson must be extremely careful of the amount of exposure they allow when they have a current record or tour, for fear that if people see or hear them too much and too soon, their interest will peak long before the record or tour has had a chance to maximize its sales potential.

What I'm getting at is this: Packaging and the creation of an image are both important, but the image has to be one that can endure the test of time. Not many people are betting on a long career for the New Kids on the Block; that is, not a lot of us think that people will be buying boxed sets of this group's records in twenty years. Granted they have made an enormous amount of money in a short time, but musically they have not yet issued any music that appears to have staying power. Tiffany has all but disappeared, and Debbie Gibson's popularity seems to be tied to each new release and is not enduring like that of Sting or Bruce Springsteen.

In the nineties packaging will work, but it may be a short-term fix unless you can find a way to convert and control it, rather than having your package control you.

Many acts wonder if it is possible to recover from a mistaken image. Just ask John Mellencamp. Early in his career, John signed with managers who decided that "John Mellencamp" just didn't have a rock-star ring to it. So they decided to change his name to Cougar. A nice idea; it probably would have improved his chances of getting tour sponsorship from a car company. Well, after his hit "Jack and Diane," John started to get troubled and after a few more hit records, he got downright upset. He decided to go public with the news that his name was really Mellencamp and that he was damned proud of it. It took guts to insist on using his real name. But, in truth, his name wasn't the issue at all. What John was trying to say was that he had had it with all the phony-baloney rock-and-roll life-style and that he was just a singer from the Midwest. It was no accident that his publicist pushed the fact that he recorded his album in his home studio or that he released a single called

"Pop Singer," which was kind of a put-down of the whole "rock-and-roll stud" persona.

For John, it was a credibility issue that revolved around his name. For him, using his real name worked like a charm. He gained a kind of credibility that an artist named John Cougar might never have had. But the trick is that ever since he made the change, he has delivered great music and has never wavered from the new image that he created. You can recover from a mistake in image or, as in the case of Kiss, transform a gimmick into a legitimate career, as long as you deliver musically and in performances and you don't waver from your chosen course.

But I want to talk a little about my two favorite image artists, David Bowie and Madonna. These are possibly two of the smartest people in music to have ever walked upright on the Earth. Bowie is so creative that it's scary, and Madonna could have given Machiavelli lessons in control and manipulation. Each has done it his or her own way, but both have capitalized enormously on the concept of image.

David Bowie began to make his mark musically in the late sixties and early seventies, and he did so in an extraordinary fashion. With the release of each new album, he adopted a new persona. From "Ziggy Stardust" to the "Thin White Duke" to his current incarnation, Bowie has always been able to alter his image while maintaining the musical and personal qualities that have made him a virtual living legend. What Bowie has done is to challenge his audiences intellectually to accept the new persona and to understand the music that comes with it. When video came into fashion, most acts rendered exact replicas of their song lyrics on the screen. For instance, if the song said, "I was driving down the road," you saw a shot of a guy driving down the road. But Bowie's videos were different. In an interview that he gave in the mid-eighties, he said that when he made a video, he made a conscious effort to create a whole new storyline with the pictures, so it could stand on its own even without the music. This took Bowie's videos to a new level of interest and intelligence.

A modern Renaissance man, Bowie has extended his creativity beyond music to film and has won critical acclaim as an actor in

Merry Christmas Mr. Lawrence and *Into the Night.* The keys to all the manifestations of his image are intelligence and control, accompanied by outstanding and memorable music. No amount of image can make up for a bad record, but an interesting and arresting image added to a good one can turn a star into a superstar, as in the case of David Bowie.

Madonna is the bad girl everyone loves to hate. But in just the first four years of her career, she has earned over $100 million selling constantly reinvented versions of herself to an ever-growing legion of fans. What Madonna has done is to bring us all into her house to have a look around. What we believe from things like her film *Truth or Dare* is that she is showing us everything, with nothing held back. What Madonna is really doing is showing us everything that *she* wants us to see, and showing it in a way that shocks, titillates, and downright offends. Madonna takes us right to the edge and then pulls us back again. And not only are we relieved, we're grateful. We've been manipulated, and we love it. She is incredibly obvious, but she does it with such style that we can't help but love her.

Like Bowie, Madonna constantly reinvents her character. She grew up in a different era than Bowie, so the changes have come more quickly. Madonna understands that her fans, who are still largely young girls, have the attention span of hummingbirds and that she has to keep moving and changing to remain interesting. So she has gone from Boy Toy, to Bitch Goddess, to Slut Feminist, to Marilyn Monroe, and so on. Like Bowie, she backs up these changes in her image with entertaining musical performances. If Madonna lacks anything musically, she more than makes up for it in her performances, both on and off the stage. Hardly a week goes by that the Madonna press machine doesn't churn out some story about a new lover, an outlandish quote, and on and on. Madonna has clearly replaced my favorite quipster, David Lee Roth as the Mae West of rock and roll.

You can learn two things from Madonna: manipulation and control. Madonna controls her situations, image, and music. Every detail is designed and executed by her. And she is a master (or mistress) of manipulation. Whether it's a crowd in a concert venue or the media, she has developed the knack of making them do exactly what she wants. When it comes to Madonna, you could say the media have her right where she wants them.

So the whole discussion of image comes down to the two C's: consistency and control. You must create an image that is consistent with who you really are and one that you can consistently maintain, even through alterations and modifications, throughout your career. And you must control it, every aspect of it, from photos to statements to how you are publicized, promoted, and sold to the public. If you remember the two C's you will find that your image concerns are relatively easy to deal with.

HOW VIDEO HAS CHANGED ARTISTS' IMAGES

> *When I'm in the studio and I'm creating beauty I'm six foot nine and look like Cary Grant. And then I see that reduced to this nebbishy little guy with a double chin.*

> **—BILLY JOEL**

The advent of video, and particularly MTV, has had a dramatic effect on artists' images at the early stage of their careers. It used to be that the only places that anyone would see a new act was on their album cover and onstage. There was little pressure for an artist to have a well-defined image for his or her first album or single, since image was something you grew into, something that evolved over time as you matured. Nowadays things are different. Just after signing your first record deal and making your album, you are generally called on to make a video, in most cases your first real video, and all of a sudden, you need an image and you need it fast.

For most acts, even rock, metal, or rap acts, image is tough because the image you choose for the first video is probably the one that will stick with you, especially if the song in the video becomes a hit. So now, with no time to grow into an image, bands are forced to choose images when they are probably not ready to do so.

But since this acceleration has occurred over a period of years, not weeks, bands that formed a few years ago and those that are forming today have a much more well-defined sense of packaging than did, say, the bands that got together in the sixties and seventies. Bands like Kansas, for example, had virtually no visual image. They were all good old boys and looked pretty much like mountain men. Today rock bands sometimes work on their images before they work on their music (and, unfortunately, they sound like it), but in the age of image and packaging, your image on video can determine a lot about your future career.

And what do the video guys say about image? Mostly they believe that bands understand the importance of image and they believe that image consciousness among bands has grown over the years, along with the popularity of video and video channels. So I guess it's safe to say that video has had a dramatic impact, at least as far as a band being forced to decide on its image, and as long as we maintain this accelerated pace of the popularity of songs and artists, image concerns will be preeminent.

IS IMAGE TRANSFERABLE TO OTHER COUNTRIES AND CULTURES?

The Sex Pistols were one of Britain's most notorious bands. They enjoyed enormous popularity for what was not a mainstream act and had quite an impact on the British music and fashion scene. In the United States, however, radio stations wouldn't go near their music, video had not yet really come on the scene, and the punk movement was relatively small. Besides, the anarchy and political turmoil that the Sex Pistols were espousing had a lot to do with the turbulent political climate in Great Britain at the time, but the same culture didn't exist in the United States. As a result, in the eyes of the masses, the Sex Pistols were never really much more than a novelty.

In general, an artist's image is transferable to countries and cultures, at least those that share a language or a cultural concept. Europe, Australia, North and South America, and, to a point Japan, all are fascinated with the *Billboard* Chart type of acts like the

Rolling Stones, Elton John, and Madonna. But some acts just don't make it in some cultures. Although British rock acts can gain enormous popularity in the United States, U.S. bands that play what is referred to as "corporate rock" have a hard time in Great Britain. In the past, acts like Journey and Boston had small success there compared to that which they enjoyed in the rest of the world. Today, even bands like Mötley Crue and Poison are not as well received in Britain as they are on their home shores.

Sometimes language can be a barrier. Only the really big North American acts have managed to break through in non–English-speaking countries like France, Germany, and Spain; however some newer British acts who record in English may fare better because musical styles in England are closer to those of Europe than U.S. musical styles are. And although Japan is primarily interested in its own domestic artists, the big acts have prospered there as well.

But the real question isn't whether the act does well in other countries. The real question is, "Is the image transferable?" The heavy-metal image of bands like Mötley Crue and Poison does well in Japan. There are numerous metal music magazines and a variety of nightclubs that cater to the metal crowd. Moussed hair, leather, and chains are hot fashion items in Japan, and the heavy-metal life-stlyle is alive and well. In Europe it's different. The American heavy-metal look is most popular in France and Germany, but its popularity is limited. Italy and Spain are little interested, and in England the U.S. heavy metalers are seen as downright silly by most music fans. The look and presentation of heavy-metal groups are too contrived for European fans, who are more interested in unique, funk-based acts or the more "honest" Americans like R.E.M.

All-American acts like Huey Lewis and Wilson Phillips usually live from record to record. There is nothing particularly memorable about their image, or lack of it, and they sort of fade into an "All-American" tapestry that is essentially meaningless to a world audience who may respond to their music but not to their image. Unlike Americans, who seem to buy just about any artist's image from anywhere in the world if the act has a hit, some cultural

prejudices prevent certain looks or ideas from crossing international-
al boundaries. As an artist it's useful to know what you are getting
yourself into when you travel to another country, and if you are
interested in breaking the territory, it's a good idea to talk with your
label in a particular country and get some suggestions about how to
fit better into the local scene.

ANTI-IMAGE ARTISTS

> *Listen, I might be an antique, just like the Stones,*
> *but antiques are of value.*
>
> —*BILLY JOEL*

A stocky build, short, around forty years old: This sounds more like
a description of somebody's dad than of a rock star, yet several contemporary stars fit this description. As the sixties stars have aged,
the definition of a rock star, which used to be young, skinny and
good looking, has changed considerably. Many of these older stars
are still skinny, and most are still good looking in a grown-up kind
of way, but incredibly, they are popular with fans who are half their
age, as well as with their contemporaries. These artists' popularity
is somewhat tough to understand for those of us who came from a
generation with song lyrics like "I hope I die before I get old" and
whose slogan was, "Don't trust anybody over thirty."

How, then, do artists who do not fit the pop-idol mold manage to
have such success? The answer is, it must be their music. Even
though a large portion of the grown-up yuppies and former flower
children continue to buy music and attend concerts, it's not enough
to explain the large number of records sold by the Rolling Stones,
the Grateful Dead, or Paul McCartney, so younger fans must be
buying their records and enjoying their music. If the public likes a
song, it is apparent that it makes little difference to them that the
singer does not fit the star stereotype; what matters is that the
songs are good and that they enjoy them and want to hear them
again and again.

But not only older stars are anti-image acts. Artists like Hammer and Ice-T reek of image, but what about artists like Michael Bolton or Wilson Phillips? Bolton and Phillips do not have a particular image or a special look, and their music is enjoyable but not especially unique, yet both enjoy great success with their records and tours. And that seems to be a recurring theme. Image is important, but it will most likely never outstrip the music in terms of importance to the public. Without good songs, good recordings, and good performances, image is not going to buy you the success or longevity that Bonnie Raitt had before her big hit record or that the Stones have enjoyed for over a quarter of a century. Anti-image acts have one thing in common: good music. It is what brings them to the attention of the fans and the media and it is what allows them to continue with their careers.

CHANGING YOUR IMAGE

At various stages of your career, you are going to encounter pressure to change your image. You may feel this pressure early, when a record label or manager believes that your image should be different from what you think it should be. It may come later, when you are trying to find an elusive hit, or it may come from a corporate sponsor or someone in another business deal who believes that you should change who you are to suit a business purpose. There is a simple answer to all these situations, and that answer is "Don't." I can almost hear what you are thinking: All through this book I've been telling you to play by the rules that I've been giving you, but here I'm telling you to dig in your heels. Well, yes and no. The other rules are really the means to get things done. Knowing who does what and how they do it and why gives you the information that you can use to maneuver through the system and even make the system work for you. But your image, well, that's different. Your image is who you are. It's that little voice inside we all of us that tells us what to do, and what choices to make, and every time we don't listen to that voice, things screw up. Well, that little voice is the only voice that you should ever listen to about your image and what you do with your talent in the business.

Some artists like John Mellencamp have spent years trying to recapture their identities after managers tried to manufacture images for them. The Rolling Stones, Bruce Springsteen, Sting, Paul Simon, and a host of other artists, those whom we all hold in regard as having integrity, have always maintained the same public persona throughout their career. They stood up for the causes in which they believed, and refused to do things that they considered out of character or downright wrong—even, I'm certain, at the risk of having their label, manager, or some other business entity turn against them. The trick is to realize that you are the one who has to live with yourself and that all the business types around you are merely marketing your product. But to you, it must be more than a product. It has to be real. So, of all the questions that you need to consider in your career and of all the decisions you have to make, this is the easiest. It's what I call the Popeye principle: "I yam what I yam, and that's all what I yam."

PUBLICITY

To say no is a snub they find very hard not to take personally. And revenge shortly ensues.

—MORRISSEY

So what good is being the new rock-and-roll genius if nobody knows about it? In addition to airplay, the best way to tell everybody is through what we call the media. There's only one small problem here. Invariably, the media seldom write or broadcast what you want them to publicize and, in fact, they usually write what you don't want them to publicize. If it wasn't so serious, it might almost be funny. But it is serious and it isn't funny. Ask Gary Hart, the former presidential candidate; he'll probably tell you the media aren't too funny.

Mr. Hart is a sterling example of what not to do with the media.

He dared the media to follow him. They did, and he not only didn't get to be president, he didn't even get to run. You might say that he was six inches from the presidency. Baiting the media is like waving a red flag in front of a bull or poking a pit bull with a stick. The chances are that if the media decide to get on your case, they will win. They will win mostly because they have control of the means of communication, and all you can do amounts to standing on a street corner and hollering.

Although it difficult, the media can be handled. But you need to know a few basic rules. Memorize them; they are important to your survival in the media jungle.

1. Never trust the media with a secret.

2. There is no such thing as "off the record."

3. The media know what they believe and don't want to be confused with the facts.

4. Once something appears in writing or on the air, it is truth.

5. Any attempt to get back at the media is suicide.

6. Letters to the editor are a sign of weakness.

7. There are two kinds of "fair": state fair and bus fare. The media, on the other hand, are seldom fair. Don't expect it.

8. If something can hurt you, the media will find out about it.

9. If you lie to the media, they will try to destroy you.

10. The media eat their young.

You may think I'm exaggerating, but next time you are in a supermarket, take a look at the tabloid papers. What you see in them is an exaggerated form of the kind of exposure you have once you are in the public eye.

But your best weapons for dealing with the media are communication and information. Tell the truth whenever you can or at least keep the lines of communication open. By controlling the quantity and subject matter of the information that the press receives about you, you can virtually program them to help you with your career. If you don't give them information, they will go looking for it, and if they can't find it, they will make it up. It's better that you should be the one who controls what they get and when they get it. And to do so, you will need some basic materials. This goes for those of you who are just starting out, as well as for any recording artist who is in the public eye. It's never too early in your career to start thinking about the power of the press.

PRESS MATERIALS

The first thing both new acts and established recording artists need is a press kit. New acts will find the kit useful in a number of areas: with agents, clubs and schools, and, of course, the media. Recording artists, on the other hand, usually have a new press kit with each album release that includes up-to-date information on their activities since their last recording, as well as any awards they have won, successful tours they have played, and any interesting personal information. The press kit should include three key components: a biography, a photograph, and press clippings.

Biography

> *They'd really be happy if I weighed 400 pounds and had a one-inch dick. Then they could say, "He's very successful but he weighs 400 pounds and has a one-inch dick." But they can't say that about me so I have to live with all this other shit.*
>
> —DAVID GEFFEN

The first impression that you will make on a large segment of the media community will be your biography (or bio)—a thumbnail sketch of your personal and professional history that will give some sense of you as an individual and as an artist. It is here that a lot of artists, both professional and novice, make mistakes. As devastating as this may sound, no one really cares where you went to high school, how many people were in your graduating class, your current hobbies, or your favorite movie, unless you can figure out some way of introducing these subjects so they will be amusing to the reader. The media have no interest in such intimate details of your life until you become a big star, at which time they will want to know all the above plus what you had for breakfast and how many times a day you go to the bathroom. For now, however, keep the materials that you put in your biography relevant to what you do.

If you are the long-lost daughter of some internationally famous personality or if the high school groups that you played in included Bryan Adams or Sting, people in the press will definitely be interested. Otherwise, try to restrict your information to these facts: your name, age (maybe), musical education (if any), professional accomplishments, and a general view of you as an artist and as a human being. Avoid pontificating. Don't dwell on glowing quotes about your "distinctive vocal style"; just be sure that they are highlighted in the press kit. Things like that speak for themselves.

Present your biography in a brief (one typed page should be enough) comfortable style that informs, rather than hypes. For a group biography, you should take a slightly different approach. Don't bother with the biographies of individual members; just concentrate on the formation of the band, how you came together (people are curious about this and bands seldom discuss it), the group members' names, any information about other bands the members have belonged to (only if these bands have had some level of success), and some idea of where your new band is at musically. Here you may want to use a quote or two as a point of reference for the reader, but go easy. A quote like "crisp, top-notch rock and roll" from the *Los Angeles Times* is infinitely preferable to "the best band on the planet Earth" from the *Oakville Beaver.*

Keep the bio interesting, but remember to keep it consistent with your image. If you are a straight-ahead kind of person, stay away from exaggerations or hype in the bio. If you tend to be more flamboyant, include some items that will stir up a little controversy. Be careful, however, not to confuse controversy with fiction. A famous rapper got himself into some trouble early in his career by claiming that he had achieved certain things that he had not, in fact, achieved in the area of motor cross-racing. It's one thing to stir things up a little; it's another thing to mislead the press. They don't like it and they will get even.

Press Clippings

Clippings are usually included, so the media can see what their colleagues are writing about you. These clippings may be feature articles in prestigious publications or charts from _Billboard_ or other publications or reviews of your performances or recordings. Whatever the content, it is all designed to give the media a favorable impression of you through other materials that have already appeared.

No one has ever been able to tell me whether good articles convince writers that they should write something good about you, too, or if they challenge the writers to disagree. I once knew a heavy-metal band who put only their worst reviews in the press kits. It sort of sent a message, "Go ahead, slag us; we've heard it all before." And interestingly enough, the press were charmed by this tactic and generally wrote about how witty and clever the band was for doing it. And that, students, is the point of today's lesson: Whatever you decide to do, plan it. Make it your idea that gets into print, not the media's. The media receive so much of the same old thing every day that when they do receive something unique, they generally deal with it. But keep something in mind: The media, particularly writers, are a relatively intelligent lot, and your "gimmick" or "hook" should appeal to their intellect or sense of humor, as in the case of the metal band's bad reviews. You've got to stand out from the crowd, so be sure that the clippings that you include are interesting ones that have something to say about you and your music. Be smart when choosing your clips; use only a few of them and make them work for you.

CRITICS

> _There is nothing that a critic can tell me_
> _that I can learn from._
>
> **—PRINCE**

Most musicians hate critics. And sometimes it seems like most critics hate musicians. Although radio and television programs occasionally review albums or concerts, it is writers for magazines or newspapers that are the targets of most musicians' wrath. You spend months writing and perfecting the songs and then hours, days, weeks, and months perfecting them in the studio. And when finally you release them on an album, some jerk in a magazine or newspaper wipes you out with three sentences in an article in which he is reviewing three or four new albums of acts that he thinks are like yours. So you're toasted, and not even in your own review of your album.

Or worse, you spend months and mountains of money preparing your new show, and when you take it on the road, some idiot in Nowhere, Nebraska, tears the show apart in the *Daily Bugle* the morning after your first gig. It's enough to make you want to kill somebody. So you 1) scream at your publicist, 2) scream at your manager, 3) write a letter to the editor, 4) make fun of the writer in your next interview, 5) make fun of the entire state of Nebraska in your next interview, or 6) punch a hole in the wall of your hotel room.

But do you want to know what you should do? Make a list. That's right, a list. Buy a small notebook, and every time critics slag you, write down their names for the day when you are the biggest act in the world and any press person would crawl on his or her knees over broken glass to talk to you; then you can make sure that no matter where these critics are or what they are doing, they won't be able to talk to you. Not ever. In fact, you can talk to everyone else but them; they will be the only writers on the planet who don't get to talk to you. The Eagles had a list, as do several other artists. It sounds silly, but it's good therapy. There's no point getting stressed over a bad review. It's over. Generally, bad reviews don't do much damage. Your fans will still come to see you and radio stations will still play your records. So instead of getting all tied up in knots, just buy the notebook and keep the list.

DO'S AND DON'TS

There are some basic publicity do's and dont's that you should keep in mind.

Do's

1. Be entertaining in your interviews. Charm the interviewers if you can.

2. Be consistent. Try to remember what you said yesterday and repeat it. You should have two or three major points about yourself, your music, and your band, and you should make those points in every interview. You can add different anecdotes or vary your topics to keep it fresh, but consistency will let you do your job with the media best.

3. Be cooperative. If your press agent sets up a bunch of interviews, remember they are to forward your career, not the publicist's. If you don't cooperate, the press agent will work with another act who does. Remember, to a record label, bands are like buses; another one comes along every half hour.

4. Be grateful. If a press person has written good things about you and you meet him or her, say thanks and maybe you'll keep getting nice things written about you.

5. Stick to your plan, answer the questions, and don't ramble. If your answers in an interview are precise, they make for a much better interview, and rambling on usually gets you in trouble.

Don'ts

1. Don't get put into "gang" stories or reviews. Writers like to take three or four new rap releases, for example, and do one piece on rap in which they review the four records. In such reviews, you will be compared to the other three, either favorably or unfavorably, and you will not get nearly as much space and focus. In particular, don't let yourself be interviewed for these pieces. The writers will talk to you for an hour and use one sentence.

2. Don't make up stories. The press will check you out and if they think you are lying, they will go after you. Unless there's some reason not to, tell them the truth, or at least stick to the story that you and your team have devised.

3. Don't get into running battles with certain writers, shows, or publications. I've seen more acts let their pride get in the way of their good business sense. You may think you're getting even, but all you're doing is missing an opportunity.

4. Don't bait the media unless you've decided on that as a strategy. They really do have control of the means of communication, and it's a battle you can't possibly win.

5. Don't change your position on issues too abruptly. If you appear to flip-flop, the media will criticize you for having no clear direction or integrity. Be consistent with your answers and your ideas when the media are involved.

As I said, the media can be managed. It's your job and that of your publicist, manager, and record label to ensure that you make all the necessary moves proactively to make the press work for you. If you wait until they write the story or review and then complain, you'll have no one to blame but yourself. But if you get out there preemptively and work the press, you'll be able to turn the effort into positive results or, at least, minimize the downside of any negative press.

HOW TO MAKE A RECORD
COMPANY LISTEN

*I was dismayed with the lack of response to my music
in Nashville. It was suggested to me that the west
coast was a little more ... open environment for my
form of music ... but I was out there for nine and a
half years before we finally got signed to a record
deal. It took a long time but, in a way, it's like going
to medical or law school.*

—DWIGHT YOAKAM

My guess is that over 50 percent of the people who pick up this
book will turn to this page immediately. I am constantly asked:
"How do I get them to listen?" "How do I get their attention?" and
"How can I get to them?" But the question that I am seldom asked
and the one that is much more important, is "Am I ready to make a
record?" What? you say. "Of course, I'm ready to make a record; I
made a demo didn't I? I rehearsed, I sound good, why not?" Good
question. Why not? If you aren't ready and you go too soon, you
could be wasting a shot. Being ready is more than simply having
your demo finished. It is being able to listen to your tape critically
and to decide a few things, namely,

• Is this the absolute best I can do?
• Is this stuff unique and world-class enough to get signed?
• Am I ready to make the mental and physical sacrifices, and
do I have the maturity to handle a music career right now?
• If I were hearing this for the first time, would I be impressed?

•And, finally, does it make any sense to wait a while, work on our material, and look for the unique hook that will make it impossible for us not to get signed?

These are hard questions, but really relevant. A lot of musicians, and I mean a lot, send tapes out as soon as they are finished recording. Sometimes after the band has been together only for a week or two, they look for a record deal. This is anything but a realistic way to get a recording contract. If you aren't ready to make a long-term commitment to make your music as good as it can be, why should you expect the record companies to make a long-term commitment to market it? All you are doing in this situation is setting yourself up for a no from the record labels.

There are, however, two kinds of no from a label. The first is a complete dismissal—No, not good enough now and no indication that it will ever be good enough—and the second is, No, not yet. The second no is the beginning of a relationship. It means that the A & R person hears some potential but think it's a bit early for you to record; you're not ready. All I'm saying here is that the old story about never getting a second chance to make a first impression is, in large part, true. If you think you are ready, then go for it. But if there is any doubt in your mind about whether this is the best that you can do, then wait. And spend the waiting time constructively polishing your material and your performance. A little self-control here will pay off later.

Like I said, making the contacts and making a label listen to you aren't easy. It takes a lot of perseverance and hard work. You have to deal with the frustration and anxiety, and you're vulnerable, always waiting for someone to stomp all over you; yet you have to keep a goofy smile on your face while you keep going. It's hard, but remember that a lot of bands were there before you and they made it: They got signed, got the hits, and are now enjoying the goodies that come with success. Get out there, talk to everyone you can, and make your presence felt. You'll never know where your break is going to come from, so don't miss a trick. Remember, success is where luck and hard work collide. However you decide to handle it, the key is a well-planned attack. There is no mystery here, no secret backroom meetings, no secret codes—just good music in the right hands, in the right circumstances, at the right time.

But now back to the question, "How do I get the label to listen?" The answer is simple. It isn't easy. Record-company executives, whether they are local promotion representatives, salespeople in Cleveland, or the vice president of A & R on the beach in Los Angeles (just kidding), are very busy people. There is a popular misconception that the music business is all parties, lunches, and fun. Certainly, because the business is a very social one, the incidence of parties and social events is high. However, it is a business, and like any other, its employees are under pressure to produce. To this end, recording-company executives try hard to budget their time where it will do the most good.

Few record-company employees in the sales and promotion field work a nine-to-five day. They are generally at the office early in the morning; put in a full day working either in the office, on the telephone, or on the road; have dinner with an artist's manager, radio programmer, or sales account; and then make the rounds of the local clubs and concert halls to check out their acts and the other national and local talent who are in town that evening. With that kind of schedule, it's difficult to catch up with them, so, once again, the approach is the key. To plan your approach properly, you should understand the workings and positions within a record company and how each employee can help you in your quest for a recording contract.

ARTIST AND REPERTOIRE (A & R)

All an A & R man is really here for is to offer an opinion. You listen to something, see an act and say, "I think … I think this is a hit song or act. I think it's worthy of signing." It's just an opinion.

—DON GRIERSON,
FORMER VICE PRESIDENT OF A & R,
EPIC RECORDS

For the new artist or band, this is the most important department in a recording company. A & R is the department where all the new, aspiring talent is first previewed and considered. This job used to be done almost exclusively by the presidents of the recording companies, but, as the companies grew larger and the business became more complicated and competitive, they relinquished this vital function to specialists whose job it is to stay aware of the newest trends in music and radio and to parlay this information into signing hit artists. It is a difficult job in that they must not only be aware of what is currently in vogue, but must also be able to predict accurately what the public will be demanding in the future.

Some small record companies still handle the A & R function through one of the upper-level executives of the company, since a full-time A & R person at some of these labels is a luxury they cannot afford. In most cases, however, artists or their managers will find themselves dealing with individuals whose full-time job is to audition and select new talent for the label.

Because A & R is ultimately where you want to end up, let's get to know the A & R person's functions. A & R is an abbreviation for *artist and repertoire* department, which is responsible for signing new acts and for performing the vital function of liaison between artists and the record label. It is standard in most companies that the A & R director works either directly with the artists or with the artists' producers on the choice of songs, studio, musicians—generally the creative process. This is the department that will listen to your tape, and because it is deluged with material on a daily basis, you must be sure that your approach will have the desired effect, that the staff will be interested in you and your music.

The key is to be sure that the quality of your presentation is excellent, both technically and creatively. Most important, however, you must ensure that your tape ends up in the hands of the right person. Many artists, when they send a tape to the A & R department of a company, have the attitude, "I don't want it to end up in the hands of some secretary, so I'm going to pester the A & R director to death on the phone so he or she takes my tape personally when I drop it off." Well, guess what, folks, A & R directors are people, too, and nobody likes to be pestered. If you get on the A & R director's nerves before he or she has even heard your tape, I can assure you that it will not add up to points in your favor when it comes to listening time.

You can be sure of one other thing: All tapes that get submitted to record companies get listened to, and most companies maintain a log of all the tapes they receive. If they have any interest, they keep a file on the artist for future reference. This file serves two purposes: first, to maintain good public relations with the artistic community and possibly to discover hit talent and second, to provide protection against charges from songwriters that the label has stolen their songs. Generally, if your talent is not suitable for the company's label, your tape will be returned with a letter informing you of the bad news. If you want your tape to be returned, you should make it known in the letter you send with the tape and enclose a stamped, self-addressed envelope.

Sometimes, the company will keep the tape around if there is any interest in it or if one of your songs is suitable for another act on the label, at which time you will have to decide whether to let someone else record your stuff. It's a judgment call, but publishing royalties are something to live on until that big break.

How to Get the First Listen

Competition on signing bands, that's the easiest part.
Breaking bands is the hardest part.

—DEREK SHULMAN, CEO
ATCO RECORDS

There is a popular misconception that if your demo isn't of master quality, the A & R people at the label won't listen to it. That simply isn't true. A & R people get a lot of tapes that are finished masters for licence or purchase, and some bands with good financing may go right to the masters, but you certainly don't need a master-quality demo to get a listen. As I said earlier, one thing you can be sure of is that labels listen to all of the tapes they get. No one can afford to miss a hit, and it's pretty easy to tell from just a few minutes of listening whether the band is ready to make a record.

Now for the good stuff. First, there is a general consensus among my friends and business associates that it is easier to get signed now than ever before. Although most of the rules about how to get signed have not changed in the past decade, the proliferation of independent labels has made a difference. Simply put, musicians now have more labels to approach, and those labels, as a group, are able to sign more acts. For a while in the seventies and eighties, the only way to get signed was to make a multiyear deal for several albums. There was little or no room for a singles deal because with rock and roll as the dominant musical form, singles simply made no difference. But now with rap, hip hop, house, and even several varieties of heavy metal, there are more singles deals than ever. There is a market now for singles, and those singles deals are leading to album deals if the singles become hits.

So if it is easier to get signed these days, how do you go about it, that is, how do you get the record labels to listen to your tape? There are several ways to have your tape listened to. The first, and most standard method, is to have your lawyer, agent, or manager take the tape to the A & R department of a label. Now when I say the A & R department, what I really mean is that it *eventually* gets to this department. If, for example, your lawyer is familiar with the president of the label, the president may be the first one in the company to hear the tape and, if he likes it, he will pass it along to the A & R department. Whatever the case, your tape will end up in the hands of the A & R department. Here's what the A & R people need from you to listen to your tape.

Most A & R people are concerned first and foremost with the songs. No offense, there are a lot of good singers and players out there, but good writers are a rarer commodity. A & R people receive hundreds of tapes every year and a lot of them are good, but if the A & R people hear a good song, their interest will definitely be piqued. So, when you are recording your demo, focus on the song and be sure that it showcases all its hit benefits, from lyrics to hook to interesting changes.

The next thing that the A & R people will look for is a unique element that makes you something special. This element may be something as obvious as a different voice like Bob Seger or Bono or something more subtle like the special quality of Sinéad O'Connor. Your job is to discern what it is about you or your band that makes you unique and feature it up front in your presentation to the label. Next, they will look at how the band is connected. Who are the manager and the agent? Where has the band played? Does the band have a following? If you've done your homework in building your team and your following, you'll have all the answers to these questions. Finally, the A & R people will want to see your act. That introduces you to the wonderful world of the label showcase, that is, a gig arranged by your manager or agent so the label people can have a look at you.

A showcase for a label follows basically the same rules as does a showcase for an agent. Just ensure that all the details of your performance are worked out, that technically everything is in good working order, and that you give 100 percent at the audition, and you'll be heading in the right direction. It's sort of like an oral exam in school and it does, in fact, make up about 50 percent of your grade for the A & R people.

Another important connection for getting your tape to the record company is the publisher. A tape from your publisher, especially if it is the publishing wing of the label that you are approaching, will carry a lot of weight, particularly if your material has been recorded by other artists.

These are all the established or traditional methods within the business of having your tape presented. If, however, you're not fortunate enough to have access to this network, it doesn't mean that you don't have a chance, only that you are going to have to be a little more creative in your approach. It is here that the secretary who you've been ignoring becomes important.

Handle your submissions in a businesslike manner. Contact the A & R department by telephone and speak to the secretary or coordinator of the department. This is the first person who will see your tape. Make your name and the name of your band known to this person. Tell him or her that you are sending a tape and ask to whose attention it should be addressed. Enclose a tape, a copy of the song lyrics, a biography of you or the band, and a short letter explaining your reasons for submitting the tape at this time. "I wanna be a star and make a million dollars" is not what I have in mind, by the way, but more like, "We've been together for a year and a half, have written and recorded this material, and believe that we're ready to make a record" and some information about where you can be contacted.

Otherwise, after speaking to the A & R secretary and sending your tape, allow reasonable time to elapse and then telephone again to make sure that it has arrived. Don't ask a lot of questions about whether the A & R people have listened to your tape or liked it or whatever. If they have, they'll tell you. Otherwise just ensure that they received it and ask when would be a good time for you to call back for more information. Follow-up is the key. Don't badger them, but if you phone once a week and keep your conversations brief, polite, and friendly, you may find that you have an ally in the secretary or assistant to whom you speak, and he or she may begin to work on your behalf.

You may even ask if the A & R assistant has heard the tape, and if not, send one. This will not only stroke the person's ego, but if he or she likes it, it will put one of your fans in the record company camp. For example, when Rik Emmett, formerly of Triumph, was looking for a solo record deal, the A & R secretary of one label was a big Triumph fan. She played his demo tape in the office so loud and so often that it finally caught the A & R director's attention, and he offered Rik a contract. A little promotion at this level can go a long way. Once you get them to listen, the rest is up to the quality of your material. But assuming your material is good, an ally at the label can go a long way.

A pervasive attitude in the business is that unless you have a heavy-hitting lawyer or some other inside connection to present your tape or negotiate for you, you have no chance of getting signed to a deal. This simply isn't true. Not all the deals in the music industry are made in the back room, and this kind of talk is generally just "sour grapes" from someone who's had no success. Keep a positive attitude, and if you have the goods, you'll make the deal.

But what about the band who lives in Fargo, North Dakota, can't afford to go to Los Angeles or New York, and doesn't know any of the hot-shot lawyers or managers who could get them a deal? So, what's the problem? It's a little harder, but the basic theory is the same. What you are trying to do is to get your music into the hands of someone who can get you a recording contract. If you live in Fargo, the trip may be a little longer, but you can get there just the same. You've got five options if you live outside one of the major music centers:

_1._ Move (not practical, besides the last time I looked, not all bands came from New York and Los Angeles).

_2._ Make a contact through the local promotion representative of the record company.

_3._ Make a contact through the program director or music director of your local radio station.

_4._ Make a contact through a local booking agent or concert promoter.

_5._ Get seen by a big-time manager or agent at a local concert.

Five Options! and I bet you thought you didn't have any. Here's how they work:

1. Move. Not an alternative early on. In other words don't move to make the contacts. Rather, move after you have made the contacts. A lot of bands or artists travel to New York or Los Angeles stone cold, not knowing anyone, and expect they will schmooze their way to some meaningful meetings. Brave, yes. Smart, no. It's a better idea to work from your local market, make some contacts, and then go to meet them. And New York or Los Angeles may not be your first stop. You may go from Fargo to Minneapolis and then to Chicago and later to New York. You go where you have to go, but go with contacts and a purpose.

2. The local promotion rep. These are my favorite guys and girls. For a long time, I was one of them, and I can tell you it is one of the most exciting, personally rewarding, and thankless jobs on the planet, but damn it's fun! What local reps do is phone or visit local radio stations in their territories to try to convince them to play the records that they are working. They also take care of artists when the acts come into their turf. They set up interviews, take the artists to the stations, arrange dinners between the artists and the key radio people in the area, look after the station's contest winners if they are supposed to meet the artists, and a lot of other stuff. (An outline of the local rep's job appears later in the record-company section.)

In any event, these local guys and gals are everywhere. They live, love, and listen to music. And they have the ear of the people at their head office when it comes to new talent. Time and again I've heard record-label presidents and A & R people telling me about some new band they were going to see who was recommended to them by a local rep. And these bands aren't in New York or Los Angeles. They are in St. Louis and Cincinnati and Denver. Record labels will go anywhere to find a hit act.

Find out who the local reps are. Look in the phone book for the number of the record company's branch office or call the head office in New York or Los Angeles. Then call the rep, introduce yourself, and ask if you can send a tape or if he or she would like to come out and see you at your next gig. A & R people get hundreds of tapes a year. Local reps get about five. And the chances are that if they like your tape, they will come to see you, and if they like your performance, they will get on the phone to their boss asking for someone to come out and see you.

Another thing you should know about the politics of a record label is this: When the promotion department likes a record or a band and recommends it to the A & R man, the act usually gets a serious listen. After all, it is promotion to put the record on the radio, and if they are already motivated, there is a good chance they will work their tails off to make it a hit, which, in turn, will make the A & R people look good.

3. *Local radio stations.* As you will learn in the section on radio, stations employ several people who have regular, weekly contact with record labels and who would be in a position to mention your band or even send a tape for consideration. These people are the program director, the music director, and the promotion director, although just about anyone at the station can help. And you would be surprised how easy they are to get to. Just call the station, ask for each person by name, and ask if you can speak to him or her. Explain why you are calling and ask if the person would take the time to listen to your tape. If you are playing a show in the area, invite the person out to see you; it won't hurt to invite the entire on-air staff of the station and try to get to know them. The point here, and in fact the point of the entire music business, is to get a buzz going in the marketplace about you and your music.

Contrary to what you may think, the radio station personnel will be anxious to help out if they think that the tape is good and that you are ready to record. Every city takes pride in the rock stars who have come from it, and the radio people are anxious to increase the number of stars who come from their town. Your most enthusiastic response will probably come from the AOR stations and country stations in your city or town that are interested in developing new talent. CHR and AC stations are more interested in hit talents who have already made it because they concentrate on hit product for airplay. They will be the least likely to get involved in a new project, but it doesn't hurt to try them as well.

4. *A local booking agent.* Earlier I talked about finding an agent in your area to get work. The process here is the same. Ask other musicians, club owners, and managers, all of whom deal with agents in some capacity and can probably recommend one to you. To spread your music and influence outside your city or town into the surrounding area, you will need the help of a local booking agent who books the region in which you live. Since the agent probably spends a great deal of time trying to get some of his acts to appear as opening acts for local promoters who buy the big tours, he often makes contacts with the important promoters and agents. If the local agent has ever worked with an act who has gotten a recording deal, he may have made some record contacts as well. Whatever the case, when you feel you are ready, you should utilize the local agent as another conduit to the labels.

5. *Big-time managers or agents.* If you are fortunate enough to get an opening gig for a national touring act in your city or a nearby city through your agent's relationship with a local promoter, you have a good chance of being seen not only by that important promoter, but by the national agent who represents the national act. Also, the local promotion rep for the headliner will definitely be there and, possibly, someone from the head office, maybe even the A & R guy. Sounds good doesn't it? Well, it won't happen by itself, you have to make it happen.

Push your local agent to make the connection with the local promoter. Make the connection as well by sending your tape and bio to the promoter with a letter asking to be considered for a gig. Be sure to tell the promoter how much you have played and where and the extent of the crowds that you can draw because his prime interest is to sell tickets. If you have made the radio connections that I talked about earlier, add them as references. If you have already connected with the label's local promotion rep, ask her for a plug to get on the tour. Chances are she will talk to the manager or to someone at the label who will.

If you are lucky enough to get the gig, find out who the agent is for the headliner and write or call him to tell him that you are opening and would like him to see you. If the agent is looking for a place to see the headliner and he has the time, you may get lucky. Meanwhile you should get in touch with the A & R person for the headliner's label and those from other labels and tell them that you will be opening and would like them to see you. Contact the promoter and ensure that you can buy a block of good seats for your guests. If you think a small party after the gig would help, arrange one; in fact, if you can manage to play a gig at a local club where the A & R guys can see more after your opening set, it's even better. Yeah, it's a hell of a lot of work, but you ain't seen nothing yet. Wait until you get signed.

You can get signed if you live outside the big cities if you plan your attack. Since you'll have several players in the marketplace talking about you and your act you'll have to direct traffic to ensure that people aren't tripping over one another. But if you orchestrate it correctly, you'll have the beginning of a good buzz that you should be able to parlay into some solid contacts with the labels.

REJECTION LETTERS

> *Basically, record companies don't want a new artist.*
> *A new artist means a new file, means you have to*
> *convince radio. So as an A & R person, if you sign*
> *an artist you better realize that you're going to go*
> *through meeting after meeting where you have to*
> *convince people that this person or band is great.*

> —*PETER KOEPKE,*
> *FORMER DIRECTOR OF A & R,*
> *ATLANTIC RECORDS*

Once you've made the contacts, you'll want to begin to use them to get a deal. That means you will send tapes, try to set up meetings, and try to make the connections that will result in a deal. In the course of all this activity, you will begin to receive the dreaded rejection letters. No matter how long you are in the business, a rejection letter is tough to swallow, that is, unless you can tell a flat no from a no that is the beginning of a relationship with the label.

You need to keep a few things in mind about rejection letters. First, what the labels are rejecting is the tape you sent them—not your band, your live show, your music, your family, your ethnic origin, or you. They rejected only what they heard on the tape. And the reasons they rejected the tape could be numerous: They have no budget left to sign acts this year, they have too many new developing acts on the label, they're not looking for a rock band now, they already have a female vocalist, and on and on and on.

Signing a band is an important financial commitment for a label, or at least that's how you want it to be, and it won't be done casually. Most people don't think of the music business in terms of inventory, but inventory is a word that you'll hear regularly. What I mean is that you are always competing for shelf space, just like a can of peas or a box of soap powder in a supermarket. Almost every aspect of the business that you encounter will have some quota— for the number of acts that can be signed (a record label) or the number of songs that can be played (a radio station) or the amount of product that can be stocked (record stores). Usually, the reasons for the quota are financial. Labels have to be sure that there is enough money to record and promote all the acts on the label and enough staff to serve them. Here are a few examples:

Record Company

As much as they would like to, labels cannot sign every band that they like. If they did, they simply would not have the resources to pay for recording, video, marketing, and tour support for all the acts. Therefore, they have to choose from among all the tapes they receive and can sign only a reasonable number of acts each year. To that end, they must be aware of the kinds of acts they are signing to keep a balanced roster of acts, unless, of course, they specialize in a specific type of music like heavy metal or rap. But in general the major labels try to keep a balance among all the different types of music.

If you are in a heavy-metal band and you send a tape to a label, there are several things you need to consider. First, the label may like your tape and be interested in signing your brand, but if it already has one or two new heavy-metal bands it is trying to break, it may not have the resources to support a third. Therefore, the label will send you a rejection letter. The letter may or may not tell you that is the reason you haven't been signed, or if the people at the label are interested in you, the letter may ask you to contact them before you sign anywhere else. As I said, it's a question of shelf space. Right now that label has too much heavy-metal inventory and simply does not have the shelf space to include you.

If you had a new kind of soap powder and were trying to retail it, you might go around to the stores and find the ones that seemed to have shelf space or that had the biggest shelves and could make room for you. That would be the logical place to try to start your product. Well, the same goes for getting a record deal. If you are trying to get your tape listened to and your band signed, it may be worthwhile to study the labels that you are soliciting and figure out their shelf space for an artist of your type. In this way, you at least begin to eliminate potential reasons for them to reject you.

Radio Stations

The inventory business is the same for radio stations. I go into this in some detail in the radio and record-company sections, but here are a few things to think about now. Every station has a finite number of slots for records that can be played each week. In some cases, up to half are reserved for gold records or past hits. That leaves only half the playlist for new records. There are two types of new records—those from established stars who are following up previous hits (and there are a lot of them) and brand-new artists who have never had a hit in their lives (there are also a lot of them). Guess which ones the radio stations play first. So that leaves a small number of slots for new artists.

This situation gets complicated by the fact that some records simply won't go away, that is, the listeners never get tired of them and they hang around the playlist forever taking up slots. Sometimes these records are put into a category called *recurrent,* which means that they're not current enough to be considered new and not old enough to be called gold. A recurrent record takes up half a space, but it takes up space nonetheless. So on radio, you have shelf-space problems again, only this time it's when you are trying to get your record into an open slot. Since there are literally hundreds of bands on the chart or waiting in the wings that also play your kind of music, shelf space could be a problem. Radio stations need variety; they simply can't play all heavy metal or all rap. In the situation that I just described, labels may be reluctant to sign you solely because there is simply too much of your kind of music already fighting for space on radio, and they need to create something fresh and new.

Record Stores

Record stores feature only three kinds of records: star product that sells out fast, sale product that sells at a marked-down price, and new artists whom the record companies pay them to push. By "pay them," I don't mean payola (we'll talk about that later), I mean that the labels promise to buy advertising to push certain records (which creates customers for the store), in-store appearances by the artists, and extra discounts to put the records up front in the feature racks. Other than that, you again run into the shelf-space problem. There is only so much space in a record store, and the store owner has to make sure that this space is maximized to sell the most product.

This shelf-space phenomenon holds true for becoming the opening act on tours, booking dates in certain buildings, getting songs placed with big-name artists for covers, and on and on. You will be fighting for a space in each area of your career. So to maintain your position, you have to ensure that your preparation, approach, and closing of the deal are all as good as they can be. Although the label people probably won't tell you any of these problems in their rejection letter, these are just some of the reasons that a label may choose not to sign an act that has otherwise submitted a good-quality demo tape.

On the other hand, the record-company people may have decided that, in their estimation, you are not ready to make a record. If you are lucky, they will include some of their specific criticisms in their letter. You should pay attention to these critiques, especially if you find that they are repeated in letters from different labels. For example, if all the letters say that the songwriting is unfocused or the lead singer has pitch problems, you should take an objective look at what you are doing and, if you agree, make some adjustments. Too many artists receive a rejection letter and immediately get angry, writing off the A & R person as a jerk who doesn't know what he or she is talking about. Don't get mad; this is business, and emotions will just confuse you and prevent you from making smart business decisions. As I said before, there are two kinds of no. If you suspect that your letter is the second kind of no, that is, "not now but later," write to the A & R person, thanking him or her for listening to your tape (this is a good idea no matter what the response) and saying that you're working on new material and will send another tape shortly for his or her opinion. In this way you have done two things: You have shown some class and you have indicated to the A & R person that you realize music is an ever-changing process and one in which you intend to include him or her. When you have a new tape ready (not a week later; spend some time on it), send it along with another letter telling the A & R person what you think is different from the last tape and, if the person has made specific criticisms, tell him or her what you have changed or why you chose not to. Whatever the case, make the A & R person part of the process, your process for getting your label deal.

DO'S AND DON'TS

I've talked about some of the specifics of making contact with the labels through a number of channels, but now I'd like to address some of the key positives and some of the potentially disastrous negatives that you should keep in mind as you solicit labels.

Do's

1. Make your contacts through professional channels and show them that you mean business.

2. Conduct yourself in a businesslike manner; save the theatrics for your show.

3. Keep up on what the labels are doing, who they are signing, which products are becoming successful, and the like. This goes for the A & R people, too. Keep an eye on which of their signings are winners so you can compliment them and watch for the stiffs, so you don't bring them up and embarrass both of you.

4. Demonstrate a good working knowledge of the business.

5. Read the trades, other books like this, magazines, and anything else that will educate you about how the business works.

6. Be aggressive and seize every opportunity to make contact with anyone from a record label.

7. Talk to as many bands with label deals as possible and get their side of the story, from how they got signed to how their labels treat them.

8. Spend your money wisely. Doing so will ensure that you have enough money to finance the making of demos, sending out tapes, traveling to visit labels, and so forth. All the planning in the world can't help you if you run out of cash.

9. Make friends—from people at the record label to agents to other bands to promoters. After all, who would *you* rather help: a friend or a stranger?

10. Be positive and always wear clean underwear (my mom made me put that in).

Don'ts

1. Don't compare yourself to other acts that have been signed, as in, "You signed them and we're better, so why won't you sign us?"

2. Don't lose your temper. Keep your emotions out of it.

3. Don't criticize other bands, labels, or A & R people. You *never* know who you are talking to.

4. Don't change things in your music or your act if you don't agree just because some label guy tells you to. If you don't believe in the change, don't make it.

5. Don't sign the first deal that comes along if it isn't right, especially a singles deal with an independent label and if publishing is involved. If you got one offer, you'll get more. Sign only what is right.

6. Don't spend a fortune changing your tape for A & R people. If they are really interested, they will offer to pay for the changes. If they don't offer, ask them to pay. If they decline, then see Item 4.

7. Don't rush. That means don't rush your recording sessions to get the demo finished. Don't rush to send the demo out, don't rush the people you send it to to respond, and so on. You can have it fast or you can have it right; you have to choose. By the way, if you rush the decision from the label, remember no is an easier decision to make than yes.

8. Don't lie. More than one band has told a label that they have other bids, forgetting what a small business it is. Just tell the truth and get on with your business.

9. Don't let your ego talk; make sure it's your brain that does the talking. A & R guys know big stars and they know up-and-comers and they are in the thick of it in the business, so they can spot bullshit coming a mile away. Save the hype for the interviews. Talk business when you're doing business.

10. Don't get discouraged. It's a tough business, but if you believe in what you do and stick to your creative guns, you'll do OK.

TOP TEN MISTAKES THAT BANDS MAKE ON DEMO TAPES

While I am doing the David Letterman–type list, let's take a look at the top ten things that bands do wrong, as compiled from my conversations with some of the country's top A & R people.

1. Unprofessional Presentation

There is a right way and a wrong way to submit your material to a label for consideration. The right way is to use good-quality tape, properly labeled, with song titles, times, copies of the lyrics, and a brief bio on the act. The wrong way is to use poor-quality tape that makes the music hard to listen to, give no information about any of the material, and leave it up to the A & R person to guess what you are singing about. If you want to be considered a professional, your materials have to present you as one.

2. No Reason for the Submission

"I want a record deal" is really not a reason for submitting a tape, at least not in the eyes of the folks I talked to. There has to be more than that. For instance, how you came to this point in your career where you believe you're ready to submit a tape. Why you chose that particular label. Where you have been and where you see yourself going. All this information is important for the A & R person to have some context in which to listen to your tape. Don't shortchange yourself by simply firing off a bunch of tapes. Take some time to make a proper presentation, and you'll increase your chances of a serious listen.

3. Lack of A & R by the Band

An A & R person expects you to do some A & R work on your own before sending your material to the label. Be selective and objective about your music. Just because you've recorded four songs doesn't mean you should send all four to the label. Choose the best stuff that you recorded, even if it is only two of the four songs, and send it, or if you like the other two but don't think they are quite ready, wait, fix them, and then send all four. Basically, what I'm saying is that you need to present your strongest material to make your best impression. Put your best foot forward.

4. Band Isn't Ready to Record

A band that doesn't yet have a manager or agent and that hasn't really played anywhere but simply got together to record has to be awfully good to get a record deal. Labels are looking for acts that have a team and some experience behind them.

5. Bad Arrangements

Minute-and-a-half-long intros before the vocal, endless guitar solos, songs with six or seven different parts or tempo changes, all are the sign of poor arrangement to an A & R person. In a demo a label is looking for a clean, crisp, focused presentation of your material, so good, professional arrangements will make a big difference when listening time rolls around.

6. Lack of Image and Direction

John Alexander of MCA Music gave me the best quote to illustrate this point. He once received a tape from a band that said, "We can do everything from country to heavy metal, just pick a style and we can do it." If *you* don't know who you are, then who does? A label wants to know what kind of act you are, to whom you will appeal, what radio format or formats your record can be sent to, and what sort of concerts you will play. Before you send your tape to any label, you should be able to answer all these questions definitively.

7. Band Didn't Do Its Homework

Sending your tape to "To whom it may concern" or "Capitol Records" is no way to begin a relationship with an A & R person. I suspect that if the label returned your tape addressed to "Rock Band," you'd be pretty insulted. Well, it doesn't cost much to pick up the phone, call the record company, and ask for the A & R person's name. Then you address your tape and letter to that person. Simple, ain't it? But you'd be surprised how many artists haven't figured that one out yet.

8. Wrong Style of Music for the Label

Dance labels don't release a lot of heavy metal. And metal labels don't put out much rap. And a gospel label won't release either one. Again, do your homework. Don't just get some music industry directory and send a tape to every record label listed. It's a waste of time, tapes, and postage. There are probably only ten or fifteen labels at the most that you should pursue. Spend your time finding out what those labels are doing, what sort of bands they are looking for, and who the appropriate people are to talk to. Another thing, if a label is already committed to a new, young act of a specific type (solo female, a country-rock band, or whatever that is very much like your act and it is spending a lot of time and money to break that act, hold off until the label has some success because the company will be reluctant to work on two projects that are so similar.

9. Blank Tapes

Believe it or not, this issue came up quite a few times. It's a real good idea to listen to every tape that you send to an A & R person before you send it. Also be sure that the tapes are rewound and cued up to the first song. Nothing is more annoying than having to wait for the tape to start.

10. Including Too Much Junk in Packages

A & R people don't want piles of stuff in the package. As I said before, all you need is a tape, titles, lyrics, a photo, and a few press clippings accompanied by a letter telling them

- why you are submitting the tape
- who your management/agent is
- how long you have been together
- how long you have been working

Also, be sure that you put a label on both the cassette box and the cassette. Most A & R people have a few hundred tapes around their office and if they like your tape but don't know who you are, then ... (scary thought, eh?).

Now some of you are probably sitting there saying to yourselves, "What a bunch of prima donnas!" Well, consider this: The average A & R person probably gets several hundred to a thousand tapes every year. The good ones try to listen to as many tapes as possible. They have taken the time to tell me what bugs them, and now I've told you. So, the way I see it you have two choices: First, you can call them a bunch of jerks or second, you can realize that you now have some inside info and use it to your advantage. The choice is up to you. (I recommend Number 2.)

RECORDING CONTRACTS

In the early days of rock and roll in the fifties, there was an onslaught of managers, small labels, publishers, and artists racing to put records into the marketplace. Music recording was not even considered a legitimate business by some, and the idea of ethics once you got beyond the major labels was laughable. While Columbia and RCA and the others were turning up their corporate noses at rock, men like Sam Phillips at Sun Records and Berry Gordy at Motown were signing acts almost as quickly as they came through the door. The only problem was that they were signing them to contracts that were horrendous. Some of the clauses were unfair, and some were downright crazy. For example, the Motown contract of the sixties made it clear that if the artist decided to leave the Motown label for any reason, he or she could not make records for any other label for five years! Motown called it a non-competition clause. Royalties, if paid at all, were minimal, and advances were out of the question. In comparison to today's deals, these contracts amounted to nothing short of slavery and made the difficult Hollywood film-studio deals of the thirties look like a walk in the park.

Nowadays things are different, but again, that goes for the major labels and does not always hold true for some smaller labels or individuals who will sign you up forever on the strength of a few dollars. The first and best advice that I can give you is to get a lawyer immediately! Recording contracts aren't something for a layperson, especially an inexperienced musician, to fool around with. You can bet that the recording company will have an attorney or two, and unless you ensure that your rights are adequately protected, your dream can quickly become a nightmare.

So the following discussion of contracts is not meant to send you off to negotiate with a label or producer. Rather it is intended to give you a small amount of information that will allow you to speak intelligently with your representatives when they begin to discuss your business arrangement with a label or independent producer.

Recording contracts are personal-service agreements and are predicated on the idea that you are being contracted by the company or producer to provide the service of performing music for the manufacturing and sale of records, tapes, and compact discs and that you will be compensated financially by them for doing so.

The contract breaks down into eleven major areas: term, advances, royalties, type (production or direct signing), recording commitment, budgets, tour support, accounting, termination, and default. Here's how each area of the contract works and the effect that it can have on you as a musician.

Term

The *term* of the contract outlines the number of years that the company or producer thinks it wants to be involved with you. It is always at the company or producer's option and can be outlined in various ways. Traditionally, the term of the agreement is expressed in an initial period of X years to be followed by X number of consecutive one-year options to a total of one, three, or five years.

The term of the contract is a tricky decision. On the one hand, you don't want to tie yourself up for a long time with some person or company that may let you down (remember, it's the person's or company's option to renew). On the other hand, you don't want the company or the producer to think that you have no any long-term potential and therefore to concentrate on another artist with whom it has a better contract.

A three-year total, consisting of one initial year and two consecutive one-year options, is best. Remember, it's your life and art that are being bargained for, so be careful!

Advances and Recoupability

Advances are lump sums of money representing royalties that will be due an artist when records are sold, but are paid to the artist by the record company before the actual sales. Advances against royalties, that is, against the percentage of the retail or wholesale price of the record that goes to the artist are, in most cases, *recoupable*, that is, are recovered from the sale of records before the artist receives any payments. They function much like an interest-free loan.

Advances are defined in most recording contracts as money that the record company spends for recording costs, videos, deficit financing of tours, and contractual option payments, that is, the payments made by the record company to the artist when it decides to extend the term of the agreement by one or more of the option years.

In some contracts *tour support* money is also recoupable. Tour support money is any money given to an artist or group to offset the costs incurred in performing live to support an album but before the band can command a large-enough fee to meet its expenses. The record-company people don't do this because they are swell guys; they do it because it has been proved time and again that live appearances stimulate record sales.

Other costs, such as manufacturing, promotion, and marketing, are not recoupable expenses. In some cases, but not often for new artists, a band may negotiate a *percentage of recoupability*, in which case only a portion of any advances is recoupable.

Bear in mind that an advance is money paid out before it is earned. Even though a record company does not view it as a loan (that is, it generally bears no interest and if your contract terminates for any reason before your sales earn back the advances, you do not owe the company the money), while you have outstanding advances, you will not be paid any royalties from the sale of your records until, in most cases, the advances are totally earned back.

In the current economic climate, the large advances of days gone by are but a memory, except for a handful of superstars. Today's advances come mostly by way of album budgets and tour support, not in lump sums of cash to the artist.

When it comes to royalties, you need to watch out for something called *cross-collateralization:* when the record company looks around for other places from which your advances can be recovered besides record sales. For example, a good lawyer for a record company will probably try to cross-collateralize your record royalty advances with your mechanical royalties, that is, the publishing royalties you receive from the use of your compositions on the record. If you encounter cross-collateralization in a contract, try to have it removed because it could definitely have an adverse impact on your cash flow. If you allow the label to get its hands on your mechanical royalties, you will not have access to that money. And an advance on mechanicals may be the only money you see from your records for a significant period, since as it will be some time before the label sends you any money for royalties even after you sell the records.

Here's what I mean. If you sign a deal on January 1, get an advance of $50,000 plus the costs of making the record, and deliver the record to the record label on May 1, the record probably won't get released until at least July. The record will be shipped to the marketplace in July and August and may begin to sell in September or October. The label probably has to account to you only twice a year. In June your record hadn't even been shipped, so no royalties were payable. In December you may show as having sold some records, but the label has to do two things before you receive royalties. First, it has to recover the recording costs, video-production costs (if they were recoupable and they probably were), and your advance and withhold a reserve for returns (see the section on Royalties). If you get any money at all, which is doubtful, it won't be much. By the way, the label may have as much as sixty days after the accounting period to pay you—on March 1 of the year *after* you signed your deal. The company won't account to you until June and won't pay until August. Now unless you have gotten real lucky and have sold a lot of records in your first year, you are going to need some money to live on, and that money will come from your publisher in the form of an advance on mechanical royalties. So if you give those royalties away, you'll be taking a substantial amount of capital out of your cash flow—a disaster for any working band or artist.

Type

The *type* of deal that you negotiate with a record company can vary as well. To oversimplify, there are only a few kinds of deals that an artist can make.

The first type of deal is a *direct signing* to a label. This deal takes place when a record company hears your tape or sees your act (usually both) and decides that you are a marketable commodity. In this case, you are usually approached with a contract that specifies a term, advances, and other such items that I have just discussed. The distinction is that you are, in essence, an employee of the company, performing a service for pay. By going this route, you give up a certain amount of autonomy since the record company retains certain rights in your contract, in the areas of material, studios, and so on, because of the nature of the agreement. As a new artist, you can expect to get 12 (which is about average) to 15 (great) percent of the retail selling price of the record as a royalty.

The second type of arrangement is a *production contract.* Under the terms of this agreement, you or an independent producer are responsible for the recording and delivery of albums to the record company. The record company may advance portions of the recording costs while the project is under way, but withholds the final payment until the finished tapes are delivered. The key element in this kind of arrangement is the freedom you retain for your songs, studio, approach to your music, and the like. Most of these deals contain a clause that allows the company to reject the album for certain reasons, but in a large percentage of cases, the company does not do so. A label will do a deal of this type if the artist they want to sign is already under contract to the production company and this is the only way they can get him or her. Under the terms of a production agreement, you will receive essentially the same royalty as with a direct signing, although the royalty may be slightly higher in some cases to allow some money for the production company.

As an artist, you will have a deal with the production company for a split of royalties, which may be fifty-fifty, sixty-forty, or whatever the best deal you can negotiate with them at the time of signing.

The next type of deal is a *master lease.* In this type of deal, the label essentially rents the master from you in exchange for royalties. The royalty rate is higher because the label doesn't have to spend any money on production, since you are delivering a finished master to it. Depending on your individual arrangement with the label, the label may give you an advance on these royalties in the form of a lump sum.

The next type of deal is a *pressing and distribution* deal (or P & D, as it is known). In a P & D deal, you, the artist, make an arrangement with the label whereby it does three things for you: (1) manufactures your records, for which you pay; (2) markets and promotes your record, for which you pay a fee; and (3) distributes your record, that is, makes sure that it gets to the record stores.

The fee for marketing can be anywhere from twenty cents to a dollar a record. The cost of manufacturing depends upon the configuration, that is, whether it is a cassette tape or a compact disc. This is the type of deal you may make if you haven't been able to make a direct signing or production deal, but have interested the label enough that it is willing to work with you. You will need to put a lot of time and energy into this kind of deal, but if it is the only kind of deal you can make, it's worth it because you still have all the benefits of being with the big label, and as far as the outside world is concerned, you are with the label.

The last deal is what is called a *buy-sell* deal. These deals are not nearly as prevalent as they were some years ago when the independent distributors were more active. A buy-sell deal works like this: If you had decided that you were going to record and manufacture your own record, for example, the distributor would buy the records from you at an agreed-upon price and would then sell them to record stores at a price that was marked up to include the manufacturer's profit. In this kind of deal, as in all record deals, the retail store has the right to return unsold records for credit, and you have to absorb these returns. In most cases, the distributor "buys" the records from you, but he wouldn't start paying you for them until the record stores paid him for the records that they sold. This is the way a lot of records and bands got started in the sixties and seventies; for instance, Heart were signed to a small independent label called Mushroom Records, which had a buy-sell deal with many of its independent distributors. In this sort of arrangement you become the record company and you have to do all the promotion, marketing, and publicity for your recording; however, it is a way to get your records into the marketplace. It is the kind of deal that you will probably end up making if you record and release your album independently. It's a good first step in your recording career, for if you are able to create some interest, even in just one or two regions, and sell some records, the major labels will look more seriously at signing you and may make a deal.

Royalties

Here's the part you've been waiting for. It's the part where you get paid for making music. Royalties, or points, as they are sometimes called, define the amount you will be paid for each piece of product that is sold. There are four key elements in the discussion of royalties:

1. Royalties are computed on either the wholesale or retail price of the product. Generally, there is an artist royalty and a producer royalty, and the percentages differ from contract to contract. There are no real norms, so it is up to you to negotiate the best possible deal. The percentages are 5 to 20 percent of retail (simply double that figure if your royalty is based on wholesale) with two or three points (percent) going to the producer.

2. Royalties are paid on net sales, that is, a certain percentage of the money that is due an artist and producer is held back by the record company against records that are returned unsold from the record stores. This is called a *reserve clause.* Every record company allows record stores to return a certain percentage of unsold records for credit. Instead of holding back the entire royalty payment, the company retains a reasonable (or sometimes not-so-reasonable) portion as protection. Through complicated accounting procedures, the full amount is eventually paid, but only after the number of records returned for credit is deducted from the number of records shipped to the stores for sale (which yields the *net sales figure,* that is, the actual number of records that have been sold and paid for); the net sales figure is the basis for the full amount of royalty money released to the artist.

Promotional copies are not paid for; therefore, no royalties are paid to the artist on these records. A promotional record a record is one that a record company gives to a radio station to play, to a reviewer for a newspaper or magazine review, or to the public in contests or other promotions. No royalties are paid on these records because the company receives no revenue from them. The quantity of promotional records given away by the record company is monitored closely because the company must account to the artist not only for how many records were sold, but for how many were given away at no charge; if the numbers differ radically, it can become a serious point of contention between the label and the artist.

3. *Free goods* are records given to record stores in place of discounts. For instance, a record company offers a 10 percent discount on your new record as an incentive for stores to buy larger quantities, to advertise it, or even to buy it at all (not every record that is released gets played on the radio or carried in every store). When the invoice is made up, instead of giving them an actual 10 percent discount from the money owed, the record company gives them extra free records valued at the amount of the 10 percent discount; that is, for every ten records the stores buy, they receive eleven. If they buy a hundred they get ten free; if they buy a thousand, they get a hundred free; and so on.

These free goods become the property of the stores to do with as they please. They can sell them, return them for credit, use them as extra incentives for people to buy records by selling them at greatly reduced prices, or whatever. The thing to remember is that these free goods are given in place of a discount; therefore, rather than see them simply as free records, you must view them as lowering the unit price of all the albums purchased by the retailers by the applicable percentage, in this case, 10 percent. No royalties are paid on free goods, for as in the case of promotional records, the record company receives no revenue for them. The quantities of free records are reported to the artists, however, so they can be aware of the quantities of their product that are in this category. Most contracts restrict the amount of free goods that the record company can distribute for a given album.

4. Certain conditions affect royalty payments and the amount paid to the artist. As I mentioned in the section on Advances, no royalties are payable to an artist whose advances, or a portion thereof, are recoupable until these advances are earned by the artist's sales and are paid back to the record company. In other parts of the world (referred to in most contracts as *International Territories*), a lesser royalty is paid because of increased manufacturing costs and limited sales potential, currency differences, or the inclusion of either a branch operation of the artist's record label or an independent distributor, who must also receive a percentage of sales for handling the record in that territory. If the record is sold at a reduced rate through a mail-order record club or is sold as a *delete* (a record that has been removed from the company's catalogue of current releases and sold at a reduced price), the royalty paid to the artist is reduced.

5. The artist is paid only when the record company is paid for the product. Even though the money may be advanced to the artist, if the record company is not eventually paid for the product, the artist is put into what is referred to as an *unrecouped,* or unearned position, and royalties are not paid to the artist on any future recordings until he or she catches up. Some artists have beaten this system by insisting that each album is a fresh start in the contract and therefore that the record company can withhold royalties only on each individual album that is not in an earning position, rather than withholding all money.

Recording Commitment

When you sign a recording agreement, you will have to guarantee that you will record and deliver a certain number of albums and singles within each contract period. Since an album usually includes ten to twelve songs and singles are generally taken from albums, the delivery of an album usually satisfies the recording commitment for albums and singles in most contracts. This commitment usually reflects the minimum number of albums that an artist can deliver during a contract period. The status of additional recordings is determined on a record-by-record basis.

The record company places the following restrictions on the recording commitment to protect it from certain abuses that could occur:

1. Most contracts stipulate that the *master recordings* that are delivered must consist of previously unrecorded material. They do so to avoid a situation in which an artist, wishing to change labels, delivers rerecordings of old songs, saving new material for a new deal.

2. A *live recording*, that is, a tape of a concert performance, usually does not qualify as a delivery unless specified in the contract.

The recording commitment exists so the record company can be assured that the artist will not do a first album and then, if successful, stop recording for a long period or attempt to capitalize on his or her success and change labels for a better deal. In many cases, this situation occurs even with the recording commitment, and it becomes a case for the courts. At this point, the recording company *suspends* the artist's contract. During a suspension for *nondelivery*, no time elapses on the contract and if an artist is three months late in delivering an album, for example, the entire term of the contract is extended for three additional months. This clause of the recording contract, known as the *suspension clause*, has been tested in court many times (once by a band that I managed), and each time the record company has won. It's hard to imagine how any court could rule in favor of the label. Compared to other occupations, a musician's career is short, and to allow a label to extend a contract arbitrarily may seriously jeopardize any chance the musician may have to realize the full potential of his or her talent or to establish any kind of financial security. Even though the suspension clause doesn't seem fair to the artist, the courts continue to come down on the side of the record labels and uphold it.

Tour Support

Artists who were signed to recording companies sometimes receive advances from the companies known as *tour support.* Most record companies believe it is good for the band or solo artist, and for record sales, to be seen in public performances. In areas where the group cannot make enough money to support the cost of touring, the record company makes up the difference between what the act is being paid and the expenses that they are incurring on the road.

In 99 percent of the cases, however, this money is recoupable from royalties. Many bands run up big recoupable advance tabs with their record companies and then sell thousands of records, but make no money. It is a good practice early in your career to make your tours financially self-sufficient so that later, your record sales earn you money and don't simply pay off your deficit. This means smart, tough booking practices and an almost fanatical obsession with financial details. In the end, however, good sense will pay off in dollars.

Budgets

There are many costs connected with the recording of an album. Studio rental, musicians, arrangers, engineers, all must be paid for, as well as tapes, rental gear, and the like. Budgets for albums can run anywhere from ten thousand dollars, which is considered low, to a half a million or even a million dollars for the supergroups. No matter how much is spent, however, most contracts stipulate that the record company must approve the budget before the recording session starts. For the supergroups, this approval is often a mere formality because the record companies know that even if these albums are expensive and go overbudget, they will at least be able to recover the costs from sales.

This section of the contract is important to the record company in the case of a new or relatively unknown artist because the sales potential of the act is unproved and, therefore, the company must be careful not to spend more than it can reasonably expect to recover from sales. This is often a serious point of contention between a new artist and the record company, for when you get to the end of the budget and the album is not quite up to the standard that the artist has set for himself, a decree from the record company that the budget is exhausted and thus that the recording session is over can be hard to take. This is the point at which good representation and negotiation, as well as a good relationship with the record company, are invaluable in convincing the company that the extra dollars to complete the album will be well invested.

Accounting

Whenever I appear at a seminar for young managers, music marketers, and musicians, this is the point when their eyes glaze over or when they suddenly get thirsty or need to use the bathroom—anything to get out of the room. But remember, boys and girls, this is your money I'm talking about, and you should be paying close attention. As I have already said, royalties are money paid to the artist for the product that is sold. Record companies employ large staffs of accountants who accurately log these sales and ensure the prompt payment of royalties that are due.

Prompt is the key word here, in that all contracts stipulate payment dates for royalties, and unhappy artists often cite nonpayment of royalties (or *failure to account*, as it is called) in their bid to leave a label.

The company can account to an artist once, twice, or four times a year, and all contracts allow the artist the right to audit the record company's books on demand.

Termination

If a record company believes you haven't been a productive signing for them, it may, at the end of the contract period, decide to terminate, that is, not pick up your option. With termination, there is no penalty to the artist, and the money that was advanced but still unrecouped is not repayable in cash.

However, in most cases, the company retains the rights to your recordings in its catalogue and can recover its advances from future sales of the product. After the advances have been recouped, that is, after your record sales have paid back all outstanding advances, the company will continue to pay you royalties for as long as the records remain in its catalogue, just as if you were still signed to the company.

Default

This is a key area in most contracts. If an artist *defaults,* it is usually for the nondelivery of a product according to the recording commitment and, as I said before, that artist's contract would be suspended for the time during which the album remains outstanding to the record company. The record company can default in many areas, from the failure to release the product or to promote it (tough to prove) to nonpayment of royalties or the failure to account. In most contracts, the defaulting party has thirty days in which to remedy the default to avoid legal action. A serious default by either party can result in the termination of the contractual relationship.

Certainly this is an oversimplification of the basic recording agreement, but it will give you some idea of the intricacies involved. There is such a thing as a standard recording agreement that any music-business lawyer can give you. Take some time to read it, not, as I said before, to become a hard-nosed negotiator, but to be informed so that when your lawyer or manager is discussing *points, term,* or *default,* you'll know what he or she is talking about. A good understanding of both sides of the recording agreement will make your life with the record company easier and more productive. Remember, a contract is an agreement between two people to do business for "mutual" benefit—yours and the other party's, and that's how your contract should work. One other point on contracts. I have always believed that once you sign a contract, you should put it away and get on with your business, which should be based on the mutual benefit I just mentioned. If you have to take out the contract, it means that the communication, and therefore the business relationship, is in trouble. The best contract is the one you sign and never see again.

"The Deal" in the Nineties

The record business is changing in the nineties, and it's changing dramatically. Along with the new corporate look of many labels, brought on by acquisitions, new infusions of capital, and a cautiously optimistic attitude about the business, megadeals are changing the way artists, labels, managers, and lawyers look at their relationships. First, a little history.

In 1986 a West German media conglomerate, Bertelsmann, Inc., purchased RCA Records, once home of Elvis Presley, for $300 million. In 1988, Japan's Sony Corporation paid $2 billion for CBS Records in a deal that was described by New York music-business attorney Allen Grubman as "the day the record business was 'bar mitzvahed.'" In 1989 Time, Inc., and Warner Communications signed a $14 billion deal that brought together two of the world's largest communications giants—a deal that included the Warner Brothers, Reprise, Atlantic, Elektra, and other labels that were owned or distributed by Warner labels. That same year PolyGram purchased Chris Blackwell's Island Records for an estimated $300 million. Also in 1989 Phillips, the European electronics giant, acquired the Los Angeles–based A & M Records for $500 million, and in 1990 David Geffen became one of the richest men in the world through the sale of Geffen Records to MCA for $550 million in cash and stock. That same year, MCA Records was itself purchased by Japanese giant Matsushita for a reported $6.6 billion in cash and securities.

These big-money acquisitions and deals have started a new round of negotiating for artists in the business. In an excellent article published in the June 16, 1991, issue of the Los Angeles *Times Calendar Magazine,* Robert Hillburn and Chuck Philips compared these new negotiations to sports figures. "Suddenly the recording business is looking like baseball with its escalating contracts," said Don Engel, a well-known Los Angeles music-industry attorney, "When the biggest star in the league suddenly gets $10 million, then all the $3 million guys want to move up the ladder to $5 million."

In March 1991 two record deals were signed that are likely to change the face of the music and recording industry forever. On March 12 Janet Jackson signed a $40 million contract with Richard Branson's Virgin Records. On March 21 her brother Michael Jackson signed a deal worth a reported $65 million. These megadeals touched off a round of renegotiations with superstars throughout the business. The Rolling Stones signed with Virgin Records for an estimated $45 million, Mötley Crue signed with Elektra for $35 million, and Aerosmith signed with Sony Music for $25 million. In the months following the Jackson deals, Don Engle was swamped. "In the last couple of months I've been retained by eight artists and entered discussions with about ten others. What we're talking about here is major artists trying to break contracts." The mentality goes like this. If you are the manager of a superstar like Madonna or Bruce Springsteen with a contract worth $10 million or so and you see the Jackson deals go down, you immediately want to get the same kind of deal for your act. Now maybe your deal with the label doesn't end for several years and in several years circumstances may have changed and with it your chances of making a megadeal for your act. What do you do? You hire a high-priced attorney to try to get you out of your existing deal so you can get a better one.

Regardless of who ultimately gets what, the Jackson deals sent a shock wave through the $7.5 billion-a-year music industry. On the one side are the managers who are looking to get as much as they can from whomever they can get it. On the other side are the record companies, which are faced with a real problem, articulated by Al Teller, chairman of MCA Music Entertainment Group: "It just won't work. If the components of these deals became industry standards, the record business as we know it would not be able to function." The lawyers, who stand to make big fees for making and breaking the deals, are, of course, disagreeing with the label presidents and lobbying for a new order. Allen Grubman put it this way: "The executives who were involved in restructuring the record business a few years ago now understand that the stars should be compensated for their true value."

Here's what's making the record companies nervous. Let's say that lawyers suddenly start to challenge all the big artists' deals in court, break them, and then make new megadeals. First, having a superstar on the roster is prestige for many labels, so they will be very reluctant to lose them. Also, since many of these companies are traded on the stock exchange or are owned by companies that are, losing a major act can have a negative impact on the price of the companies' stock that could run to tens of millions of dollars.

And finally, there is the issue of hit records. Superstars tend to make them, and hit records sell, which is the entire point of the exercise. But the real problem is this: If labels have to make enormous payments to superstar artists, it is going to have some impact on the companies' ability to operate. The money will have to come from somewhere, and, although they may deny it, the cutbacks will be seen in staff, new signings, and the like. In a way, it's like buying a Mercedes Benz if you make only twenty-five thousand dollars a year. You may be able to scrape enough money together to buy it, but you won't be able to afford to drive it. And if something goes wrong and it breaks down, you don't have enough money to fix it. It's like that for the labels. If they pay too much to get the acts, it will force them to cut back on promoting them, and if the superstar acts don't deliver the megahits, then, there will be real problems.

Irving Azoff, former head of MCA Records and onetime manager of the Eagles and Stevie Nicks, compared superstars to fine art: "When you're talking major artists, it's like auctioning a painting. There are only so many of them and you need at least one to hang on the wall. ... The deal isn't just, 'Can I ever hope to make back the money on signing this artist?' It's also about what will this do for the worth of my company and the morale of my employees." Well, certainly, the prestige of having a superstar on your label is one thing, but if it gets in the way of other business, is it really worth it?

And more important, if it affects the signing of new, young acts, then you have a real problem. Since the superstars are not going to live and remain popular forever, record labels constantly need to replenish their supply of talent. Major-league baseball teams have farm teams to develop tomorrow's talent, realizing that they can't simply rely on signing free agents for huge sums of money. Organizations like the Toronto Blue Jays, for example, have developed the farm system into an art, finding good young players, bringing them along slowly, and then reaping the rewards either from stellar performances by the young players on the Jays or by giving the team strong young players for trades to support their roster.

Whatever the case, the record business is no different: Without new blood, it will stagnate. Clive Davis, a record-industry legend who now runs Arista Records, agrees: "Experience has shown that major dollar guarantee deals that people have made—whether it was for Paul McCartney or the Rolling Stones—have lost money. ... I've always felt that the only way to have a successful company was to sign artists from scratch or to reach out for artists who might be [underachieving] at another label." Al Cafaro of A & M Records, who lost Janet Jackson to Virgin Records, is more direct: "The time, energy and money spent on these megadeals detract from new artist development. ... Not only do they cause severe morale problems with other artists on the label, they can end up with the superstar being viewed more as a profit and loss statement on the company's ledger sheet than as a creative human being."

Even Richard Branson, who made the Janet Jackson deal, agrees: "Over the years Virgin has built a reputation for developing new talent ... people from out in the streets who we feel have a unique talent." Sounds good, but it works only if there is enough money around to support the new artist program.

What if a major act wants out of their label to make a new deal but owes the label two or three more albums? Madonna, for example, could no doubt command a Janet-, or maybe even a Michael-size deal, but she reportedly owes Warner Brothers four more albums. Well, one way for an act to get out is to invoke what is called the seven-year statute. Don Engel explained: "Artists looking for better terms who still owe the company five albums after seven years come to me and they say 'I'll be dead and in my grave before I finish this contract'"

The seven-year statute was introduced into California law to avoid just this kind of situation. It says that entertainers cannot be tied to any one company for more than seven years. It was introduced about fifty years ago to free Hollywood movie stars from long-term studio deals. Record companies are afraid to challenge the seven-year law, so they are usually willing to renegotiate with an act to avoid a court fight that may prove that the seven-year law can stick and will open the floodgates to artists, signed in California, who are trying to break their deals. About four years ago, the courts gave the record companies a bit of a break on the seven-year statute. The Recording Industry Association of America, which represents most of the major labels, asked the courts to extend the seven-year statute to ten years. Although the courts refused, they agreed to allow labels to sue artists and recover damages for records not delivered by artists who invoke the seven-year statute.

Some labels are getting smart. To avoid the free-agency trap, MCA negotiated a one-album deal with Boston, which worked well enough for both of them that they signed another one. What this all means is a new level of sophistication for the music industry in the nineties and beyond. Armed with high-priced legal talent, the artists and their managers will continue to storm the bastions of the corporate bank accounts to try to get not only their fair share, but as much or more as the next guy or girl superstar. From the early artist agreements, which were true nightmares, to today's superstar leverage, the balance of power seems to be shifting in the direction of the talent for the first time, especially if you've established some level of success.

THE DO'S AND DON'TS OF RECORDING CONTRACTS

Next follows what I believe to be the definitive list of do's and don't's for a new artist signing his or her first recording agreement. If you pay attention to this list, the other stuff in the deal is minor.

Do's

1. Find yourself the best attorney you can, someone you trust and you know has made successful deals in the past.

2. Insist on reading the agreement yourself and ensure that you have any questions answered by either your attorney or the label with which you are signing.

3. Ensure that the label has an obligation to release your record no matter what, and if it doesn't, that it has to return the rights and the masters to you within a reasonable time to allow you to find another deal. Also ensure that the label will allow you to buy out of the contract for what the label has invested in the actual recording and nothing else.

4. Maintain as much creative control over the choice of material, producer, packaging, and the like as possible.

5. Be sure that the label has to exercise any options in writing on or before a specific date.

Don'ts

1. Don't let the label cross-collateralize anything with anything, especially recording royalties with publishing royalties.

2. Don't let the label include anything other than the actual production costs of your records or videos or tour-support funds as recoupable against your royalties. Be sure to have your lawyer include specific definitions of what constitutes tour support and the percentages of video costs the label will recover.

3. Don't let the label talk you into leaving anything out of the contract with a promise that there is no need for it to be contractual, since it will be done anyway.

4. Don't even think about doing a deal without a competent attorney.

I know that all this is pretty heady stuff—big-time guys talking about megadeals for superstars and contracts worth millions—but that's the strange thing about the music business. If you think, "I'm just starting out, that stuff is way above me," you could be in for a weird surprise. So many acts, especially today, struggle along and then release the perfect record for the perfect time and are suddenly in the big leagues, often before they are ready. You may think that the big deals are beyond you right now, and maybe they are, but it's important that you know the issues and answers just in case you get that elusive hit record and you go from being the Nobodies to the Ultimate Somebodies almost overnight.

TWO

Your Debut Album

RECORDING YOUR FIRST ALBUM

When the time finally comes to record your first album you are going to encounter some interesting phenomena and some very unique people along the way. In this section I talk about what and who you will run into, both to prepare you for the experience and to give you some clues about what to watch out for. I focus on four important things; (1) how recording your first album will differ from your demo experiences, (2) how to prepare for your first real recording session, (3) who are the key people in your recording experience, and (4) why sometimes your demos are great and your masters stink: how it happens and how to avoid it.

How the Process Works

Budgets
I'm probably getting a little too corporate here by putting budgets first, but believe me, money is going to be a recurring theme throughout your career, so you may as well get used to it. Think of it this way, anytime you do anything in the business, you are going to be doing it, one way or the other, with your money. In this case, it's the budget for your first recording session, which will be a recoupable expense in your contract. You've got a choices here: to work out the budget and stick to it, so you bring your record in for the amount of money that has been allocated to do it (give or take a little bit) or to forget about the budget, spend forever making the record, and not recoup until you sell triple platinum (assuming that you ever sell triple platinum). You don't have to become an accountant to record an album. In fact, once you take a look at the budget, you probably don't have to worry about it again (that's your manager's job), but you should at least be aware of what the budget is and how close you will be at the end of the project to delivering

your album on budget. If you know the story at the end of the session, you won't get an unpleasant surprise when the royalty statements arrive without a check.

Choosing Your Producer

The next thing you have to do is to find a producer. It sounds easy, doesn't it? Well, it isn't, or at least it shouldn't be. If you're a new act, the A & R people at your record label will want a lot of input in choice, as they will be familiar with different producers and their styles. More established artists will make the choice themselves.

The producer of your record is one of the most important people in your life. He or she is going to take your music and try to put it on a record in a way that is going to make radio stations want to play it and people rush out to buy it. It's a very personal thing, like letting someone go through your underwear drawer. After they get over the initial rush of signing a recording contract, a lot of bands find it hard to give up the creative reins to a stranger. And as an act becomes more successful and begins to develop a unique sound, it becomes even harder, especially if the producer suggests that the act should go in a new direction or try a new sound.

The key to a successful relationship with a producer is the same as it is in any relationship, and that's trust. You have to have a good feeling that the person with whom you are dealing really respects who you are and what you are doing, and you have to be willing to trust the person with your songs. Make no mistake about it, there are some egotistical jerks out there producing records who have the attitude, "Hey kid, I'm doing you a favor by even showing up here," and if you encounter one of them, you should do whatever is necessary to get rid of him or her. You cannot possibly create in the atmosphere of tension that will arise at the sessions, so you may as well get rid of the producer early and find someone with whom you can make a record that you all agree is the right-sounding record for you.

Preproduction

Now we get to the music part. In preproduction, you will want to begin work with your A & R person on the choice of the material for the record and with your arranger and your producer on how you are going to treat individual songs and the album as a whole. In preproduction you may do some eight-track demos of the songs in different tempos, with different instruments or treatments. A large part of preproduction is rehearsal and experimentation. It's the time in which you begin to conceptualize the music. Once you get into the studio, your main job is just to get it down with all the emotion and enthusiasm you can muster. But in preproduction you can stretch, experiment, and turn the songs into living things, ready to be captured on tape.

Recording

Next comes the actual recording session. It's tough to tell you how you should act or what you should do in your first session. Everyone is different and everyone handles the session differently. Some artists immediately take to the studio, find it comfortable, and dive into the process. Others find the whole scene intimidating and have a tough time relaxing and making good music. All that can really be said is that the studio is just a tool—a way to get your music on record—nothing more. It's private, personal, and secure from the outside world (especially if you are like an artist friend of mine who locks the door from the inside and pushes the furniture up against it). Your first session is bound to be a little intimidating, but if you remember that it is your first session and that you will never have another first session, you may be better able to relax and enjoy it and concentrate on what is most important: working with your team to make the best record you can.

GETTING READY

Producer

I talked about what kind of relationship you need to have with your producer to make the project work. Now I'll tell you what the producer does. Your producer is the one who makes a lot of decisions about how you and he are going to make a hit record. These decisions include everything from the choice of material for the record from among your songs and other songs that have been presented to him, to what some of the sounds will be on the record, to what studio and engineer you will use, to suggestions for other musicians who may be brought in to play certain parts, and even to the instrumentation in the studio versions of the tunes. Remember it is the producer's job not only to make the record sound right, but to make it as commercial as possible while remaining true to the sound of the band.

Producers come in all shapes, sizes, and temperaments. Every producer has a personality and a style, both of which will end up on your record, so keep this in mind when you choose. Do not, by the way, be overly impressed by reputation. If a producer did a good job for one act and they sold a lot of records, that doesn't mean that he is right for you; after all, people sometimes get lucky. Also, bear in mind what kind of deal has to be made. Some producers who have had one hit suddenly decide that they deserve a figure just short of the national debt plus a half a dozen points on your record for their services. Pay them what they are worth, nothing more. Your lawyer should know what that amount is and, no matter what, don't let anybody railroad you into an overpriced "prima donna" producer.

I guess I should take a minute here to explain how a producer gets paid. Producers usually get a fee plus a percentage of record sales. Sometimes the fee is just that—a flat sum of money plus the percentage points—and sometimes the fee is an advance on these points. The percentage, or "points," as they are called, are negotiable. The hotshots get five or more points, that is, 5 percent of the retail price of every album sold. Others get 2 or 3 percent, with 3 percent being about average. Some producers' deals include variances based on sales, that is, a five-point producer may get five points on the first 2 million records, and then four points on the next 2 million records, and three points on the rest, whereas the three-point guy's percentages may go up. That's all negotiation between your lawyer and the producer's. So while you guys are talking music and songs and drum sounds, the two lawyers will be bashing each other over the head with their Gucci briefcases to work out the deal. That's how the producer gets paid, and that's what he does.

A & R Person

The A & R person at the record label is an extremely important element of your creative process. Yeah, yeah, I know, that ain't what you've heard. Well, I'm here to tell you that you've heard wrong. Too many bands would crawl on their knees over broken glass just to get near an A & R type before they get signed, but after they get a deal, all of a sudden they are much too cool to listen to the A & R person. What always gets me is, How did they suddenly get so smart? If you, as a new artist, are going to start ignoring people at your record label this early in your career, you had better become very big and stay that way for a very long time. Otherwise the people (key word here) who you insult, irritate, or otherwise alienate are not going to hang in there with you through the tough times (and we all have them) for any reason other than business, and in a business that is built on relationships, that is not the way to do it. Treat the people around you like people and graciously accept what they have to offer. Some of the things that the A & R person will do for you include these:

• Help in choosing material for the record. The A & R person will listen to the songs that you have written and perhaps even play them for others in the company and will make suggestions about which is the strongest. He may also present songs from publishers, other acts, or old songs that you could cover. He does all this to find the best mix of good-quality commercial material to make your project a hit.

• Help in locating the most appropriate producer for you and your music. A & R people are in constant contact with a number of producers and make it a point to keep up on the work and reputation of both the established "stars" and the new, hot "up-and-comers." They will get copies of recordings done by various producers, arrange face-to-face meetings, attend the meetings with you, and make suggestions designed to help you make the ultimate choice. And once you've made the choice, they will then work with the producer, his manager and lawyer, and your legal and management representatives to help you get the best deal.

• Help in finding the right studio. Once again, A & R people are constantly in touch with studios, keeping up on what projects are being done where; who has the new, hottest engineers; what studios have installed what new equipment; and where the best financial deals can be made, all things that will have considerable bearing on your record project.

•Help in budgeting the recording project. A & R people will not only help you decide on the budget, they will monitor that budget so you don't spend so much money that you will not recoup until just after the next ice age. At the same time, they will get you the extra money you need to complete a project that needs only a little more to make it right.

A & R people also act as your creative link to the record label and to the industry at large. They act as cheerleaders for your project in the company and to the business. Many A & R people have good relationships with radio stations, especially in the larger markets, and the radio people respect the A & R guys and look to them for the new material they will play in the future.

My advice is to create and maintain an excellent relationship with your A & R person, to avail yourself of the things that he can provide for you, and to ensure that he understands that you know the partnership that exists between you and him, in making your records for the label.

Studio Engineer

A studio engineer is the guy who knows what all those knobs and switches on a mixing console actually do. He is a specialist in "sonics," that is, the creation of sounds and the commitment of those sounds to tape. Although many producers also understand the technical aspects of the recording studio, it is the studio engineer who has to figure out what to do when the producer says he wants the guitar sound to be "sweeter" or to have "more bite." Since these aren't technical terms, it's the engineer who has to figure out what frequency response to add to the top or bottom end of the sound, what new mike to use, or what sort of effect has to be put on the track to give it the sound that the producer is looking for. Many producers have favorite engineers with whom they work all the time, and the teamwork is the direct result of the engineer's ability to turn ideas into sounds for that producer.

The engineer will create the sounds during the laying down of the basic tracks and will then be responsible for keeping track of the various takes on various tracks of various instruments, so when the band or producer want to hear "that take where the bass plays the G against the C in the guitar solo," the engineer can find it and play it with a minimum of delay. Once upon a time, when the dinosaurs roamed the Earth, that kind of record keeping had to be done manually on different track sheets or tape boxes. The advent of computers has made the job a lot easier, but the basic concept remains the same. Once the tracks are down, the engineer will work with the producer on mixing each song. Often the engineer will be left alone to do the first few passes at the mix; then the producer and band will get involved in subsequent takes leading to the final mix. But it's the engineer who is involved at all stages.

There are a lot of music-business schools around today, and many promise to make their students studio engineers. All these schools can do, of course, is to teach you how to run a board and work the gear. The real engineer is an artist, and it is the "feel" that takes years to master. The engineer is a key player in your session. Buy him coffee every now and then.

Remix Engineer

Once you've completed the album project, it will be time to think about a single or a club mix. In some cases, the same engineer who worked on the recording session will create the remixes for these specialized uses. But sometimes a fresh set of ears can help. Since the disco craze of the seventies, a new type of engineer has emerged: the remix engineer. These guys specialize in creating sounds that are specific to the club atmosphere. Drums, bass, or other instruments that work well in the nightclub atmosphere are enhanced. Songs are lengthened with numerous edits and are made interesting in other ways, all targeted at keeping dancers on the dance floor, enjoying, requesting, and eventually buying the recording of a particular song. To capitalize on the club craze, some radio stations began playing these club mixes on the air.

After a while, though, they began to have second thoughts about playing twelve- or fifteen-minute versions of the same song. So their record companies hired the remix engineers again to make shorter versions of the club mixes specifically for radio, and the circle was complete. Rock and roll records are seldom remixed for club use in North America. Rap, hip hop, and other dance styles, though, are constantly remixed, sometimes by a variety of different famous mixers or DJs, all of whom add variety and therefore longevity to a song by keeping it fresh and interesting. If you make rhythm and blues or rap music, the remix engineer will figure prominently in your recording sessions.

Arranger

If you remember, among the top ten mistakes made by bands on their demos supplied to me by a number of A & R people, "poor arrangements" was cited as one of the major problems. Arranging is an extremely important part of your recording process. When a writer creates a song, she often tends to concentrate on the verses and choruses, lyrics and melody, and little else. An arranger tears the song down and rebuilds it, adding the subtleties that will take it from a song to a composition. Here's an example. Let's say you are a songwriter and singer who plays the guitar. You write a song that has an interesting guitar intro, a good verse, interesting chorus, and, it is hoped, a unique bridge. You decide to go into the studio and put it on tape. You make your recording with you and your guitar and maybe a drummer and bass player. You listen back, and it sounds okay, so you send it off to a label. About two weeks later, you get a letter saying that the song is OK, but it needs an arrangement. Now you're a little baffled because you thought you had one. The song has all the requisite parts, and two other musicians are playing and singing parts that flesh out the song and make it interesting. Well, here's the problem. Unless they are arrangers, most songwriters hear their material in a pretty straightforward way. When they write, they write for content, not for texture.

So you take your song to an arranger, and he or she begins to fiddle around with it. After a while you go back to see the arranger, who plays it for you with a new intro that's no longer guitar but piano and that now leads into the verse, which is no longer just you singing a solo vocal but has an answering chorus that comes back at you after certain lines. The arranger may have brought the hook in sooner and, may have even introduced the melody from the hook into the intro. The choruses are musically the same, but much bigger. The arranger may have added more voices and changed some of the parts that your musicians will play, perhaps adding some interesting voicings to different instruments to increase the texture of the song. Perhaps he or she has sped up or slowed down the tempo or changed the rhythm entirely from funk to reggae.

Arrangers add the finishing touches. If your song was a house, the arranger would be the interior decorator (don't laugh). He or she would choose the colors, arrange the furniture, and make sure that everything matches and flows from room to room throughout the house, so nothing seems out of place. Now I'm not saying that arrangers clean everything up and make it nice and neat—quite the contrary. If an arranger thinks that a song is too neat and boring, he or she will shake it up a little, throw something in where it appears not to belong just to make it interesting, and then bring it around again in context. Arrangers make the song come to life and give it focus and interest. When an A & R person talks about the lack of arrangement on a demo, what he or she is really talking about is the lack of focus and of interesting changes or ideas in the music.

Arrangers are generally brought in by producers, who are sometimes arrangers themselves. Independent arrangers usually get paid by the song and receive no ongoing percentages on the album. A good arranger can turn an average song into a hit and an average album into a creation.

Musicians

The Beatles used Eric Clapton and Billy Preston, the Rolling Stones used Bobby Keys and the Manhattan Horns, and Bruce Springsteen used "the Big Man," Clarence Clemmons. All bands, at some point in their careers, bring in additional players to perform in their recordings or on tour. Usually, they do so for a specialty. For example, the Rolling Stones brought in Bobby Keys because no one in the band played sax. The Beatles brought in Eric Clapton because they needed a great guitar performance, and no one in the band was capable of providing one. The difference here, of course, is that the Beatles didn't credit Clapton (*White Album*, "While My Guitar Gently Weeps," there ya go Eric!) on the liner notes, while the Stones obviously did.

Additional musicians are an important part of the recording process. If you reach a point in the recording where you need that interesting extra sound suggested by your arranger and no one in the band can do it, you'll have to bring in an extra player. We all know about studio players and how great they can be. They are the hired guns of the business. Guys like Jeff "Skunk" Baxter, Jeff Porcaro, David Paich, and even Glen Campbell became famous performing on the recordings of others. Each then found fame on his own, Campbell as a pop country star, Baxter with the Doobie Brothers and Steely Dan, and Porcaro and Paich with Toto.

Good session players can make a huge difference in your ultimate product and should be utilized as a tool whenever they are needed in the recording process. Let's talk about that process for minute. There is one instance in which most bands are reluctant to use a studio player and they really shouldn't be. Not every player in every band is a virtuoso musician. Some may be great writers and great singers, but just average players. Those average players should not be expected to be anything but average players in the studio, and yet there is some kind of stigma attached to bringing in session guys to handle some of the tougher parts, especially if someone in the band plays that particular instrument. There is no loss of face connected with using a studio player for a hard part in the studio session. What you are trying to do in the studio environment is to get the best possible performances and sounds and, if this means that you need to bring in some help, I suggest that you set your ego aside for a time and use somebody who you know can do the job.

There are a variety of reasons for using studio players. First, of course, you will get the part down and played well, and it will make the song better. Second, you will save a lot of time, aggravation, and probably argument. Here's what I mean. If the producer wants a specific part and one of the band members tries and tries to play it but can't, you will waste a lot of time that could be used more productively on other things. And if the band member can't cut the part but keeps trying, everyone will get frustrated, tempers will start to get a little short, and all of a sudden you'll have World War III on your hands all over some stupid guitar part. You wouldn't have a problem using a sax player if you don't play sax or, for that matter, using a producer to make the record. Studio players are the same thing. Just think of them as a device to help you get the record finished and to make it as good as possible. You can always learn the part later and play it when you perform live. After all, it's your band and your record and your song, and that should be enough.

Manager

And finally, your manager. Now what can a manager have to do with a recording session? The answer is, "plenty." While you are trying to make a record, nothing—absolutely nothing—should get in the way. There should be no annoying problems or hassles that will cause you to get stressed out so you cannot concentrate on the business of recording. While you are making a record, your manager needs to protect you from the outside world. You shouldn't be doing interviews or benefit concerts, attending meetings, or doing anything else unless you, yourself, feel like it. In addition, since few records come in on budget, it will be your manager's job to negotiate the increased dollars with the label. Although you may be willing simply to take the money from the label on whatever terms just to get the record finished, your manager will make sure that you don't have to give up anything in your contract—something labels are not above doing when you need more money to finish the project. For example, people at the label may say, "Sure we'll give you the money, but we want some publishing to recover our investment." Or maybe they will want to cross-collateralize royalties with your publishing money until they are paid back, something that I told you never to do. It's your manager's job to get the money with no strings and to keep you out of it.

It's also your manager's job to settle any problems that may arise between the label, the producer, and you. If some kind of trouble comes up, you should stay out of it and let your manager handle it. For example, if you are having a problem with the producer, you shouldn't be the one who confronts him. Chances are you will work out the problem, but the tension that could be created by the confrontation could carry over to the remainder of the session and screw up the record. As an artist, you have to remain above that kind of thing and leave it to the business types to handle. Your manager should go to the label and talk with the A & R person; together, they should go to the producer and solve the problem or get rid of the producer. In the same way, if the producer or A & R person has a problem with the record, you should be told properly, and you should hear it from your manager, who should help remedy the problem and get things back on track. Things like artwork for the packaging, photos and publicity materials, and touring plans all have to be handled while the record is being made, and it is your manager's job to get those activities under way, bringing you in later when the preliminary decisions have already been made, so all you have to do is make the final comments. Clearly, this is not to say that you should abandon your entire career once you set foot in the studio. Rather, I'm suggesting that while you are in the studio, you will need someone who is willing to take the weight of business off your shoulders, so you can be creative. Even though many musicians don't actually feel it, the making of a record is a particularly stressful activity, and your mind should be left clear and free of hassle so it can focus all its energies on making the best possible recording.

So that's the list of characters in your little album-making drama. As you can see, each makes a considerable contribution to the process, and without any one of them, your foundation begins to weaken. This is the way it is usually done and, of course, there are exceptions. But it never makes sense to reinvent the wheel. Unless you have a strong reason for wanting to change the process, it's a good idea, especially in the early stages of your career, to do it the way it has been done for three decades and utilize your creativity in your music instead.

HOW GOOD DEMOS BECOME BAD RECORDS

... the world needs substance. The world doesn't need more "hip." "Hip" is dead. The world doesn't need more "cool," more "clever." The world needs more substantial things. The world needs more greatness. We need more Picassos, more Mozarts, ... not more Milli Vanillis. Not more haircuts.

—BILLY JOEL

We've all heard stories about bands who submitted great demo tapes to labels only to go into the studio and come out with records that were not only terrible, but bore no resemblance to the demos that got them the deal. How in the world could that happen? you may ask (which I'm sure most of the bands that it happened to asked as well). Well, it can happen in a number of ways, ways that are worth mentioning so you can avoid some of these pitfalls if you see them coming. There are three main culprits. Here's who they are and what they can do to screw things up:

PRODUCER

Producers have egos, some of them have great big egos, and those egos can sometimes be a disaster for a new act. I've seen a lot of situations in which a new band is put into a studio with a big-time producer with the expectation that the producer's expertise and track record will produce a first-time hit. But what often happens is that the big-time producer takes the gig only for the money because nothing better is around at the time or to fill in some time between major projects. If this is the case, there are dozens of ways that the record can get screwed up and a variety of reasons.

To start with, the big-time producer may have little or no respect for the young band; he figures they are lucky to have him and that they should simply shut up and do what they are told. I heard of a producer who refused even to listen to the demos, saying that they were irrelevant, since he had nothing to do with them. In a case like this, the producer will then try to make the band sound like he wants them to sound, which is usually like whatever band he had his last hit with. He probably won't take into account what the band actually sounds like, and that's where the problem starts.

After a while, the producer will probably get bored with the gig or will look for another job. In this case, he will usually send the band into the studio with the engineer to do most of the work, and he'll occasionally drop by to listen to the material and make comments—and he'll do so through the entire project. Later, when he gets another job, he will inform you that his new project with a big star starts before your project ends and he'll propose taking your tapes away and mixing them somewhere else (which he will probably hand over to someone else) or suggest that you and the engineer do the mixes and send them to him for approval. In the end, the project is a disaster, the record is a stiff, and you have just paid some egomaniacal idiot a fortune to set you back a few years, which payment is recoupable from the royalties you will never get because you can't even give the record away. Nice story, eh?

STUDIO ENGINEER

Okay, now here's how an engineer can screw it up. You and the producer show up and start to work on the project. The engineer has no respect for you, since you are brand new, and hates the producer because the engineer thinks he is better than the producer and should be producing records himself. Every time the producer asks for a specific sound, the engineer does what he thinks is right, rather than what the producer asks for. After a while, one of two things will happen: Either the producer will flip out and fire the engineer or the producer will just give up in frustration, keep the engineer, and try to work around him as best as he can. Ultimately, when the record is finished, it's OK, but nowhere hear what it could have been if the producer and engineer had been in synch.

THE ARTIST

And finally, there is suicide, that is, creative death by your own hand. The music business can be a real jungle, and some bands seem to have an insatiable appetite for self-destruction. Once they sign a deal, they are suddenly the creative geniuses of all time. They will hire a producer and engineer, go into the studio, listen to their demos, and then announce to everyone that the only reason that the demos sound the way they do is that they were produced for no money in a crummy studio with some idiot engineer, and they are generally crap. But now with all this high-priced talent and equipment, the band can make the record they really want to make.

The project usually end up being about a year late and is about 100 percent over budget. Sometimes this will happen on the second or third record, but in the career of bands who just don't get it, it invariably happens. The project wears on with the producer and engineer doing the best they can. Sometimes the band will show up, sometimes not, and when they do, it's usually to criticize what is going on. The producer and the engineer try to get some mixes done, and the band may well tell them that the mixes are OK to their faces, agreeing among the band members, however, that the mixes stink and that they want to redo them themselves. The producer is either fired by the band or completes the project, but in either instance, the band insists on remixing themselves. Meanwhile the release date has been delayed, the manager is at war with the label, the producer is telling anyone who will listen what a bunch of jerks the band are, and the band is busily screwing up the record. This is the ego method of making a record, and it is a clear demonstration of the fact that you don't have to pass an IQ test to get a recording contract.

So that's who screws it up and how. Now, here's how to avoid the screwups.

Producer

If the label wants to put you with a big-shot producer, your manager needs to insist that the A & R person gets some assurances from the producer:

•That he will meet with the band and A & R person, listen to the demos, agree on a direction for the record, and *stick* to that direction.

•That he will meet with the band and A & R person to discuss any major change in direction for the project and ensure that everyone involved agrees.

•That he agrees not to take on any other projects until he has satisfactorily (to the band and label) completed your project. This includes mixing or tracking of other acts.

•That he will work on and complete the project himself and that completion does not consist of giving the tapes to someone else to finish under his "direction" or listening to mixes done by the studio engineer.

If the producer intends to work seriously on your project, then these conditions will not present a problem. If there is a problem, don't use the producer. Finding someone else at the early stage of recording is much easier than and preferable to the alternative of trying to replace a bad producer in the middle of a project.

Studio Engineer

If you have a cranky engineer, fire him! No ifs, ands, or buts. If the studio manager says you have to use him, use another studio. Don't cave in and don't let your producer or label talk you into caving in. In a lot of ways, a studio engineer is just another piece of gear (no offense), and if something was broken and you couldn't fix it, you would change studios. Well, if the engineer is a jerk and is going to get in the way of making your record, he is broken, cannot be fixed, and must either be replaced or you must move. That's it; there's no compromise.

THE ARTIST

How do I say this tactfully? Well, I guess I can't. Look, if you can't
work like a pro, then drive a cab. Artists get a lot of space in our
culture to be more temperamental and idiosyncratic than the rest
of us mere mortals. In general, I am a big supporter of artists'
rights. But just as I would take a sharp knife away from a baby so
he wouldn't hurt himself, I would step in, in a minute and tell a
band when I thought they were hurting themselves. Smart artists
have long careers; dumb ones don't. Don't choose a bunch of flash-
in-the-pan psychos as role models, no matter how much money
they have made or fame they have achieved. If artists don't act like
intelligent human beings, they won't be able to deal with the
money or the fame and will lose both. The truly successful people
in the business got that way by being smart and by listening to others who made it. Some acts get a lot of publicity and appear to be
megastars, and then one day you read about them dying on a bathroom floor somewhere from an overdose or, worse being such jerks
that one day the business decides that they are over and, believe
me, if that happens, you are over. Make the best music that you
can, listen to the pros, and add your own ideas, and you'll come out
on top.

DOING IT YOURSELF

*I've always felt that I've had to fight to get where I
am. People always say you won't make it, and nine
times out of ten artists don't, but you may be that
one. And if you don't try, you'll never know.*

—CYNDI LAUPER

But let's say that you do all the stuff that I've told you and nothing
happens, that is, you don't get signed. Well, then, obviously you
haven't done it right because I couldn't possibly be wrong, could I?
Unfortunately, the answer is yes, I could be wrong. Or at least what
I've outlined here could be wrong for your band. And that's possible. As much as I would like to think that the music business is a
science, things happen in it every day that remind me that it is
very much an art. And to that end, you may find yourself in the
position of feeling that it's time for you to release your own record
independently. If that's the case, let's talk about how you can do it
and what you should do once it's out there.

WHEN TO DO IT

The first thing you will have to decide is when to put out your
own release. A lot of factors can contribute to this decision: You
can't get a deal with a label or you've been playing at a lot of
clubs, have a good following, and people keep asking you for a
tape or something, and you don't have one to sell to them—lots
of stuff. But the most important question is this: "Are you ready
to do it?" It takes a lot of patience and focus to put out a record
the right way, so caution number one is not to take it lightly; it's
expensive and should be done only if you're serious about having
something in the marketplace to lead you to that eventual major
label deal. If you're just screwing around (which is okay, too),

you may find yourself spending a lot of money that you otherwise would spend on something else that you really want.

RECORDING

OK, so you've made the decision to go ahead. The first thing you've got to do is to record the sucker. You'll find the specific details of the recording process at the beginning of the next section. Meanwhile, earlier in this chapter I listed all the details of a major label session and, oddly enough, it all holds true for your session as well. You may not need a high-priced producer or arranger but you will need a budget, an engineer, and a band. Try to find a studio that will give you a package deal instead of an hourly rate so that the meter isn't running every time you walk in. Having done that, create your recording as you would any other session, but remember it's going to be a record, so keep the commercial side of things in your brain while you're busy being an artist.

MANUFACTURING

How do they get the tape into those cassettes anyway? Now you're getting to the fun part, where you actually have to figure out how to get these things manufactured. And when you are making the decision, you need to keep something else in mind. Although you may not have thought about making CDs, radio stations don't play cassettes, so you're going to have to make a decision: Either you'll have to make some CDs as well as cassettes or, at least, you'll need to press some twelve-inch vinyl records for radio play. Anyway, back to manufacturing, here's how it goes:

• First: You'll need a master tape from the studio, 15 1/2 ips stereo, non-Dolby.
• Second: I'm not going to talk about records for general sale here because nobody uses them anymore, although most radio stations still have turntables to play records. Instead, I'll talk about tapes and CDs. You'll need to make a dubbing master, which means that you'll have to pay some attention to the equalization

because high-speed dubbing will have an effect on what the mass-produced tape will sound like. The same goes for your CD master.

Some manufacturing facilities will offer to make your masters in house. I don't recommend it. Instead you should find a mastering facility in your town or out of town (they are usually affiliated with a recording studio) and have your masters made independently. The engineer at this facility will pay a lot more attention to setting up the equalization of your tape for mass production to ensure that the final product sounds great than will the technician at the manufacturing plant, who will simply set the equalization of your tape at frequencies that will allow the machines to mass-produce it without overdriving the highs or lows. Technicians at manufacturing plants are not renowned for their artistic sensibilities; in fact, the manufacturing plant rejected the original tape of "My Generation" by the Who, thinking that the feedback at the end of the song was unintentional distortion.

In the factory they will set the mastering up to the frequency tolerances of the manufacturing equipment. They won't boost the bass or roll off at certain frequencies because the average machine tolerances tell them not to. In a professional mastering facility the engineer will push the frequency limits of the masters, which will result in a hotter, better-sounding product.

•Third: Demand that the manufacturing facility give you test copies to listen to before it begins the actual process of manufacturing. Take the test copy to the mastering facility and compare it to the master. If it is too far off, you'll need to find out whether the mass production is causing the problem or the master itself, which means you will need to remaster. Spend some time on this stage, since it is the most important part in making your own high-quality indie recording.

•Fourth: You will need to hire an artist to create some kind of graphics for the package. Don't spend a lot of money on it, though. You don't need full-color graphics, and there is no sense trying to compete with the majors in packaging. If you want to spend the money on full-color production, go ahead, but a well-done two-color cover will work just fine. After all, they don't play the cover, do they?

•Fifth: Have the factory package your product in twenty-five-count boxes because that is probably the number you will be able to convince any record store to carry, and it's easier to count boxes than individual tapes or CDs.

PROMOTING YOUR INDIE RELEASE

Sending out a press release is a waste of time. You are just one of a hundred bands who put out their independent records that day. It's better to spend your time getting your record into the right hands. Make a list of all the new music radio and TV shows in your area and nationally, as well as all the magazines that review new music and, most important, the campus papers and stations in your area, especially those campuses where your band has played.

We all know that campus stations can be as snobby as the commercial stations, but here's what I suggest. Invite the program director or music director from the college station to your recording session. If there are five colleges in your area, invite the program directors at different times or on different days, so that they don't know that you are inviting the others. Tell them how much you like their station and if they have a show, how much you like their show. Tell them how much their opinion means to you and get them involved in the process of making the record. In this way, you are building the team that I talked about earlier and bringing people in to help you, rather than simply knocking on their doors asking for a favor.

When the tape or CD is ready, send the music directors a copy with a letter and bio of the group. Send a picture if you like but it isn't necessary. After about a week, phone all of them to find out if they received the recording and if they are going to play it. If you want to try something a little different, do a special run of the recording for press and radio, including an interview with you. You need only a couple of questions to make up about a ten-minute interview. Then record just the answers at the end of the master tape and put them on side two if your music is on side one of the cassette or at the end of the music on the CD. Write the questions on a piece of paper and include it in the letter. In this way the radio stations can ask the questions themselves and fill in your answers. It sounds like you are being interviewed and gives the station one more reason to play your record over the others they've received.

Once you've made some headway and gotten a little bit of airplay, write a special letter to the big stations in your area and send it to the music directors along with your recording. In the letter tell them where and when the record is being played, if there has been any audience reaction, and if the record is selling in the stores. Mail it or hand deliver it to the stations. Follow up a week later and ask if the music directors have listened to it. Keep calling each week until they do. At the same time, send the record to all the on-air announcers at the stations in your market that would play your kind of music. Tell them what's happening with you, invite them to a show, and tell them that if they like it, they should mention it to the music directors and that you would appreciate any help they might give you. If you have T-shirts, send them one with the record.

Once you begin to get some airplay, not before, take the record to whatever local record stores you know handle indie releases. Tell them that you are getting airplay and that you'd like them to stock your record. Give the store managers a free copy as well as one to play in their stores. The reason you should wait until you are getting airplay is easy. The store managers are constantly approached by bands with indie releases, most of which never sell, so the managers are conditioned to believe that indie releases don't get played and don't sell. If you handle it the way I suggest, the managers will know two things: First, the record is getting played and some demand has been created and second, you have an idea of how the business really works and you will help them sell the product. Also, make the managers sign for the product and work out your payment terms and pricing. If all the other indie releases are five dollars, make yours six. A higher price tag makes you look special and sets you apart from the crowd. A lower one makes you look like a mark-down and a loser that the record stores are trying to dump.

USING YOUR INDIE RELEASE TO GET A RECORD DEAL

Record companies look for two things when they consider an act: the potential for airplay and the potential for sales. If you are able to generate both with your independent release, then you have a story to tell when you submit your indie release to the major labels for consideration.

The actual approach to the labels using your indie release instead of a demo tape is basically the same. You will no doubt be a little more sophisticated in your pitch simply because of the experience you have gained, but the key things you want to concentrate on are the airplay and sales you have been able to generate. Understand what I'm saying here: No label is going to be astounded by the fact that six stations are playing your record and it has sold eight hundred copies. It's not the volume that counts, but the fact that you have an endorsement of sorts from certain people in the music business community, combined with a demonstrated ability to get airplay and sales, which have prepared you to sign a deal. Earlier I talked about being ready to get signed. If all you have done is made some tapes, played some gigs, and sent the tapes to labels, you really haven't learned much. If, on the other hand, you have been through the process from recording to manufacturing to promotion to sales, you've picked up some valuable experience that could be just the thing that convinces the label that you have the maturity and initiative to warrant their investment in you. Your indie release, if properly presented, can be a real turning point in your effort to get that important record deal.

HELP FROM INDIE ORGANIZATIONS AND CONVENTIONS

The *New Music Seminar,* held in New York each summer, began as a small get-together of new artists, representatives of indie labels, and others who were interested in the business. It has grown to a week-long meeting of literally hundreds of people, from representatives of major labels, to new acts looking for deals, to people in the media. In the past, bands have been seen and signed at the seminar through showcases arranged throughout the city that seminar delegates can attend. In principle it seems like an unsigned act's dream. He or she has the opportunity to see dozens of industry big shots, get his or her tape auditioned by them, and interact with them at the conference on a one-to-one basis.

The amount of information you can pick up from the meetings

and simply from meeting people is considerable. The musical styles vary as widely as do the delegates. Rap, jazz, pop, and heavy metal are all represented, as are acts and labels from all over the world. The seminar's speakers are always top-notch, and so are the meetings and presentations, all of which are designed to keep delegates up to date on the most recent radio and record trends, production and recording techniques, promotion and publicity ideas, and a lot more. If you know nothing about the music business before you attend, you can leave just a few days later with a good idea of how it works and some important information to move you toward your goal.

The New Music Seminar has its share of critics and there are other regional music meetings, but no conference is as specifically aimed at the indie band and label as is this seminar. And it gives bands the chance to participate in its showcases to some of the most important people in the business. The New Music Seminar and events like it are a must if you want to gain the contacts and up-to-date information you'll need to turn your indie release into a deal.

THE RECORD COMPANY

SMALL VERSUS LARGE LABELS

I earned $367 million in sixteen years. I must have done something right.

—*BERRY GORDY, FOUNDER*
MOTOWN RECORDS

There are essentially two types of record labels: majors and independents. The major labels are:

Warner Brothers: The only one of the major labels to remain

American owned. Warner Brothers and its associated labels, Elektra and Atlantic, boast a stellar roster of artists, including Prince, Madonna, Paul Simon, Robert Plant, and the Cure.

PolyGram: The PolyGram group of labels includes Mercury, Polydor and PolyGram, Island, and A & M Records. Its roster includes John Mellencamp, Bon Jovi, U2, Sting, and Bryan Adams.

Sony Music: In 1990, CBS Records, which includes the Columbia and Epic labels, was acquired by Japanese electronics giant, Sony Corporation. The Sony Music roster includes some of music's biggest-selling acts including Michael Jackson, Mariah Carey, Bruce Springsteen, George Michael, Billy Joel, and Michael Bolton.

MCA Records: In 1991, MCA Records joined the list of companies to be sold to international conglomerates. Matsushita Corporation, the parent company of Panasonic and Technics electronics, purchased Universal's music division. MCA's strength was once primarily in the area of dance and film soundtracks. With the acquisition of the Geffen label, however, MCA was able to bolster its position in the rock marketplace with acts like Guns N' Roses and Aerosmith.

BMG Music Group: Formerly RCA Records, BMG was acquired by Germany's Bertelsmann AG. RCA made its mark with Elvis in the fifties and sixties and established dominance in the country music field. In the eighties, BMG acquired the Arista label. BMG's list of artists includes Whitney Houston, Hall and Oates, and the Grateful Dead.

Capitol/EMI: British-owned Thorn/EMI is the parent company of Capitol Records, which also distributes the highly successful SBK label. SBK enjoyed enormous success in 1990–91 with Wilson Phillips and Vanilla Ice. In addition to ownership of the entire Beatles catalogue, Capitol also boasts a roster including Hammer, Bonnie Raitt, Tina Turner, and country superstar Garth Brooks.

Virgin Records: Owned by British adventurer Richard Branson, Virgin Records in 1991 set the business buzzing with its $45 million dollar deal with Janet Jackson, which was followed shortly by another $45 million arrangement with the legendary Rolling Stones. In March 1992 Virgin Records was purchased by Thorn/EMI for more than $900 million.

Motown: This label, a partnership between Motown and Boston Ventures, home of the sixties' top soul artists, continues to name Stevie Wonder and Diana Ross on its roster of talent.

These companies are the dominant forces in the industry and have considerable influence on the business. They produce, manufacture (either directly or through independent production facilities), and distribute their own labels, plus a long list of independent labels.

These independents include a whole host of new labels that have established their presence with authority in the business, including Def Jam, Def American, Jive, Enigma, Giant, Zoo, Tommy Boy, and Megaforce. Independent labels play an important role in the music industry and have done so for the past several years. Here's why:

In the late seventies and eighties the major record labels began to consolidate their efforts behind one particular kind of music, rock and roll. The business had been through some incredibly difficult times. In the midseventies the rise of disco music was meteoric, and millions upon millions of records were sold. But the business got crazy and greedy, and in 1978 it all came tumbling down. Millions and millions of unsold records were returned to the labels from the stores for credit and, in some cases, the excesses had gotten so out of hand that the record labels had already borrowed and spent the money for the records that had been shipped, confident that they would be sold.

The "disco crash" sent a shock wave through the business that caused the entire industry to change. The free-wheeling deal makers who were running the labels were replaced or forced to report to those with business and accounting backgrounds. And, more important, the labels decided not to take chances, but to go with the safe bet, rock and roll, and focus their activity on winners. And so it went throughout most of the late seventies and early eighties.

Unable to find a place on the major labels, many acts looked to the small independent labels that were specializing in the kinds of music the majors wouldn't touch. Rap, hip hop, house, heavy metal, and new music found their way into the record stores on labels like Jive and Tommy Boy. Sire Record's Seymour Stein, one of the visionaries, began to see an emerging trend toward street music, so he signed a new pop singer named Madonna, whom he thought was destined to break out and ultimately reach a wide audience. Meanwhile the other musical forms were growing, and suddenly rap and house music had taken over the clubs and the youth of America. Not since the sixties had young people embraced so many new styles of music.

The major labels, however, realized that they did not have the expertise in-house to deal with these new musical forms and that it was easier for them simply to distribute the smaller labels and leave the A & R and some of the more street-level promotion to the experts at the indie labels. They trained their guns on getting air play on the top stations in major cities in the country through their own promotion network and tried to make some legitimate hit records out of the club favorites.

It took some time, about four or five years, but slowly acts began to break, and the smaller labels prospered along with the majors that distributed them. The fact that MTV had embraced rap and some of the other types of new music was just the impetus that the independents needed, and things got better fast. Meanwhile some of the major labels that had their own smaller affiliated labels began to listen to more of the new types of music, and many acts were signed.

And that is where we find ourselves today. The successful independent labels, which have the benefit of the national distribution and promotion clout of the majors, can make hits and, from them, find the financial resources to create more. But record sales have felt the recession, as have all businesses, and many independent labels are struggling. This is all the more reason why it is important for you, the artist, and your management team to be self-sufficient through your understanding of the business, so you do not have to rely on any label for your survival. Only by having the resources and information to control your own destiny can you be assured of long-term success that can withstand any difficulties that the industry as a whole may experience.

As in the past the major labels will always own the biggest talent. This is a fact of life for all small labels. An act may start with an independent label, but when they begin to become popular, offers start coming in from the major labels and either the small label sells the artist's contract to the major or the artist simply walks away from the small label. Sometimes the small label will sue the major label and the artist, but such suits usually end in settlements, in no small part because of the small labels' inability to finance their labels *and* major lawsuits. That has always been the way of the business and it always will be. But the fact remains a lot of small labels with creativity and energy are out there and are eager to sign, develop, and break new talent.

Caution is still very much in evidence at the major labels, which are slow to forget the lessons learned in the seventies. But the major labels are signing acts, and a fair number of their signings are breaking out and selling platinum records, providing the majors with the encouragement to continue to sign new acts. Now is a good time for you to look for a deal, and the only thing you need to be concerned about is having the talent, knowledge, and perseverance to capitalize on the current marketplace.

THE ROLE OF MAJOR AND INDEPENDENT LABELS

A very strange idea has crept into the music business over the years, and it is one that I have never been able to understand. If you talk to a lot of young unsigned bands, they will tell you that although they want to be signed to one of the major labels, they consider them to be big, clumsy, and inept. I'm not sure where this attitude comes from. I suppose it could stem from criticisms of the major labels by managers, artists, and lawyers in the press. But these criticisms are usually stories about the really big stars and the heavy-hitting lawyers and are just publicity, posturing by the talent or the label, or the latest attempt by some journalist to write an "exposé" of the music industry.

A new artist cannot afford to have this kind of attitude, particularly because it is dead wrong. Yes, major labels are big companies and yes, they may move more slowly than do the smaller independents, but when a big label pushes the button, it has the weight and resources to make something happen. Certainly major labels have more staff and therefore it may be harder to communicate with or get answers from them than it would be at the small labels, where you may deal with one or two key people, but smaller labels don't have the clout of the majors to get the job done. The thing that you have to understand as a new act on a major label is how to make that machine work for you, and that understanding comes from an understanding of the machine itself, as well as the role of the majors and of the independents in the marketplace.

First, let's take a look at the major labels. Here are the players:

President

At the top is the president, a guy who you will see when you sign with the label and at the occasional press conference, unless, of course, you become a big star, in which case you'll probably see him a lot. Even if you aren't yet Bruce Springsteen, it is important to establish a relationship with the big boss. The reasons are obvious, but what is not obvious is the fact that most presidents of record labels have egos that rival those of their artists. Don't compete with the big cheese for attention. Let him have the spotlight and let him bring you into it. If you handle him correctly, he'll know it, and your road at the label will be much smoother.

Vice President of Promotion

After the president you will find a lot of vice presidents. The finance, business affairs, artist relations, publicity, and A & R departments all have vice presidents, and your mission is to get to know them all and, most important, for them to know you. One of the most important vice presidents is the vice president of promotion, who directs the activities of the entire promotion department. At some of the bigger labels, there will be a vice president for each of the different styles of music: that is, for AOR, AC, and so on—you get the picture. Whatever the case, it is the vice president of promotion who will be calling the shots as to which records are priorities for the week, which records get advertised in the trade papers and tip sheets, and basically, which records get the chance to be hits.

These people are extremely busy, especially on Mondays and Tuesdays when new records get added at radio stations, and everyone at every level of promotion is on the phone trying to get *adds* (that is, their new records put on the playlist of radio stations for the first time). So pick your meeting times with this vice president carefully and make the most of them. Talk facts, not art, since most of these folks tend to be pragmatic, realistic individuals who are intent only on getting their artists to be number one.

Be aware also that a record company is a highly political environment and that the job of the vice president of promotion is one of the most political because so much is riding on his or her efforts. You will need to be sensitive to these politics when you form your alliances at the label to ensure that you remain on the right side of this key individual. You will make the vice president of promotion your friend if you help him or her to deliver a hit record; the more hits, the better friend he or she will be. So work this vice president, but work him or her smart, learn the rules, let the vice president know that you know them, and then play by them. The vice president will have respect for you if he or she thinks you are a pro, and that respect is the first step to a hit record.

National Promotion Director or Manager

Now you are getting a little closer to the trenches. It's the job of the national promotion directors to take the directives from the vice presidents and turn them into concrete numbers through the use of local promotion managers and independent promoters. Contact with radio stations, trade papers, managers, independent promoters (indies), salespeople, and others keeps the flow of information going that assists the national promotion directors to bring in the chart numbers and stations adds that their records need to be successful. Again, avoid these people on Mondays and Tuesdays unless you have specific information about your record's airplay and keep your conversations brief and to the point. You don't want to waste their time with small talk on days when they are trying to get your record on the air. If you want to see *rude* in all of its radiant splendor, drop by a national promotion director's office on a Tuesday afternoon for a chat.

Keep the lines of communication open with this director. Ensure that you include him in all the important aspects of your career, from asking his opinion of your mixes while recording to discussing your tour plans. Throughout your career, as you continue to build your team, you will find that the national promotion director is one of your key players.

Local Promotion Manager

Local promotion managers (LPMs) are the foot soldiers of the record business. They work out of the local branch offices of record companies and are responsible for promoting the labels' products in their region. Often these guys and girls have to be veritable magicians to do their jobs. First, they are the skinny end of the funnel. What I mean is, at the head office there is a vice president of AOR and a director of AOR and a vice president of CHR and a director of CHR, and so on. But there isn't a different LPM for each format; there's just one guy or girl who works all of those formats. So all the decisions that get made at the head office eventually filter down to the LPM, who is the one who has to carry them out. In addition, the LPM works on all the local live appearances of artists to make sure that records are in the stores, that all the radio people get tickets, that the records get played, and that the posters are up in the record stores. Often, when a band is in town for a concert, the LPM will also arrange for the band to go fishing, skating, hiking, swimming, sailing, or whatever other exotic activity they enjoy.

These folks are the true workhorses of the business. When a new record is released, it is the LPM who takes it or mails it to the stations in his or her region and then follows up to ensure that it gets auditioned for airplay. The LPM contacts each station, armed with information about the group, the record, the song, the producer, the songwriter, the musicians who are playing on the record, and anything else that will make the music director sit up and take notice. If the record is by an established group that has had a previous hit, the job is a little easier. Or if the record has been released for some time and has already gained a chart number, the station may be more receptive. A new record by an unknown group is the toughest, and it takes a special song and a special approach to get noticed. It's here that the LPMs can be your biggest allies because it is, in large part, their efforts that can break a new act through sheer hard work. Make these people your friends. Find out their spouses' names and their kids' birthdays and send them cards. Along with being valuable members of your team, they are among the most genuine people in the business.

Product Manager

Too many artists ignore this important person. My motto has always been, Never underestimate anyone who can sign a check. Your product manager is your cheerleader inside the company. He sets the budgets for posters, artwork, radio and TV advertising, press materials, and sometimes videos. This manager can make things happen in a lot of areas and should be among your best friends at the label. Spend time with him every time you visit the label and talk to him at least once a week. He can be your eyes and ears inside the company and can have an enormous impact on your career.

Artist Relations

These folks will be very important to your touring life and to your life at the label. It's at this level that you'll find the most sympathetic ear to your problems because next to the A & R people, it is the artist relations people are most in tune with the artists. These are the people who will make sure that when you are on the road the local branch people will look after you. In most cases, they'll call in advance and even be out there with you, to ensure that you meet the right retailers, radio people, and press. They are also the ones who you'll need to talk to about any deficit financing that the label may give you in the way of tour support to allow you to get out there and play. Within the company, they can help everywhere, from getting you more attention from the promotion department to helping convince the powers-that-be to let you spend the extra ten grand that will make the new video right. The artist relations department is an important area for you and one in which you should invest a considerable amount of time building a relationship.

Sales Staff

The company will have a variety of salespeople who all have essentially the same job: to *get the records into the stores.* Salespeople are a breed unto themselves. Although, for the most part, they are music fans, they will not be the most sensitive to your art. Nor should they be. Their job is to move the product—units, tapes, and CDs. That's it. Not a lot of glamour here, just bare facts, and that's how you and your manager need to deal with them. Like anyone else, a salesperson will respond to personal contact. Too many bands spend all their time working the promotion people but ignore the sales department. Bad move. At the end of the day, it's the sales staff that makes sure that the record is there on the front rack, displayed, reported to radio stations, and eventually sold. Get to know the names of some of their big accounts and spend a little time learning how the sales department works. Aside from being fascinating, the sale of product is also how you will make your living. The added bonus is that if you appear to be interested in the salespeople's jobs, they will respond a lot more favorably to you, and you can literally talk your way to priority status.

Publicity Department

The publicity department is very important to you in the development of your image. Promotion will get you on the radio, and sales into the store, but it is the publicists who will stimulate interest in you everywhere from *USA Today* to *Entertainment Tonight.*

I have never been able to understand artists who give the publicity department a hard time. Many times I've seen a publicist set up a whole schedule of interviews only to have an artist pull some kind of tantrum and refuse to do any of them. And it's usually the artist who needs the interviews the most who understands this situation the least. Look, it's simple. It's *your* career, not the publicist's. If they aren't setting up interviews for you, they can set them up for someone else. After all, there are lots of acts on the label's roster, you're just one of them.

Again, work with these folks. If you have some reason why you don't want to do interviews at a certain time, tell them. The key here is communication. Let them know that you are ready, willing, and able to do all the interviews they think the record or the tour needs and work out a schedule that works for both of you. Listen to them. Publicists know the press very well. They can warn you about the traps and coach you on how to handle certain writers or interviewers. They have a wealth of information to rely on, so don't blow it by ignoring their advice. Publicity is a major part of image development. Ensure that your publicists understand your image and then work with them to maximize your profile in the market-place. The results will be increased airplay, sales, and, most important, money.

Branch Managers

These are the folks who run the day-to-day operations of the label's branch offices across the country. Branch managers are extremely important to your career for a number of reasons. In the first place, they have direct contact with the stores and can *hands-on* affect the display and sale of your record. Second, they usually have a branch advertising fund, part of which they can choose to spend on your project. This money is over and above the money designated for your project by the head office and is very helpful, especially if you are a touring attraction. Over the course of an album project or a tour, these branch managers can bring tens of thousands of dollars worth of incremental advertising to your project. Get to know them, and work with them. If they ask you for an autographed poster for a sales account, *Do It!* If they want to take pictures of you after the show with their sales account's kids, *Do It!* If you don't do it, you probably won't have to worry about being asked again. Get the point? Good. These guys can be your best friends. It's up to you to make them so.

Independent Promoters (Indies)

Independent promoters do not actually work for the label. Rather, they are entrepreneurs who will, for a fee (either weekly or per station), contact radio stations to get adds on the specific records for which they have been hired. There are indies who specialize in each format, AOR, AC, urban, and country, but the most powerful and most notorious are the CHR independents. Throughout the history of the music industry, indies have come under fire for a variety of alleged abuses, from payola (providing money or drugs to radio station personnel in exchange for airplay) to ties to organized crime. In 1989 a book called *Hitmen* gathered all the facts and fantasies concerning the independent network of promotion specialists and painted a picture of big money, mafia bosses, and millions of dollars.

These days, the independents are as powerful as ever, although the excesses of the past are gone. Indies act as a support system for the label's staff. They can focus attention on a record and bring it to the attention of radio programmers for consideration. Many indies have strong relationships with radio people that are built on years of experience and favors and, since the music industry is built primarily on relationships, they can often get promotion directors or music directors to take a chance on a new record when they otherwise may not.

Indies are expensive, anywhere from $350 to $500 a week or more. But, in most cases, you will need their help. These days many record companies even make a budget available for you to hire independents. Usually, they try to make it recoupable against royalties (if you can't get it nonrecoupable, settle for 50 percent recoupable but no more). The labels maintain contact with the indies, who report to them. Don't get confused here. After a while, you may develop a relationship with some of the indies, but it is the labels who are paying them and, like all mercenaries, they'll listen to the generals who are paying their salaries before anyone else. The best way to work the indies is to find out what they need from you to get the job done. They may need tickets to your show or a phone call to a station. Whatever the case, cooperate, because these folks have what it takes to get the job done.

PUTTING IT ALL TOGETHER

Now you know the radio and record company players whom you will be dealing with. Here's a checklist of things to look for whether you are promoting your first or fiftieth record:

1. A good record.
2. A good presentation to the record company of your record

by you and your management to get the company personnel excited and to make them believe in the product as much as you do.

3. A good presentation of your record to radio stations. Personal delivery of the record by the LPM, ads in the trade magazines, and tip sheets. A call from the vice president of promotion to key stations. All these activities show radio stations that the label is committed to your project.

4. Ensurance that sufficient copies of your record are available in local record stores, so radio stations can obtain sales reports and move it up their charts.

5. Close monitoring by you and the record company to ensure that the radio stations are receiving up-to-the-minute information about your record and that they are paying attention to the positive response that they may be getting, as well as to any other national or regional trends that may support their playing your record.

6. Assurance that independent promoters have been retained to work on your project to support the efforts of the label.

7. Personal contact by you to radio stations to support your label's efforts.

8. Reviews and advertising in the trade magazines and tip sheets to stimulate airplay and sales.

9. An integrated promotion and sales campaign at the consumer level to maximize airplay, sales, and your profile in the marketplace.

10. Concert or club appearances in cities where you are on the air to support the airplay.

Obviously this is only an outline, but if all these areas are covered by you and your record label, your chances of having a successful record are pretty good. Just remember it's a people business. Get to know the people and make them your friends. It's a business of egos, from the artists to the label people to the disc jockeys to the press. If you recognize this fact and treat people the way you want to be treated, you will gain a reputation that will open many doors to success.

RADIO

I watched Coal Miner's Daughter and we did some of the same things. We put out a couple of records while I was still living in North Carolina. Joe Stampley produced the records and we mailed them out to radio stations and then got in the car and just started up one coast and down the other, going to the radio stations and trying to talk them into playing the record.

—RANDY TRAVIS

The most important elements of your career in the music industry will be the promotion, marketing, and sale of your act and its recordings to the public through radio and your record company. In the first section I discussed how you are responsible for the promotion and marketing of your act before you sign your first record contract. Well, after that happy day much of the promotion and marketing will become the responsibility of the record company, and it will become the company's job to get your records played on the radio, put your records into the stores, and ensure that they are adequately advertised and merchandised to achieve maximum sales.

A recording agreement, however, is not a magic charm and it doesn't guarantee success. A hit single, album, or group is the result of a lot of hard work by a team comprised of your label, your management, and you. This section gives you a working knowledge of the areas of radio promotion, marketing, and sales, so your conversations with and about your present or future recording company will be meaningful.

THE EVOLUTION OF RADIO

> *It's the music that kept us all intact ... kept us from going crazy. You should have two radios, in case one gets broken.*

> *—LOU REED*

When I was a little kid, I was mystified by my local radio station. I simply couldn't understand how they could get all those groups and singers to come to their station and play their music, wait a couple of hours, and then come back and play it again. I had this mental image of a diner somewhere where Elvis, Buddy Holly, and Ritchie Valens were hanging around drinking coffee until it was their turn to go and play again. At the age of seven I discovered records, which suddenly explained everything. The advent of recorded music made it possible for everyone to listen to his or her favorite songs or musicians in the comfort of their own homes. With one initial investment in a radio, it became possible for you to include not only music but sports, weather, news, and more in your daily routine.

Radio changed little as a vehicle for entertainment in the home from its inception in the mid-twenties and thirties until the late fifties and sixties, when a man named Bill Drake began experimenting with a new style of radio programming. This new *format*, or approach to programming, consisted of playing a fixed number of hit records several times per day in a regular pattern of rotation instead of the random play that records were getting at the time. Drake's format was called *Top Forty*, which referred to the number of records he chose to rotate in a fixed period.

Drake's idea was simple. People liked to hear hit songs performed by their favorite groups and would listen to the radio station that played them most often. His format revolutionized the radio industry and with it, the concept of record promotion. Prior to Drake's innovation, in the early days of rock and roll, radio pioneers like Alan Freed put their jobs (and sometimes even their lives) on the line by playing rock and roll. At the time rock and roll was often referred to as *race music* because of its kinship to the rhythm and blues recordings of black artists. In fact, before Elvis and Buddy Holly began to make public appearances, many Americans thought that they were both black musicians. Rock and roll music wasn't popular with middle America, and every organization from Bible groups to the Ku Klux Klan tried to have it banned, which, of course, only made it grow stronger. Sometimes disc jockeys would barricade themselves in the studio and play a new Elvis record over and over again fifteen or twenty times to the delight of the ever-growing audience of teenage rock and rollers.

Bill Drake's format made one significant change in the music industry that carries on today at Top Forty's descendant CHR stations. Drake rotated only forty records on his list, and to have a hit, you had to be one of the forty. This put incredible pressure on record companies and managers of the day to get on Drake's list, and that pressure still exists today.

It took about ten years, but by the midsixties, AM Top Forty radio was the dominant form of teenage musical entertainment. Since then, radio's popularity has continued to grow, but in the late sixties the accent began to shift from the AM band to something new called FM.

FM radio, which today offers classical, beautiful music, pop, jazz, and rock and roll, had its beginnings in the mid-fifties, but did not really become a viable alternative to AM until the mid-sixties when FM stations on the West Coast began playing a new, alternative kind of rock music. While AM was playing the "safe" pop records of the Beatles, Beach Boys, and Sonny and Cher, FM was playing music from the dark side by bands like the Doors, Cream, and Jimi Hendrix. This format became known as *progressive* or *underground* radio and was a reaction to the tight-listed AM Top Forty format. A wealth of new artists who were making records that could not be played on Top Forty radio because of political, drug-related, or other unacceptable lyrics arrived on the scene, along with hippies, the war in Vietnam, and the peace movement, which would combine with other factors to radically alter the fabric of contemporary society.

Today Top Forty is called CHR and underground radio is known as AOR. Along the way radio has added several new formats, including adult contemporary (AC), urban, country, new age, and more. But whether its AOR, CHR, or M-O-U-S-E, the question from artists is always the same: "How do I get *my* record on the radio?" Here's how a record actually gets on the radio and rises to the top of the charts.

RADIO PROMOTION

The first thing you should know is that the competition for airplay is incredible. Hundreds of records on hundreds of major and independent labels are released around the world each month, and regardless of their country of origin, groups and artists all seek success in the lucrative U.S. marketplace.

Think of a radio station as you would a retail store. A retail store has a finite amount of room for inventory. If the shelves are filled with products that sell well, the store isn't going to remove one of them to try out a new product, of which the consumer is unaware. Only after the store has marketed the new product and can be assured of consumer demand will it give the product a try on the shelf. To carry on this idiotic analogy (but it's working, so bear with me), after the product starts selling well, it gets more shelf space and then finally its own display in the store. Got it? No? OK, here's what I'm talking about.

Each radio station has either a chart or a playlist. This is a list of the records that the station is playing, usually in order of popularity. CHR stations usually a have chart numbered from one to thirty. At AOR stations, the chart numbers are replaced by the categories light, medium, or heavy airplay. When a record that the station has been playing for a while is no longer popular (it has fallen out of the *Billboard* Top Thirty or requests from listeners have stopped), it is taken off the *current* list. The record may still get played in what is called *gold* rotation or *recurrent* rotation, but it is no longer treated as a current song. This opens up a slot on the playlist.

The radio station then researches several records and chooses the best and adds it to the playlist, usually as a test. During a test, the record's progress is monitored. Each week the station calls local record stores to determine which of the records on the chart are selling best and which are slow, so it can rearrange the chart numbers. The station also checks to see if any of the test records are selling because even a small quantity of sales at this early stage is a good barometer of future potential. Some stations monitor telephone requests or responses. If the phones ring off the wall every time a new record is played, it's a good bet that the record is headed for the chart. (So if your record gets playlisted, be sure to get your family, friends, relatives, and co-workers to man the phones!)

When a radio station puts a record on the air, it's called an *add*. When a record is being tested, it's not really an add yet; it becomes an add only after it tests well and is put on the playlist. There are *full-time* and *part-time* adds. A full-time add gets your record on the playlist, where it is played all day long. A part-time add means that your record will be *dayparted*, or played only during certain times of the day. Let me take a minute to explain dayparts.

Radio stations divide their day into the following segments:

6 A.M. to 10 A.M.: morning drive
10 A.M. to 3 P.M.: midday
3 P.M. to 6 P.M.: afternoon drive
6 P.M. to 10 P.M.: night
10 P.M. to 6 A.M.: all night

The exact times may vary from station to station, but the dayparts remain the same. In each period a station will play different kinds of records, and it does so for two reasons: listener reaction and advertising. We all know that radio stations, just like television stations, make their money by selling advertising time to sponsors. At certain times of the day more people listen to the station than at other times. The dayparts with the most listeners are referred to as having the highest ratings. Radio stations base the amount of money they charge for commercials on a rate card that is based on the ratings of the station. Within the overall station ratings, there are highly rated dayparts. Commercials in these periods are the ones from which the station can make the most money. A station's overall ratings may place the fifth in the market, but its morning-show daypart, for example, may have the highest ratings in the city. A station does not have to be number one in the market to have one or more successful dayparts and, in fact, it is rare for any station to be number one in all periods. Anyway, back to your dayparted record.

Morning drive and *afternoon drive* are usually the two highest-rated periods for any station. At these times, most people are on their way to or returning home from work and are usually listening in their cars or on radios as they get ready for work. Stations stick to the hits during these periods, along with the news, weather, jokes, and traffic. New records seldom make it to this daypart, unless they are from established artists or a novelty types of records that fit well with the comedy orientation of most morning shows.

The *midday* time slot is much more laid back, because during this daypart the radio functions as background music in the workplace or at home. Artists like Phil Collins, Joni Mitchell, and Gloria Estefan see a lot of action here, and if your music is along those lines your record could well be dayparted to middays.

The *night* daypart begins to rock a little heavier, since research shows that more teenagers and young people are tuned in at this time. If your record is rock oriented, you'll probably be tested in this period. *All night* is not really a daypart; it's more like, well, the twilight zone. Granted, airplay is airplay, but few records break big from airplay between midnight and 6 A.M. If you are dayparted to all nights, somebody is trying to tell you something.

Most radio stations live by the credo, "You can't get hurt by the ones you don't play." If there is any question in their minds about your record, most stations will pass on it until that question is resolved. Stations believe that if they play a bad record, listeners will *tune out* (change to another station), and this, of course, is a disaster for any station. So you have to ensure that your presentation to them is convincing, that it makes them feel confident enough to add your record, and that you close the sale once your record is on the air. A little later, I'll tell you more about how to handle things once your record gets added.

Earlier I mentioned research as a part of the process of getting a record on the air. Radio stations rely on a variety of different types of research to help them make their decisions about what new records to add. Trade magazines and tip sheets both play a role here, as do airplay on other stations, retail sales, live touring, publicity, and previous hits. Research allows a station to determine which records to add to their list, to gauge the progress of those already added, and to decide when a record should be taken off the air in favor of another that may perform better. What these all add up to is the fact that getting the add is only the beginning, and continued promotion once the record has been added is not only advisable but vital.

Earlier I mentioned closing the sale once your record has been added. It's essential that you take the appropriate steps after the add to ensure that your record *converts* to a chart number and then moves up the charts, it is hoped, to the Top Ten or (dare I say it?) number one. One of the most important elements of this promotion is making sure that there is a stock of records in local stores. As I said before, radio stations call stores to check up on sales, and if the store managers report no stock, or worse, are completely unaware of your record, it does not do much for you at the stations. In the old days we used to call this *lubricating* the market. Once he had gotten the add, a good local promotion manager would visit the key stores in the market and give the store managers a box of singles at no charge. This gift would accomplish two things: First, the managers were made aware of the record and had copies of it to sell if it was requested and second, since the store managers got to keep the money from the sale of the record, they owed the local promotion rep a favor, which usually came in the way of good reports to the radio stations. Yes, this was shady and yes, it worked. These days, with singles no longer a viable sales barometer, the record labels use other methods, but the aim is still the same: to get copies of the record into the stores and to ensure that the store managers are aware of the record and report the sales to the radio stations.

If the record gets a good phone response from listeners and has even modest store sales, it has a good chance of making it to the chart. Some stations have a step between the playlist and the chart that they call *hitbound.* Hitbound is an indication that the record is doing well, but cannot chart yet for one of two reasons: It hasn't done quite well enough to earn a chart position, or there is simply no space on the chart and the new record hasn't done well enough to dislodge any of the current chart records. If, on the other hand, a record is on the playlist for a week and gets little or no response from either listeners' calls or sales, most stations usually leave it on for another week and keep watching it. If the record isn't showing any signs of life after two or more weeks, however, it is usually dropped from the playlist to give another record a chance.

As you can see, the playlist system gives stations some leeway to experiment with new records, so they can get a feel for which of them is really destined for success.

So, to recap:

1. A record is *released.*

2. It is *serviced* (mailed or otherwise delivered) to radio stations.

3. Each station auditions all the new records each week and then researches each one to determine which have the best potential for success.

4. One or two records are added to the playlist as a *test* or in a specific *daypart.*

5. The new record is monitored by the station for phone responses from listeners and for sales.

6. If the record does well, it is added to the chart. If not, it remains on the playlist for a while longer and then is either charted or dropped from the list.

Before I talk about the players, there are a few other things about record promotion that you should be aware of. This is the really important stuff, so please pay attention. Everything that I have told you so far has been pretty basic information, sort of Promotion 101. But there are some nuances that make the difference between good promotion and great promotion.

Compare Apples to Apples

One of the weapons in a promotion rep's arsenal is knowing which other stations are playing a record. A good promotion person will do his or her homework and will be able to quote call letters from sta-tions in other cities that are having success with a particular single. This is a good strategy because stations feel more secure if other markets are playing a record and it is performing for them. You have to be a little careful here that the cities you quote have something in common with the city in which the station you are talking to is locat-ed in. For example, *don't* tell a New York radio station that the record is doing well in Lubbock, Texas, or you'll be laughed out of the station. *Do,* however, tell a Detroit station that your record is doing well in Philadelphia or Chicago. Those cities have something in common, and success in them is a big plus for you.

Don't Ever Leave a Station Hanging Out There Alone

Sometimes a station will add a record for you and, for whatever reason, the record just doesn't work anywhere else. Try as you might, you just can't get any other stations to play the record or, if you do, you get only a few of them. After a couple of weeks you should phone the people who have added your record, tell them the truth, and give them the option to take your record off the air. That's right, I said *you* give them the option to take your record off the air! This is not as crazy as it seems. If the record clearly isn't working, there is no point leaving your friends who added the record to twist in the wind with a *stiff* (unsuccessful) record. Before they make the decision to drop your record, and, by the way, they will probably be a little ticked off that you convinced them to add it in the first place, give them a call and do the right thing. They will have a lot more respect for you if you respect them, and maybe they'll stick with your record a little longer, even if it isn't working. In any event, you will probably have made friends for the next time and instead of hiding from the station that added "the hit that never was," you'll make them your first call when the next time comes and, in the record business, there is always a next time.

Don't Trash Your Record Label

Whatever they may say to you on the phone or in person, radio and record people are buddies and will always back each other up. They may agree with you that your label is horrible and the promotion staff is lame. They will then tell the label what you said, and you will be in trouble up to your eyeballs. Don't get me wrong, the radio people aren't out to get you. It's simply that radio stations share a business relationship with the record companies, and the product they have in common is artists—lots and lots of artists—with new ones coming along every day. Artists come and go, but the labels are always there, and as long as the labels are there, radio stations will have records to play. You, unfortunately, cannot make the same guarantees to stations. So if you have a problem with your label, tell your manager or your lawyer or your label, but don't drag the radio stations into it. If they sense a problem between you and your label, they will assume that your records will no longer get support from the label. To them that means, if they play it, the label won't put records in stores, support your tour dates, arrange promotions with the stations, or do any of the things that they rely upon to support their investment of airplay in you and they will be very hesitant to play your product.

Record promotion is a tough and precise business and its practitioners are some of the most creative people in the business. Let's take a look at the cast of characters involved in your recording project.

THE PLAYERS

Program Director

A program director (PD) is equivalent to the captain of a ship. He is responsible for ensuring that all the elements of the station are working together. He coordinates music, news, sports, special features, and other elements into the station's programming. He also handles the on-air talent (not an easy job) and acts as the liaison between the station and the community, media, and music industry. He generally chairs the station's weekly music meetings, at which the new records are added to the playlist. At most stations, the PD has the final say about which records do and do not go on the air.

Music Director

Each station employs a music director (MD), whose job is to sort through all the new releases, research them, and decide which of them will make the cut for that week's music meeting. The MD is also often the station's link to the record companies. It is the MD who talks to the local promotion people in person and the national promotion staff, as well as independent promoters, managers, and artists by telephone about the releases currently being worked in the marketplace. The MD makes the calls to local record stores to check sales and is usually the one who gets out to see the new acts when they come to town. It's an exhausting job, and one that is vital to the station and to your record.

At most stations an interesting dynamic is at work between the MD and the PD. The MD is generally the one who has to deliver the news to the record rep that a record is not being added or is being dropped from the chart. Since most record reps have a relationship with the PD as well, they will, more often than not, call the PD to plead their case. You may think that MD would view this as going over his head, but, in most cases, the opposite is true; the MD often encourages you to go to the PD, especially if he likes your record but was voted down at the weekly music meeting. It is imperative that you get to know the PD and MD of the important stations in your format and work them on the phone and in person as often as possible.

Consultants

My ol' daddy used to have a saying about consultants. He said, "Consultants are guys who know a thousand ways to make love, but they don't know any girls"(no offense guys). Consultants don't actually work at a radio station; they simply advise stations how to program to become successful in the marketplace. They study a station's overall sound, music, announcers, news, and commercial mix and will, for a fee, adjust these elements according to a formula that they have designed with the intention of creating a more successful station. Consultants are important to the promotion of your record in that they are generally in contact with a large number of stations each week.

Although they usually cannot actually add a record to the station's playlist, their recommendations carry considerable weight. Many consultants distribute music lists to their stations each week, so it is important that you and your label ensure that your latest release is on their lists. Consultants can be valuable allies to your marketing effort.

TRADE MAGAZINES
AND TIP SHEETS

> *Climbing for me is like music in that it's at once a*
> *completely liberating experience and yet requires*
> *absolute discipline and focus. I've never seen any-*
> *body check out early, but I've seen plenty of them*
> *fall off the charts.*

> **—DAVID LEE ROTH**

There are two types of publications in the music industry: *trade magazines* and *tip sheets.* Trade magazines are generally filled with industry news and trends about corporate mergers and formations, sales, staff changes, and new innovations in marketing and merchandising. They cover all types of music, from classical to country to rock and roll, as well as videos and live touring. And they contain the radio airplay and sales charts that indicate the relative success of records in the marketplace. *Billboard* magazine is the oldest trade publication in the music industry, first appearing in the late 1890s as a news magazine for the outdoor billboard and poster industry. *Radio and Records* and *Cashbox* are the other U.S. trade magazines. *RPM* is the oldest recognized trade magazine in Canada. In Europe, it's *Music and Media,* out of Amsterdam, Holland, another Billboard family publication and Europe's only pan-European music journal.

The second group of music-industry communicators are tip sheets. They are used primarily by radio stations, record labels, and record retailers to assess, in their early stages, which singles and albums appear to be breaking out, that is, gaining immediate industry and consumer acceptance. These stations and retailers can thereby be at the forefront of new hit material and can capitalize financially by being the first with the newest—an important aspect of a business that deals in minutes and seconds, rather than in days or weeks. Tip sheets contain industry news, comments from radio programmers, record company ads for new releases, record reviews, *picks* (reviews and recommendations of new records that the editors think will be most successful), and radio airplay charts.

Some examples of tip sheets are the *Friday Morning Quarterback, Hits, Hitmakers,* the *Album Network, Monday Morning Replay,* the *Gavin Report,* and the *Hard Hundred.* In Canada, the sole tip sheet is the *Record,* which follows trends in the music industry north of the forty-ninth parallel.

PROMOTION THROUGH "TRADES" AND "TIPS"

Trade magazines and tip sheets play a major role in the establishment of a hit single or album. In most cases, records first appear in the tip sheets mainly because tip sheets follow the progress of a large number of records, while the trade magazines track fewer new releases.

Just after the release of a single or an album to the radio stations, the promotion staff of the record company begins the long and arduous process of contacting every radio station across the country that may play that type of record (they wouldn't call a jazz station to play a country record, for example) in an attempt to get the new record added to the station's chart or playlist. Each radio station reports its list of records to the tip sheets and trade papers, and as more and more stations add a particular record, the record begins to show up on their charts. The object is to get the attention of other stations that may not yet be playing the record to add it to their list, based on the success that the record is having elsewhere.

Tip sheets base their charts primarily on airplay, while trade magazines combine this information on airplay with reports of sales by the retail stores to create their chart numbers.

There are many theories about which trade magazine or tip sheet is the most accurate or influential. For example, some believe that the *Billboard* magazine sales and airplay charts have the greatest impact internationally, that is, record companies, publishers, and record retailers around the world accept the *Billboard* information as the most accurate barometer of a record's success. *Billboard* is distributed in more countries around the world than is any other music industry publication, which most likely accounts for its international influence.

A favorable report, a good chart number, or a pick in one of these publications is extremely important to the life of a record. Therefore, record companies maintain good relationships with trade magazines and tip sheets and advertise frequently in these publications in an attempt to keep their artists and product in the industry's eye.

To the layperson a tip sheet may look like a blueprint for a nuclear reactor, but, after some study, it becomes relatively easy to comprehend. Trade magazines are somewhat more obvious, but the subtleties and nuances of their charts take quite a bit of study and experience to master. And the oldest and most influential charts are those found in *Billboard* magazine.

THE BILLBOARD CHARTS

There are a lot of people out there ... who are given
credit for being totally about the art, whose main
thrust is "Let's write a hit." There are a lot of people
who get credit for being unswerving individualists,
but, if you really knew the truth, you'd be surprised
at how much **Billboard** *comes into*
their conversation.

—BRUCE HORNSBY

Billboard magazine publishes nineteen charts in its weekly industry magazine, including charts on dance, jazz, and country music, plus top-selling videos, but the two charts that receive the most attention are the Hot 100 Singles and Top 200 Albums. Why these two? Easy. It's from these charts that a large number of record retailers across the country decide how many records they should order for their stores. A good chart number, debut, or bullet can mean the difference of thousands of records worth tens of thousands of dollars to the label and the artist.

The Hot 100 Singles Chart

For the Hot 100 Singles chart, *Billboard* compiles the information from both its radio monitoring and retail reports and determines the changes in its chart, that is, which records will move up, down, or off the list. A record that has done particularly well in a given week receives a *bullet*, that is, an indication that it is a record that is fast gaining popularity with radio stations, retail stores, and consumers. A bullet ensures that other radio stations that are not presently playing the record will consider it more seriously for airplay.

If a record has a strong *debut* (its first week on the chart), it has a better chance of success. If a new record comes on the chart at number 99, nobody but the artist and his mother will notice. If, however, a new single debuts at number 53 with a bullet, the industry sits up and takes notice. To debut at such a high number, the single has to have been played by a large percentage of the radio stations and to have enjoyed some success in the retail stores. The rate at which a single moves up the chart is another key issue. If a record moves too slowly, that is, not enough local stations add or move it up their local charts, the single can lose its bullet or get stuck at the same chart number for several weeks in a row, both of which are bad situations because they send out a signal that the record is in trouble. Radio stations or retailers who may have been considering the record for play or purchase will then hesitate. Their hesitation, of course, causes more trouble for the record as it begins to move backward and, eventually, off the chart.

The other problem is, when a record moves up the chart too quickly. That's right, moves *up* too quickly. This may not seem like a problem, but it can be. If a single gets a lot of action in its early weeks and roars up the chart, it is bound to hit a point at which the records ahead of it stop its momentum. Superstars can jump over records that are ahead of them, but even they sometimes have trouble doing so. If your record hits a wall and the *traffic* (other records) ahead of it won't move, it may stop at number 11 and never get a chance to get into the Top Ten, which psychologically makes a big difference to tours, the press, and future releases. If, however, through its relationships with radio stations and retail stores your label can control the upward movement, slowing it down and speeding it up as necessary, then it can watch the Top Ten, find an opening, and rush through.

Working the charts is a lot like a good football offense. You don't keep running into the line, you look for the holes and capitalize on the openings. All these strategies, by the way, are planned in the promotion department of the label, where one person is usually charged with working the *Billboard* charts. I highly recommend that you find that person and make him or her a good friend.

The Hot 200 Album Chart

The album chart is based on sales. Recently, *Billboard* reached an agreement with a company called Sound Scan, to institute a new sales-tracking system through which sales of specific titles are automatically indicated at cash-register transactions. This system creates an accurate picture of a record's action at retail. From this information, the weekly Top 200 Album Chart is created, and the movement of a record on the chart is paramount to its survival. There is little flexibility to these charts, and some record labels have a problem with that. In the past, if a label shipped only a small number of the new album in the first week, *Billboard* would hold the record off the chart for a week, add up the sales of the first two weeks, and give the album a higher debut number for its first week on the chart. No one was hurt by this practice because the label did legitimately ship the quantity of records it reported. The new system does not allow for this type of activity, so records either sell enough copies to make the chart or they don't; it's that simple. The system, however, tends to skew in the direction of established "hit" acts, and thus new and developing acts have a hard time making it to the Top 200. In response to this problem, *Billboard* created a new section of the magazine called "Heatseekers" that tracks and profiles new acts and releases. The traffic situation, as well as most of the other things that I just discussed, also holds true for the album chart.

The *Billboard* album chart is also important for another reason. Many major and independent labels outside North America watch the progress of a new artist on the *Billboard* chart and determine whether they will release the record in their territory on the basis of the record making it to the Top 100 of the chart. This is extremely important to your international success and can make the difference between sales and royalties worldwide or only in North America.

RADIO AND RECORDS

Another industry publication that exerts a lot of influence on the success of a record is the trade paper *Radio and Records. R & R,* as it is called, is published in Los Angeles and is the key to the radio-promotion industry. A network of radio stations across the United States and Canada send weekly reports to *R & R* about current releases. Each week *R & R's* various editors in CHR, AC, country, AOR, and other formats compile this information and create the charts for the week. The *R & R* charts are based solely on airplay and are a most influential barometer for many stations to add a record or move it up their charts.

R & R created a method of identifying an apparent hit record through something it calls a *breaker.* When a record achieves airplay on 60 percent or more of the reporting stations in a particular format, it becomes a breaker. A *CHR breaker* means that 60 percent of all the *R & R* stations in the CHR format have added the record to their playlists in the first week. These records then appear on charts on the back page of *R & R,* from which record labels plan their strategy for the coming week. If 60 percent of all

AOR stations and 60 percent of all CHR stations play a record, it can become a *double breaker.* Another double breaker occurs when an AOR track is a breaker on both the *R & R* Hot Tracks chart and on the *R & R* AOR album chart. Confused? Good, because if you understand the *R & R* system after just one read, when it took most of us in the business weeks, months, or years to figure it out, you're obviously too smart for your own good. But seriously, this should give you an indication of the incredible strategic planning and thinking that goes into the life of just one record. Promotion people at big record labels work dozens of releases at a time, each with its own special characteristics. They are a special breed, living in a world of call letters, numbers, and telephones every week of the year.

PAPER ADDS

I should mention a situation in the business that causes a lot of grief and aggravation for the trade papers that rely on radio reports to create their charts. The phenomenon is known as a paper add. A *paper add* is the radio stations' practice of reporting to a trade paper that they are playing a particular record that they are not, in fact, playing.

Record companies or independent promoters ask radio stations to do paper adds and the stations comply, so the record companies can get "breakers," "bullets," or other types of recognition for their records. If a station simply doesn't have room that week for the record to go on the air, but the label needs the add, it will report the record but not play it. Or, in some cases, it never intended to play it, but report it to maintain their relationship with the label. This practice drives the trade papers crazy. "How can we build a legitimate chart if these people have no respect for what we do?" one trade employee asked me, and he is right. Other radio stations rely on these charts to make their decisions, and it simply isn't right for a station to report a fraudulent add.

There is an ominous undertone to the paper add as well, and that's *payola.* Reporting a record that you are not playing seems to be the kind of activity that one may take money to do and, even if one doesn't, it seriously affects the credibility of that station and of those working in its music department.

The trade papers and tip sheets view themselves as important links in the industry's communication chain. They inform the business of the key news and information that are required to carry on business in a profitable fashion. They communicate information about what radio stations are playing what records and provide an objective link between the two. They advise the business through their charts about what records are doing, as well as interpret the charts to indicate the records that are breaking out nationally and regionally. They are an invaluable information service upon which the industry has come to rely heavily. In addition, they see themselves as advocates and lobbyists for the business itself. In the face of censorship activities, copyright legislation, or other such activities, the trade papers ("trades," as they are called) are at the forefront of comments and activities on behalf of the business as well as of communicating the details of these activities to the industry at large. In a sense, the trades provide the crucial business-to-business communication that is vital to any industry.

TIP SHEETS

In general the tip sheets are targeted at radio station programmers, and they provide early, inside information on new and breaking records. Tip sheets differ from trade papers in that they cover a lot more records, both regional and local breakouts, and include comments from both radio station programmers and record executives about new releases.

The view provided by tip sheets is much more grass roots. While trade publications try to give a national overview, tip sheets provide the local flavor. The tip sheets are most valuable in the early stages of a record. If you get only one or two adds in your first week in the marketplace, the trade papers won't know you exist, but you will show up in the tip sheets. If you have an independent release and radio stations report that they are playing it, your record will show up in the tip sheets.

There are various tip sheets for various formats. For example,

CHR has *Hit, Hitmakers,* the *Gavin Report, Friday Morning Quarterback,* and *Monday Morning Replay.* AOR has the *Album Network,* the *Hard Hundred,* and *FMQB Album Report.*

The tip sheets also include charts, record reviews, and picks. They aren't always right (in fact, often when they choose an unknown act, they are wrong), but that isn't really the point. The point is that the tip sheets exist to communicate immediate and fresh information to the marketplace. There are dozens of reasons why they would pick a record, from an editor's personal belief that it is a hit, to information that the label has a major commitment to the act, to feedback from some radio people who have heard advance copies of the record. Whatever the case, a tip sheet's picks can be influential and are instrumental in helping a record get off to a strong start.

The music industry *works* (promotes to) the tip sheets. Record company executives, managers, agents, and even artists all maintain a constant dialogue with the editors of tip sheets to help identify and support records and artists who have the greatest potential for success.

It is the immediacy and informality of the tip sheets that make them so effective and important in the business. The editors of the tip sheets have close relationships with radio stations, labels, and managers and are always at the forefront of new artists and action. The tip sheets are where your record will get started, and they provide a platform upon which to build your eventual move to the trade magazines' charts.

ADVERTISING IN TIPS AND TRADES

Each week you will see pages and pages of advertising in the trade papers and tip sheets for new artists, albums, and singles. This advertising serves several purposes. The most obvious is, of course, to entice radio stations and retailers play or buy them.

But there are a few other reasons that trade ads are important. First, if a label is willing to buy multiple full page ads for an act, it sends a message to the music industry that its commitment to the act or record is strong. This goes back to the fear of radio and some retailers that they will be left out with a new record (either on the air or in stock on their shelves) that the record company has no interest in or commitment to. If they see the full-page ads, it makes them believe that the label's commitment is both real and long term. So if you are an act signed to a label, it is important that you have several full-page ads in the trades, not for your ego's sake, but to send the clear message that the label believes in you.

Second, the ads are a message to the trade paper itself that the project is real, that is, that the record label believes in your act and is going to try actively to make it a hit. This may strike you as peculiar. You may ask, "If the band has been signed and released, why would the label not try to make it a hit?" There are many answers to this question, from politics, to other priorities, to lack of funds in the label's budget, but suffice it to say that record companies do not promote every record they release 100 percent. That's why even after you are signed, you must continue to promote your record both to your label and to the music industry at large. The trade message is exactly the same as that sent to radio stations and retail stores. If the trades think the label is committed to you and it is a toss-up between charting your record or someone else's, they will pick yours if the label commits advertising dollars to your record.

There is a third reason for ads, which I do not believe is valid but some do. Some believe that if you buy a lot of ads in the trades, it will entice them to give you a good review, better chart positions, or whatever. This has never been my experience.

Different trades are used for different reasons by the record business. If you want to announce an artist signing worldwide or the breaking of a new international territory, *Billboard* is the best bet. If you are announcing a new domestic release by an act you think is destined to be a hit, once again, you use *Billboard* to send a message to the industry, especially to record retailers. If you are trying to reach radio stations with the information, then it's the tip sheets or *Radio and Records* you want. These tips and trades are where the ads that show the call letters of the stations that are already playing the record or other information to try to get stations to add it are found. They perform a valuable function for artists and managers, publishers, and major and independent labels. Learning how they work is a prerequisite for a successful music career.

INDEPENDENT RELEASES

We talked about how to put out your own independent record if you are unable to obtain a release and the pros and cons of doing so. But you should be aware that unless something out of the ordinary takes place, it's unlikely that the trade papers are going to review your record or, for that matter, chart it. Here's why. The trades are concerned about backup for the record, as are radio stations and retailers. No matter how good the record is, the chances of you having the resources to attack the marketplace and lock in a hit with an independent release are seriously against you. You may get mentioned in a column somewhere or in a new-talent page, but that is about all you should expect. To get your record into *Billboard,* contact the person who handles the "Heatseekers" section and send a copy of the record to him. Find out the name of the editor at *R & R* for the radio format into which your record fits and send a copy of your record to him as well. Try to establish some kind of relationship with each publication, even if it is just a weekly or monthly written update from you that tells them how you're doing. Just get your name in front of them as much as possible, but don't expect much.

On the tip-sheet side of things there is a better chance of getting some ink. The best ways are either to have a station that is playing your record mention it in its comments to the tip sheet or have one of the writers or editors mention it in his or her remarks. They will usually do so in conjunction with some regional comment about your part of the world. Once again, don't expect too much from them.

I've seen people with independent releases buy full-page ads in *Billboard* or the other trades. I don't recommend doing so. A full-page ad costs a lot of money and really does not have much impact. The only time it makes sense to do so is if there is a special issue for an upcoming international music conference, a spotlight on your country (if you live outside of the United States), a special issue on country music, or the like—any gathering or feature that may help you make a licensing deal for your product with a major or independent label. Otherwise to buy an ad to try to get radio stations to play your record or retail stores to stock it is a waste of money. These ads cost several thousand bucks, and a good independent promotion person costs about five hundred dollars a week, so the price of one ad equals about four weeks of independent work on your record, a much better investment. When you sign a deal with a label, let the label advertise; until then, spend your money wisely on promotion. It will pay much greater dividends and may lead to the record deal you are seeking.

Before the release of your first record, you would be well advised to buy a few copies of the various tip sheets and trade magazines and study them. An understanding of this important part of the music industry will go a long way in your relationship with the promotion department of your record company and the radio community. It isn't rocket science, but it's pretty damn close.

VIDEO (I WANT MY MTV)

*I hate videos. If you wanted to torture me, you'd tie
me down and force me to watch our first videos. We
all look like assholes. With "Slippery When Wet" I
told the director, "We're going to do a concert. You
film it and cut it down to three minutes." That finally
captured the spirit of the band.*

—JON BON JOVI

As recently as ten years ago, a discussion of video might not have
appeared in this book. Video music is still a relatively new concept,
but it has grown by leaps and bounds and has secured for itself an
important role in the music industry. The introduction of home
videocassettes, pay TV, the increased capabilities of cable and
broadcast TV, stereo TV, and channels like MTV and VH-1 have
expanded the video market, and musicians and music business people must be aware of all the implications of this musical form.

For the most part, videos work promotionally; that is, if your
record company chooses to produce a promotional clip of a song and
make it available to television or cable stations, it can expose your
act to millions of people. If you are an unsigned group and choose to
produce a video to help obtain a record deal, it can be the thing that
sets you apart from all the other tapes that the labels receive. Clubs,
retail stores, shopping malls, and the fashion industry have all chosen to use rock videos as part of their marketing strategies.

The problem with videos is, well, money, and artists are faced
with two problems. First, many labels now view videos as a privi-

lege where they once saw them as a right. Second, if an act does a video, record companies now insist that all or a portion of the money that they spend be recoupable against artist royalties. Since the videos themselves are seldom sold for profit, this means that the video money must be recovered from record sales and you will find yourself getting further and further behind.

To produce a high-quality video of a group, either in performance or conceptually, can cost upwards of fifty thousand dollars. Between the cost of the crew, equipment rental, tape and film, sound recording, mixdown, audio synchronization, and other post-production costs, video productions for the average act can represent a considerable financial investment. So how do you do a video and, at the same time, not end up in the poorhouse? There are two answers: You don't, or you do, but you must try to do it smart.

Let's start with a local band trying to get a record deal. In most cities the local independent television station has a music show of its own. Approach the station on the basis of taping one of your concerts for a special on this show. The station may not agree to do your whole concert, but even one song will give you what you need. Sit with the station people and plan something special. Play a concert for a local charity, try a unique location—whatever it takes to entice them to film your show. Be sure that there is some kind of written agreement between you and the station that outlines that this is a promotional piece that is not intended for sale and that the station is not entitled to any part of your record deal or any kind of financial payback. This is one way for an unsigned group to get the product without having to lay out the cash.

Another way is to approach one of the local colleges or high schools in your area. Many of these schools have video production facilities for their communications students. It is a good bet that some of the students would *pay you* to let them do a rock video as their class project. You may need to pay for the videotape, but the rest of the facilities, as well as the crew and expertise will come to you at no charge.

If you are a recording act, you have three options: Number one is to go the same route as I just discussed. The chances are that this route will work even better for you than for an unsigned group because you are a desirable commodity. MTV or other video channels or shows occasionally film an act in concert at a club for a concert special. Your label may have to share some of the production costs, but it is certain to be cheaper than starting a video from scratch.

Number two is to investigate the possibility of a home-video deal. This way, you will have a piece of product that is available for sale and will be able to extract a clip from it for promotional use.

Number three, of course, is to bite the bullet, make the best recoupment deal you can with your label, and then do everything you can to keep the costs down.

Canadian bands have a fourth option: the VideoFACT program, which supplies funding to groups and labels to produce videos to stimulate the domestic video and recording industry. Some outstanding videos have been made through this program, many of which have been seen on MTV and Canada's Much Music video channel.

However you finance it, a video is a must for any serious marketing effort for your release.

THE PROS AND CONS OF VIDEO, AND HOW TO MAKE A GOOD ONE

Some of the more popular touring bands have expressed concern that the availability of a group on video can have an adverse effect on ticket sales. However, research indicates that this is not the case. The real danger with video is overexposure or, worse, a bad video.

As I mentioned in the sections on radio and records, if a record is heard too often on the radio, *burnout* can set in. People simply get tired of a song they have heard too many times and sometimes call the radio stations to ask them to stop playing it. Well, video accelerates the process, since people not only hear a hit song in high rotation on radio but see it in the same rotation on video. Nobody really knows how much exposure is too much, but artists must be very careful not to get overexposed to the public. This is one reason why artists like Bruce Springsteen and Michael Jackson usually have a cooling-off period of at least two years between releases.

The other situation is much worse. In the past some artists made self-indulgent, horrible videos that were either offensive, bizarre, or, worse yet, boring. By doing so, these acts flirted with career suicide. When they hear your music, listeners can create their own mental images to go along with it. But when you create the images and put them on the screen, you have to bear in mind that you are doing it for the viewer to enhance the story and impact of the song. So your images have to be chosen carefully and assembled well to produce a product that will improve, not reduce, your chances of a hit.

But regardless of questions of image, quality, and the like, video is a major part of the business, and it's here to stay, so here a few things to keep in mind when you set out to do a video:

Work with Reputable People

If you know any other bands who have done videos, ask about the people they used. Ask if they were satisfied with the way these people worked, the cost, and the final product. If you get a good recommendation, meet with those people and discuss your ideas with them. Advise them of the image you are trying to convey and discuss the concept that you want to get across in your video.

Meet with the Director

Discuss your ideas with the director and decide whether you think he or she understands what you want to do. If you decide that you want to use this director, insist that he or she see your band perform live at least two or three times to get a sense of what your act is all about. No director should come into a shoot cold, never having seen your group, and attempt to direct an entire crew to render your music artistically. This is especially true if you are doing a live shoot. If the director has never seen the show, there is no way he or she will be able to direct three or four cameras and get all the right angles and shots at the right times. It simply cannot be done.

Select the Best Venue

If you are shooting a live-performance video, it is imperative that you choose the right place to shoot it. Ensure that the place can be properly lit, that the camera operators will have the mobility to move around to get the right camera angles, and that the building has the look that you want to convey for your act. If you are shooting a concept video, remember once again that the look is important and that your image is what is being portrayed because your image is one of the most important elements of your career. Be sure that the venue manager will cooperate, since he or she may have to open up the venue early or stay late to accommodate your production schedule. You may get the manager's cooperation by telling him or her that the video shoot will stir up interest in the club or venue and will bring in more business for your appearance. You'll need everyone's help to make your shoot run smoothly.

Use an Audience

Once again this suggestion refers to performance videos. If you are doing a video of your live performance, it is advisable to use an audience, even a small one, to heighten the excitement of the piece. Sometimes a video director will want to shoot your performance onstage in the afternoon with no audience for close-ups and then shoot it again with an audience later. To do this convincingly, you have to be aware of your energy level during the close-ups or the video will look too staged. Also, you will have to work extra hard to keep the audience animated. Their performance is almost as important to the video as is yours.

Dress Like a Star

Costuming is an essential element of any video. Nothing is more distracting than the wrong clothes in a video. This goes for overdressing and underdressing. Make sure that the clothes you are wearing are right for the song that you are filming and that they don't take away from the job at hand. You don't want people who are watching the video to be so distracted by your outfits that they can't pay attention to the song. Keep your costuming consistent with the music, look, and sound of your video, and the final product will be a success.

Be "Audio Alert"

I'm sure you have seen at least one video or TV program in which the sound didn't match the pictures on the screen. No matter how serious the subject matter, a badly synchronized video will always look like a Japanese *Godzilla* movie. Be sure to be present when the audio portion is being dubbed to the images, and if there is even the slightest variance, make them do it again and again and again, if necessary, until it's right. The last thing you need is to spend a lot of time and money and end up looking ridiculous.

Images Are Important

Don't make the look of your video too busy. Your images should have an impact and be powerful and dramatic, but not overactive. A too-busy video detracts from your music and will render it ineffective, both as a promotional device and as a piece of art. This goes for what I call "window dressing" as well. Girls, dancers, cars, motorcycles, and such should add to, not distract from, your performance.

Be a Student

Before you film a video, learn as much as you can about it. Talk to people in the video business—your director, the cameramen, and others—to get as much information as you can about what they are trying to do, just as you want them to know about your work. Take the time to let them explain what they need from you. Performing for a camera is different from performing for an audience, and they can help you understand what you need to do to come up with a good product. If you work as a team, you and your production crew will be able to make the best video possible.

There are a few other things about video that you should know. If you have a recording contract and are approached by an independent video production company, be sure that you take into account the restrictions of your recording contract with respect to making a home-video deal before you sign a contract. You can't sell the same thing to two people, and home video is usually included in most recording agreements.

If your video is going to be sold for broadcast, be sure that you or the publisher issues a synchronization license. A *synch license,* as it is sometimes called, is an agreement that gives someone the right to use your music in conjunction with pictures he or she has made. If you are performing any material on your video that has been written by other artists, then you must get a synchronization license from the publisher of that material.

A synch license can be issued for one specific broadcast on a particular date, time, and program, or it can be a *blanket license* that is good for all broadcasts of the video for a specific period. Synch licenses can also be a little tricky. If your concert is being broadcast live, then you don't need a synch license. However, if you broadcast the same concert later on tape, then you do. The difference is that live, you are not mechanically linking the songs to the pictures, but on tape you are. It's a good idea to check with the publisher of your material and with your record label about the need for synch licenses before you allow any of your videos to be broadcast.

It is also a good idea to clarify who owns what. If your record company pays to produce a video, then chances are that it owns the copyright of the video. On the other hand, if the company has made the budget recoupable against your royalties, then there is a good argument that you own it. Regardless of the situation (and you can see that there could be many different scenarios), be sure that there is an acknowledgment, on paper, of the ownership of the title to each video, so if you decide to sell your videos to another label or for a video-compilation package, nothing will get in the way of your deal. If you are not yet signed to a label and are producing a video on your own, ensure that you have a written agreement specifying that you, alone, are the sole owner of the video master and the music and the pictures that are on it and that no one else but you can copy it, sell it, or authorize it for broadcast.

THE IMPACT OF VIDEO

> *MTV is essential and anyone who tells you otherwise is an idiot.*
>
> **—JEFF AYEROFF,**
> **CO-MANAGING DIRECTOR OF VIRGIN RECORDS**

There is a great story about Kiss bassist Gene Simmons, who arrived at MTV one day wearing a pair of knee pads. He walked into the office of Vice President Abby Konowitch and said, "Okay, who do I have to blow around here to get my video played?" The fact is that most artists get into the business to make records and then, suddenly, have to learn how to make movies. Making videos creates some strange situations and a lot of stress for many artists, but, as I said before, video is now a fact of life in the business, and it's important that you learn its creative and legal implications, so you can make it work best for you and your career.

I'm often asked how video has changed the music industry. In conversations with people in the business, the consensus seems to be that it has created a new marketing tool. For the younger bands, it has been effective because the core viewers of MTV, for example, are fourteen to twenty-four years old—big buyers and supporters of new music and a generation that grew up watching TV. For them to get their music on TV seems only natural. For artists with older or *upper-demographic* appeal, VH-1 has stepped in to offer pictures to a generation that got its music from radio and, in large part, still does.

Video has helped to take many new artists to a new dimension, but one of the negatives that has been caused by what many call the MTV culture is the live-versus-*lip-synch* controversy. As you probably know, when artists "lip-synch" a song, they don't actually sing, they simply mouth the words to a recording that is played. Before video, the only way you could see a band was to buy a ticket for their concert when they came to town. Today, you can see many bands on many video channels every day, often long before you ever see them in concert. Because of this situation and the heavy visual imprinting of MTV and other video outlets, acts think it's no longer enough simply to stand on stage and play, but that they have to build a show that looks almost like a rock video. In these shows it's usually impossible for the artists actually to perform while running up and down ladders, ramps, and scaffolds, so they lip-synch instead. Some believe that it's unfair and dishonest for artists to fake their singing in concert. Some states have even introduced legislation that would require advertising for the show to indicate that some of the singing isn't real. Most people in the industry, including MTV, prefer that bands really play their instru-

ments and sing onstage, but the reality is that the visual impact of
MTV has changed the way concerts look, feel, and are staged, and
the physical demands on the artists to put on a show often make it
impossible for them to sing every song. In some cases, the visuals
have become more important than the music, the form overtaking
substance, and the word *concert* should probably be replaced by
show.

Overall, however, video, in general, and MTV, in particular, has
given the music business a considerable shot in the arm. Radio is
both conservative and fragmented, focused almost totally on playing just the hits. AOR radio wants to play nothing but Led Zeppelin, and CHR radio nothing but dance music. Alternative stations are cool, but not enough people listen to them and even they
argue among themselves as to which bands are alternative and
which are mainstream. Video has brought it all together. Without
video, new acts like Living Colour and Faith No More probably
would never have been able to get as much airplay and become as
popular as they have in the same amount of time.

To protect its position in the video field, MTV has negotiated
thirty-day exclusives with the major record labels that allow them
to choose 30 percent of the labels' videos for a thirty-day exclusive
on the channel during which time no other video channel or show
is permitted to air the clip. MTV pays the labels about $15 million
(total) a year for the privilege. This practice has driven some of
MTV's competitors to take drastic action. In 1989, and again in
1991, Black Entertainment Television (BET) boycotted MCA
Records in protest of an MTV exclusive of Bobby Brown in 1989
and Heavy D. and the Boyz in 1991 that ended only after negotiations between the label and BET. BET had boycotted other labels
as well for what it called the unfair practices of MTV. Some acts
like Hammer and Madonna own the rights to their videos, so the
exclusives don't apply, but MTV gets most of the video exclusives
it wants.

It is always a good idea for artists to own the copyrights for as
much of their creative material as possible to maintain control in
just such situations. When you negotiate your record deal, try to
keep your video rights. If you can make a better deal for your

career with MTV and the other video networks and channels, then it is merely a positive by-product of the more important issue of ownership of your valuable copyrights.

Some have criticized video, claiming that it burns out records too quickly. A song that is played on the radio, in jukeboxes, and on TV it can get overexposed in a short time. Most video channels dispute this claim with what appears to be sound logic. Video channels say that the average video viewer doesn't sit glued to his or her TV watching videos for hours. Rather, viewers watch for a short time, zap to something else, and then zap back. From what is known of TV-watching habits, they're probably right. So even if a video is in high rotation, that is, getting played three times a day on MTV, the chances are slim of a viewer seeing it more than once. But sometimes even the record companies will call MTV to ask them to stop playing a certain video, claiming that they see it too much. The answer is simple: It is the song that makes the video, and if viewers-listeners like a particular song, they will continue to watch it for a long time and not get burned out. There is really no evidence to suggest that songs come and go any faster since the introduction of video channels.

One of the biggest issues that video channels have to contend with is the banning of videos from the air for moral or other reasons. Like the major networks, video channels have broadcasting standards and practices to which they adhere that are tested with certain videos. Nudity, foul language, and such require a video channel to take a second look at a video. Generally, the channel will request an edit from the band and generally the act will comply, otherwise they risk losing video support for their project. Video channels are quick to point out this is not censorship, but merely adhering to the same standards and practices of the major networks.

Over the years MTV has been criticized for having too much power because they have no real competition. I believe that this is a pretty narrow view. Face it, there are at least fifty to sixty other cable channels (soon there will be a hundred), and each of them is programming something that some MTV viewer may want to watch. Many of the other cable shows feature videos or other music programming, and there are dozens of local video shows as well. USA and ESPN networks and the other choices on the box can take viewers away from MTV. On weekends, for example, MTV has found that young men prefer to watch sports or movies or simply decide not to watch anything. In truth, the major competitor for any video channel is the life-style of the age group that is most attracted to videos. These young people are highly mobile and active, and MTV and the other networks have to fight to hold their attention. One way they do so is through promotions—in the case of MTV, outrageous promotions, like giving away an island, a house, or Axl Rose's condo complete with furniture.

On occasion MTV and other video outlets comment on video works in progress for groups to help them, but in talking to them I've found that most consider themselves more like owners of art museums where you can see the videos than art critics who express an opinion. But often the record labels like to get comments for standards reasons, especially if they think that a band may be pushing a little bit far.

MTV representatives visit the record labels every quarter to listen to their new releases (so as soon as you get a record deal and have begun to record, make sure you or your manager hightails it down to MTV, meets the players, and lets them hear some music). In this way MTV thinks it is a lot more proactive with the labels in developing and breaking new artists.

GETTING ON THE AIR

The criteria that are most important in getting you on the air on any video channel are a hit song, a great video, and your popularity as an artist. Video channels encourage creative videos and will reward good videos with airplay. Even if a song is just OK but a band makes a stellar video, MTV and the others will usually play it. Otherwise, they think that bands would not bother to make great videos, and with no videos, what would video channels program? A great video and an average song will not do as well as a great song and an average video. Although, of course, everyone should strive for both, this point is something to keep in mind. According to

MTV, R.E.M.'s "Losing My Religion" was one of the best combinations of a great song and a great video in recent memory.

Artist promotions help because stars bring people to watch the channels. Videos by Madonna, Guns N' Roses, and others are why people watch, and the fact that video channels rely so heavily on these acts for drawing power increases the equity for the acts themselves, making them even bigger in the eyes of the public. That's one reason why breaking new acts is so important for video. Take a band like Guns N' Roses: In 1987 they were virtually unheard of and now they are considered by many to be the biggest rock band in the world. Video channels have been part of this band since day one and have grown with them, and they are equity for the video broadcast business and video is equity for the band.

With all this in mind, the reality is that it is not impossible to get on MTV and other video programs if you are a new artist. Your record label, your manager, and even you as an artist can meet with them and put together a marketing plan to help get you exposed. Clearly, this will happen for a new act only after the marketplace has expressed a certain level of interest in you and your music because literally hundreds of new acts are being released each year, and there are only so many spaces on the air.

But MTV, for example, believes that it is playing more new music than do most radio stations. Some of the new music starts in special shows, but there are always at least half a dozen new acts on the air that MTV, with the labels, is trying to break. Some of the special shows on MTV for new acts are "Headbanger's Ball" for metal acts, "Yo! MTV Raps" for new rap acts, and "120 Minutes" for alternative bands. But some new videos go into normal rotation. There is also a section of the MTV chart called the "Buzz Bin," which includes five or six videos of new bands that consumers may not even know and will see for the first time on MTV. At the time of this writing MTV is in 50 million homes, which is about half of the total number of TV households in America. Worldwide it is in over 200 million homes in seventy-seven countries. Soon, MTV will be the largest single music network in the world. A worldwide ad on the MTV Network can have a dramatic impact on your recording and live-performance careers.

THE FUTURE OF VIDEO

The future of video is an interesting one. Most agree that the novelty of playing videos twenty-four hours a day wore off a long time ago. Music-driven special programs, not sitcoms or game shows or the like, but music- and artist-driven shows are the future. MTV, for example, perceives that its future role will be a life-style channel for the youth culture. It will be totally music driven, with special shows, news, or whatever all music related. For video channels and programs to work, twelve to thirty-four year olds must find them hip. Keeping on the edge and playing new music is the best way for these channels and programs to do that.

One thing is for sure: MTV and the other video channels all sincerely believe that each year one or two new acts that no one has ever heard of will break through and become stars because of video exposure.

NETWORK TELEVISION

Network TV has always been a rather strange place for music. There have been numerous attempts to make it work for rock music, but it always falls short. And yet there is no better way to reach millions and millions of people than "on the box." In the fifties Dick Clark's "American Bandstand" gave teenagers their first glimpse of many of the day's top rock attractions. Then Ed Sullivan brought Elvis Presley into America's homes, but only from the waist up, in one of the most controversial television broadcasts in history. In the sixties two shows, "Shindig" and "Hullabaloo," broadcast in the afternoon and early evening, brought all the day's top acts into the after-school lives of millions of teenagers. Meanwhile, Ed Sullivan had graduated to showing the entire bodies of such stars as the Rolling Stones, Herman's Hermits and, of course, the Beatles, but Ed still had his share of problems with the censors, and Mick Jagger was forced to change the words of "Let's Spend the Night Together" to "Let's Spend Some Time Together." In the home video "25 x 5," you can see a clip of that performance, complete with a close-up of Mick Jagger rolling his eyes every time he sings the lyric.

The advent of MTV changed the way that network and cable TV look at music, but not much. Whereas on MTV and other video channels you get a steady stream of music videos in an all-music environment, network television is different. On network TV the environment is variety entertainment and sports, and music has to accommodate itself to the format. "Saturday Night Live" started using feature performers in the seventies and gave America the opportunity to see some of the world's newer or more controversial bands, whereas other shows like the "Tonight Show" and some variety specials tended to feature the softer pop acts like the Captain and Tennille and Stevie Wonder. Through the seventies there were attempts to put music on TV with "Don Kirshner's Rock Concert" and "Midnight Special," but both shows were relegated to late-night viewing when the audience is the smallest, and both shows eventually faded away.

About the only place you could see music on prime-time TV in those days was on the Grammy Awards telecast, but even that bastion of the music industry tended to go with safer pop acts and stayed away from hard rock and roll. In recent years the Grammys have used some real rockers and telecasts of the American Music Awards and the Billboard Music Awards have brought more music to the airwaves in prime time. But these programs still tend to go for the big stars, leaving the only TV exposure for new rock acts to "Saturday Night Live" (and they usually book well-known acts). But a few new trends are changing the situation. For example, the "Arsenio Hall Show" has become the hip alternative to the "Tonight Show." Arsenio likes music and knows that it appeals to his audience. What's more, he works with the bands he presents, asking them questions instead of just having them play. Although a lot of the acts he presents are rap acts, no doubt Arsenio's favorites, the fact remains that rock music is making it to TV in a well-viewed time slot. David Letterman and Joan Rivers both added a lot of pop music to their lineups in the early nineties, and in 1991, the ABC network went back to the old late-night concert format and created "In Concert," which did well enough in the ratings to get renewed for a few more seasons. And the comedy variety show "In Living Color" became a showcase for some of the best new rap and black artists, in keeping with the overall feel of the show.

But never expect network TV to even approximate the MTV experience, for, as I said before, the two environments are totally different and until one of the major networks decides that an all-music format has the best appeal, we will have to restrict our music on network TV to guest spots on otherwise nonmusic shows. Getting on these shows is not easy. There are few of them and the competition is fierce. Usually, the show's bookers are most interested in an unique act or an act that is currently riding high with a hit. It's the record label that generally pursues the opportunity, and there are no tricks. All you can do is ensure that the publicity department of your label is aware that you want to be on the show and keep hammering away at the publicists until they get you an appearance. There's one thing to keep in mind: The shows usually make their decisions at the last minute, so you may be called on to cancel a concert date or to fly back to Los Angeles or New York, or wherever, from your tour to tape a performance. But it's worth it, especially for the "Arsenio Hall Show," and you should always be willing to make the sacrifice to do it.

HOME VIDEO

The home-video market for music videos is still in its infancy. For some unexplained reason, music fans aren't particularly interested in owning videos of the concerts of their favorite acts. Whereas they will listen to a tape or a CD over and over again, seeing an act once or twice in concert and on MTV is enough. And the rental market is even worse. Think about it; you are in the business, but how many times have you rented a concert video? A few videos have had an impact. An Elvis collection released by Disney Home Video sold several hundred thousand copies but that isn't really a music video as such, it's more of a collector's item (after all, black velvet paintings of Elvis sell, too). But in the main, home videos of music haven't made it.

But that doesn't mean that you shouldn't try to put a deal together anyway. Atlantic's A-Vision is an aggressive company, as are Disney and a few others. They won't pay much of an advance and probably won't even talk to you until you've had a hit. They want concerts, not collections of videos, and they want names that will sell. But if you are able to make a deal after your first hit, the video is an excellent promotional tool, contest prize, and introduction to foreign territories and may even be the basis for a special on MTV, VH-1 or other video channels. Whatever the case, home videos are an element of the music industry, so you should want to be a part of it, and, although a home-video won't be the most lucrative aspect of your career, it should be pursued through your manager and label.

ON THE ROAD

Let's face it, the first tours the Beatles did, the main essential thing was scoring chicks.

—*PAUL MCCARTNEY*

Everyone knows that a rock tour consists of private jets, champagne, groupies, and limousines, right? Wrong! Tours are a grueling necessity for the proper marketing of a musical act. A tour may be defined as anything from a swing through five local bars in your city to a coast-to-coast sweep of sixty cities. The goal is the same: to get out in front of as many people as possible to play your music and to make money. In the case of the local bars, the goal is it's to make money and to be discovered. In the sixty-city tour, it's to make money, but also to increase your profile and therefore your record sales and perhaps even to help you pick up a gold or platinum album. What follows is an outline of what you can expect to encounter when you hit "the road."

THE IMPORTANCE OF TOURING

It's as close to sex as you can get.

—BILLY JOEL

And this man is married to Christie Brinkley! There are two key reasons for touring, and they are two of the most important elements of your career. The first aspect is your career itself. For you to gain the necessary credibility to enjoy a long career, you have to be able to show your fans, the press, and the music business that you can perform live. Most record companies won't even consider signing an act unless the band can put on an impressive stage performance. In the age of video, lip-synching, and the like, it is even more important for you to be able to deliver the goods on stage that you put on tape.

You may think that as soon as a band's new album comes out, they should hit the road, but this is not the case. A record needs time to get on the radio, to get into the stores, and finally to get into people's heads. There's no point putting tickets on sale for a show or appearing at a club if people cannot yet identify your new music with your name. Otherwise your record will do well but because no one knows that it's yours, your concerts will be poorly attended. A minimum of eight weeks should pass after a new album is released before you go out on the road.

And your agent must be completely filled in on the record label's game plan to promote your release before he can plan his strategy. If the label is doing a large-scale marketing campaign but only in a certain number of cities or in a certain area of the country to try to break you there first, the agent has to concentrate on those areas, too. Or if the act has sold a lot of tickets when they played certain markets in the past, the label has to know, so its promotion staff can attack those markets because there's a better chance to sell more product if the band has demonstrated appeal.

One of the most coveted things for a new act is the opening slot on a major tour. More than one act has broken out from this position. In fact, some acts have even left tours in the middle to headline their own dates—a combination of their record becoming a hit and their live performances earning them critical acclaim and an audience of their own fans. Opening for the Rolling Stones in 1989 was a big break for Living Colour, and this experience has been repeated by a number of other artists.

There are two ways to get on a tour. The first is to earn it through airplay, record sales, and reputation. That's the hardest way. For example, Trixter, who record for an independent label distributed by MCA, were not initially pursued by a lot of agents because they were on a small label and were a new and unknown act. So a small agent picked them up. Their record came out and their agent booked them on a few club tours. Suddenly, the record started catching on, MTV added the video, and a lot of radio stations played their record. The band was then offered the opening slot on several tours because they now had value in the marketplace. They went on the Poison tour, the Warrant tour, and others because they had sold a lot of records and had sufficient value to draw fans of their own to the shows. Through radio and video airplay consumer demand had been created, so people would buy tickets to see them. The ability to sell tickets as an opening act is one of the most important reasons why a band is added to a tour.

The second way to get on a tour is by capitalizing on business or personal relationships. If an act or its manager has a relationship with another manager whose band is going on a tour, that relationship can give them an edge over everyone else. Most often, securing an opening slot on a tour is a joint effort by the agent and the record label. Alice in Chains, who appeared on the Van Halen tour in the summer and fall of 1991, is a good example. The band's agent had relationships with both Van Halen's manager and with some of the band members. He recommended Alice in Chains for the tour, and Van Halen agreed to consider them on the condition that the record label would advertise, market, and promote the band's appearances in the tour cities. Their label promised to do the marketing, but so did about nineteen or twenty other labels for their acts. Ultimately, Alice in Chains was chosen because they were the right act for the tour, the label agreed to promote them, and what may have been most important, their agent had a relationship with the headline act that gave them an edge over their competition.

The second key reason for touring is for your record label and recording career. Records sell for a lot of different reasons: because they contain hit singles, the artist is popular, and what is often most important, because the act has gained an audience through touring. It all goes back to what I said before. If you can do it on stage, whether you are really playing or just lip-synching (although you have to have a lot of nerve to charge people twenty-five dollars to watch you pretend to sing), you get people excited and they are motivated to want to recapture that excitement by buying your record.

Some think that videos may replace concert touring, but the industry insiders know that they will not. On video you are only as good as your next hit. Besides, no one has to buy a ticket to see your video, they don't talk to their friends all week about going to see it, they don't get together with a bunch of friends or a date to see it, and they don't buy your T-shirt or program while they are watching it. Live concerts are participatory experiences that cement your relationship with your fans. Few things have more of an impact on the sale of tapes and CDs than do live dates. Some hard-rock and heavy-metal bands, for instance, get little or no radio play, yet they sell substantial quantities of records by getting their music to their fans through live performances. If people can't hear your music, they can't be motivated to buy it, and touring is the way you make sure they hear it with all the energy and enthusiasm you can put behind it.

But for all its benefits, touring is still a tough business. Here's an outline of how you can maximize the touring experience for your own career.

BOOKING AND PROMOTERS

> *I think you should keep on playing rock for as long*
> *as you have an axe to grind, and if you haven't got*
> *an axe to grind, you should go into cabaret.*

> **—PETE TOWNSHEND,**
> **THE WHO**

Booking is the first step in the tour business. To do a tour, you have to make the deals that will give you somewhere to play. That is the role of the *booking agent*. He or she is your connection with the world of promoters, club managers, and venues.

The first step for the agent is to contact the promoters and let them know where and when you want to play. A *promoter* is the one who underwrites the costs of your live appearance and takes the financial risk for it. He pays you; prints tickets; advertises; books the hall, theater, or other venue; and handles most of the business of your appearance. Depending on your deal with him, some of his costs, including his cut, will be deducted from the gross receipts, and you will be paid some percentage of the net.

Concert promoters operate in major cities and territories around the world. In major markets, one dominant promoter usually does most of the major events. He may have one key competitor and a number of small promoters, who will do the very new or alternative acts or who specialize in jazz or other types of music. Some promoters have become legends. The late Bill Graham was one of the most famous concert promoters in the world. The acknowledged Godfather of the business, Bill began in the early Haight Ashbury hippie days in San Francisco at the legendary Fillmore West, where bands like the Grateful Dead and others got their start. In the quarter century that followed, Bill worked on the major national tours of nearly every major star of rock and roll, including the Rolling Stones and the Grateful Dead. Tragically, Bill was killed in a helicopter crash returning from a Huey Lewis and the News concert, ironically while wearing a Lynyrd Skynyrd jacket, leaving behind an incredible legacy as one of rock's most colorful and influential characters.

All across the United States—in Dallas, Cleveland, New York, Denver, and other cities—you will find many entertainment entrepreneurs who started with nothing more than a few dollars and a love of music and whose businesses have grown into major entertainment companies. In 1989 a relatively new promoter from Canada shocked the industry with a revolutionary touring concept. Michael Cohl and his BCL Group offered the Rolling Stones a deal that included a reported whopping $50 million advance for all rights to their tour. This type of deal, which is called National Tour Promotion, could possibly become the standard for the concert tours of superstar acts in the future.

In a traditional booking transaction, the booking agent contacts the local promoter and outlines the terms of the deal for the act in the promoter's market. These terms may include the guaranteed fee for the act, the percentage of the gross that the act expects to be paid over the guaranteed fee, the cost of sound and lights, and any other financial aspects of the deal. This contract is generally for only one or two markets in which the promoter may work. The agent then makes a series of these calls to as many cities as the band has indicated they want to play until he come up with all the deals the band needs to go forward with the tour. These activities are based solely on live engagements and do not include any other rights, and the only money that changes hands is the deposit money from the local promoter to the agent to hold the date, usually about 50 percent of the guaranteed fee.

In national tour promotion things work differently. First, there is no agent in the deal. The national promoter negotiates directly with the management of the act and, in effect, becomes the promoter for every date on the tour. The national promoter pays the act for the entire tour—usually a substantial amount of money, representing the guaranteed fee for all the concerts on the tour. But the national promoter acquires other rights from the band as well, including merchandising (the right to sell T-shirts and souvenirs), broadcast rights (the right to produce radio and TV shows of the tour and to sell them for broadcast), and sponsorship (the right to sell the sponsorship rights to the tour to a company like Budweiser or Coca-Cola). The fee that the national promoter gives to the artist includes fees for all these rights. This deal is attractive to managers for a number of reasons:

- •There is no agent's commission to pay on the deals.
- •The band has its guaranteed money in the bank before the tour even starts.
- •One-stop shopping. The manager can get information about all the band's concerts or deals from one source.
- •Ease of accounting. The manager settles with only one promoter, not with a string of different promoters, which reduces the irregularities that sometimes crop up in accounting.
- •The artist and manager become partners with the national-promoter on the tour and are aware of the details of all the deals that get made. Everything is on the table, and the act has a better chance to make more money.

This approach to touring is catching on quickly in the business, although agents dislike the concept for obvious reasons. They dislike it because the power they enjoy in other deals is limited, along with their earning power. Also, these limitations sometimes have dire consequences for developing talent. Here's why. In addition to their superstar clients, agents have young talent who they are trying to put on the road. In some cases, the best way to do so is to trade favors with promoters. For example, if a promoter in one region wants to book a superstar act, the agent will insist that he take a developing act as well.

It is the ability to engage in these sorts of deals that gives agents their influence, and once this leverage is taken away, it is difficult, if not impossible, for the agents to maintain their previous spheres of influence. But national touring is certainly a reality, and it will be interesting to see how agents adapt and what roles they find for themselves in this innovative approach to concert tours.

Negotiations with Promoters

Earlier I talked about the key aspects of the deal. The first is the amount of money that an act will be paid. If a promoter is sure of your drawing potential, that is, if he thinks you can fill a club or a concert hall with fans, he will offer you a guaranteed fee, or *guarantee*, that is, a confirmed fee in addition to a percentage of the gate receipts, rather than just the latter. The guarantee is generally based on past performance, the popularity of the act, competition between promoters in the marketplace for the right to book the concert, and whatever the market will bear. Agents contact a promoter, get an offer, and then take it to another promoter to try to beat the first offer, and so goes the auction until one of the promoters pulls out.

The guarantee is only one part of the equation, however. Some promoters may offer a lower guarantee in favor of giving the artist a higher percentage of the gate receipts, or *gross*, as it is called. That is, of course, for those acts for which the promoter has that kind of flexibility. In fact, it is the agent and artist, not the promoter, who control the financial arrangements, especially if the act is well known and much desired. In that case, the agent tells the promoter what the expected guarantee is and advises him of the percentage split. Generally, this split is 85 percent to the artist and 15 percent to the promoter; that is, after the expenses are paid, the artist receives 85 percent of all of the money from ticket sales that is left over. You can see how one-sided these deals are in favor of the act. It is a traditional case of supply and demand. There is only one Bruce Springsteen, Madonna, or Rolling Stones (all three, by the way, would get 90 percent or higher) and if you, the promoter, don't get them, they will either skip your city or play for your competition, neither one of which is a particularly attractive alternative.

When the gross receipts exceed the expenses of producing the show, including the artist's guarantee, it is said that the show has "gone into percentage." This means that there is money for the promoter and the act to split, as I just outlined. When the show does not go into percentage and does not even "break even," that is, ticket sales do not bring in enough money to pay the artist's guarantee or the expenses of the show, the promoter tries to renegotiate his deal with the act, but he usually ends up absorbing the loss.

In the booking process, all the other details of the show are discussed as well, from how and when the tickets will go on sale, to how much they will cost, to sponsorship and other items. The promoter supplies the agent with *a ticket manifest,* that is, how many tickets will be put on sale for the concert. The ticket manifest is important because it is used to calculate the gross on which the percentage splits are built. Agents and managers watch this aspect carefully and have been known to have their own people count seats or "take the drop," that is, take all the torn ticket stubs and physically count them and compare them to the computerized box-office printout to ensure that all the numbers balance and the promoter did not put more tickets on sale than are reflected in the box office settlement.

The deal is discussed and finally the agent issues a contract to the promoter. When the promoter receives the contract, he reviews it, notes any changes he wants to make, and discusses the changes with the agent. Along with the contract comes the *contract rider,* that is, the addendum to the agreement that outlines the technical aspects of the show, along with information on the band's dressing rooms and other specific needs and often even information on advertising and promotion. The standard live-engagement contract looks like this:

THE LIVE-ENGAGEMENT AGREEMENT

An agreement between a promoter and an act or their agent is a surprisingly simple piece of paper. First, notice that I said "piece," not "pieces" or some other word that denotes a lot of paper. The contract form, which is called a "T-2" for traveling engagements, is a one-page agreement provided by the American Federation of Musicians of the United States and Canada.

At the top of contract are the name, address, and phone number of the booking agency that issued it, which makes it clear who the agreement is with, and the fact that it is a union form makes it clear that the gig is union sanctioned. The agreement is a "personal services contract" between the promoter and the artist and the manager or agent, who contracts to provide the artist's services to perform a concert for the promoter. The contract shows the date that it was issued and outlines the details of the engagement. In some cases, the artist's name appears only after the letters f/s/o, and the listing for the artist is the name of a corporation. What this means is that the artist has formed a corporation for tax reasons and that the contract is between the promoter and the corporation "for the services of" the artist.

Venue and Show

Next comes the *venue*, that is, the building or site where the event is to take place. Usually, the agent tries to be specific in listing the name of the venue, its location, and its size. The date of the show, the number of shows on that day, and the showtimes then appear. In the case of a headline act, the contract reads "1 show." The length of the show is seldom, if ever, specified because it is impossible to tell superstars how long they are allowed to play. In the case of opening acts, it usually reads "1 show" and indicates the length of the set; for club gigs, it says "2 sets (or 3 more sets) of 45 minutes." This section of the contract also lists the number of the local chapter of the union for the city or town in which the event is to take place.

Compensation

Next the contract includes a calculation of the gross potential of the engagement based on the number of seats and the ticket prices. It will also show any local taxes or deductions that may affect the potential gross. The gross potential is then printed on the face of the contract so that both the promoter and the agent know the number on which the artist expects to be paid. This is important, for what comes next is the notice of compensation to the act. Compensation for a concert attraction is usually represented by some guarantee plus a percentage of the gross.

There are a lot of formulas used for calculating payments to the artist. Here are two of them:

1. A superstar act may receive a guaranteed payment of $250,000 versus 90 percent of the gross receipts less the expenses of putting on the show. What this means is that once enough tickets are sold to pay all of the expenses, whatever money is taken in beyond that amount will be split 90 percent to the artist and 10 percent to the promoter.

2. Nonsuperstar artists may receive a guaranteed payment of $50,000 to $100,000 versus 75 to 85 percent of the gross potential after show expenses.

Whatever the case, the number of tickets is multiplied by the price per ticket to calculate the gross. The contract is always specific about the percentage splits between the promoter and the act.

Some of the things that may affect the gross are local taxes, foreign currency exchange, and other costs. At a county fair, for example, some amount of the ticket price may be deducted and given to the fair as the gate admission. Whatever the case, all the financial dealings are be indicated on this one-page document.

Merchandise Percentage

The contract also indicates what percentage of the merchandise sales is guaranteed to the act. You may wonder what the promoter has to do with money for the merchandise. Well, as you will see in the merchandise section, every building takes some percentage, usually a pretty hefty chunk, of the gross merchandise sales. A promoter often makes points with an act by getting them a bigger percentage of the merchandise gross through negotiation with the venue. In some cities, the venues are more flexible, especially if the promoter can take the show to their competitors if he isn't satisfied with the deal they are offering.

Deposit

The contract indicates what sort of *deposit* the promoter must pay to the act to hold the date. Usually, it is 50 percent of the guarantee and must be sent or wired to the agent's bank account before the contract is considered valid. Generally, these accounts are *escrow* or *trust* accounts that ensure that the band's money is protected. The balance of funds is paid to the act on the night of the show *before* they appear. There have been more than a few tense moments backstage when promoters did not have the cash or certified check handy and bands' road managers would not allow the headliners to go on until the money was handed over. That is a cardinal rule of the business: Always be sure you get *all* your money before you play. It's real hard to repossess a show.

Generally, the only other financial element in the agreement is for *production*, that is, the payment for sound and lights. These payments are usually ten to twenty thousand dollars or more and generally are a way for the act to get more money and to avoid paying tax or commission on it, since it is essentially the reimbursement of an expense.

Other
Other things that the agent may add to the standard agreement form are these:

1. The artist's billing on marquees and in advertising.

2. The type of foreign or domestic currency in which the funds are to be paid.

3. A notice that the show cannot be taped or broadcast without a contract with the artist for those activities. What this means is that the union wants to ensure that a radio broadcast, video, TV show, or anything else besides a live performance that takes place at the engagement is indicated on the contract and the artist is compensated for it.

4. A disclaimer from the union that absolves it of any responsibility in case the show does not take place; that is, it indicates that the union is not contracting to stage or perform the show. It also provides for the admission of a union representative to attend the event, to ensure that all the clauses of the contract are being adhered to by both parties and to settle any dispute that may arise.

5. A space for the promoter and the artist to sign the contract.

THE CONTRACT RIDER

Pretty simple right? Short and to the point. Well, it would be if it weren't for a little line that appears at the top of the standard agreement: "Any and all riders attached hereto are made a part hereof." A simple phrase, which on average extends the length of the contract from one page to twenty-five, thirty, or more. But today, the scope of live events is such that you couldn't deal with all the issues that arise from a show at a stadium, arena, or even a smaller venue on one page.

Contract riders have taken a pretty bad rap over the years ever since the Van Halen "No brown M&M's" story, but they are an important part of the communication among the concert promoter, agent, artist, and manager. Riders contain specific information not only about what kind of food the band wants in the dressing room, but about all the technical, marketing, and advertising aspects of the show.

Details of the Concert

The rider includes information about the date and venue of the engagement and references the contract to which the rider is attached. Then, it lists information about contacts for the production manager and road manager for the act. These names are listed so the promoter can contact the artist's organization in advance of the engagement to discuss any of the technical aspects of the event and to address any changes in the rider that may be required. Promoters pay close attention to details of the rider because it is usually clear in all contracts-riders that the artist is not required to perform if the obligations of the rider are not met.

I've broken the rider down into specific sections for the ease of discussion. Not all riders are laid out this way, but most certainly take the same approach if they do not contain the same information.

Presale

The presale section discusses two things: the size of the stage and how that size will affect the number of *kills*, or seats, that will have to be eliminated because of the poor view of the stage. There is a lot of jargon here, so stay with me. First, the artist's production or road manager indicates that the stage must be of a certain height, width, depth, and so on and lists any risers or platforms that need to be included, as well as any draped sections and the like. The rider also includes the size of the sound system (which the band brings) and where it is to be placed on the stage. From this information, the promoter begins to make up a *seating plan* that shows what are called the *sight lines* from each seat.

Then, the promoter's production people determine that there are certain seats from which the fans' view will be limited by the sound system or other obstructions. In addition there may be seats behind the stage that the act will allow the promoter to put on sale only after all the other seats in the venue are sold. All these seats, which are obstructed views, are called *kills,* which means they have been killed or removed from the floor plan. The other kills are created by the sound- and light-mixing consoles that are on the platforms located in the middle of the floor at most concerts.

Here's why all this is important. In addition to the fact that the production manager needs to know the details of the staging requirements of the act, it is from the seating plan that the promoter creates the *ticket manifest.* This manifest is then used to determine how much money the promoter should have in the box office at the end of the sale period. This amount is called the *sale capacity,* which is different from the *venue capacity* in that it is a net figure that takes into account the number of kills caused by equipment, obstructions, and other interference with the sight lines.

Sponsorship

The next thing you encounter in a contract rider is the sponsorship section. These days, many bands allow their tours to be sponsored by a product or a company. Later I'll go into sponsorship in detail, but let's take a look at how it may be treated in an artist's agreement.

The sponsorship section usually lists all the details of the artist's contract with the sponsor as they apply to the actual live engagement. For example, it indicates how the sponsor's name or logo is to appear in the advertising and what advertising it is to appear in. It may say that the sponsor's name, logo, and slogan are to appear once in all print ads; that the name is to appear at the top of the ad; and that the name is to take up 10 percent of the overall space of the ad. It may state that the manager will supply artwork for the ad that contains the sponsor's logo and that this artwork is the only official artwork that is to be used. The sponsorship rider also describes radio and TV ads, contests, and how the sponsor is to be included in each. It may also give some information about how many signs the sponsor should get and where they should be placed.

In addition, the rider will probably say something to the effect that it is the promoter's obligation to remove all competitors' signs from the venue before the show. This requirement sometimes presents a problem for the promoter, who usually does not control the signage in the venue and thus has to come to some agreement with the venue as to how these signs will be eliminated. The rider will be specific in its insistence that no competitive product be identified in any way with the concert or tour and that the employer, that is the promoter, is the guarantor of that part of the rider.

The rider also generally stipulates that the sponsor is to be included in all the advertising for the event and that the sponsor's logos are to be shown on the video screens between acts and before and after the concert. It most likely also requires the provision of a room for the sponsor to host guests, generally called a hospitality suite, and a "meet and greet" (a reception where the band has to meet the sponsor's executives and customers— most artists refer to it as a "meet and grief").

The rider will tell the promoter how many free tickets the sponsor is to receive and where the seats are to be located. This is a very important point and is often the cause of a lot of difficulty. When a sponsor signs a deal with an act, it expects to get great seats for the executives, district-office staff, and its customers. If a promoter fails to hold good seats for the sponsor and all the good ones are sold to the public, there is no remedy except for the act to try to make it up to the sponsor in other ways. The manager and promoter are often at odds about tickets for the sponsors either because the promoter has made sponsorship deals with other companies or is reluctant to hold tickets or otherwise cooperate with the artist's sponsorship program.

The bottom line for all the items contained in the sponsorship portion of the rider is this: The act has made an agreement with the sponsor to provide certain things. Some of the things are beyond the direct control of the artist and manager and are in the hands of the local promoters. The only way that an act can ensure that the local promoter will cooperate in the sponsorship program is to make it a part of the performance contract.

Tickets and Settlement

The next part of the rider is the band's requirements for tickets and the financial accounting of the show. This section of the contract outlines the following details of the pricing, sale, and distribution of tickets and details of allowable expenses for the concert.

As I said earlier, if the act is to be paid on a percentage of the gross, the manager and agent need to have a way to ensure that the percentage will be of the actual amount collected by the promoter after allowable expenses. That's where this part of the rider comes into effect. The agent asks for a manifest or inventory of all the seats available for sale in the venue and for a printer's manifest of the tickets printed for the show. For computerized tickets, the manifest is simply a computer printout detailing the total number of seats available and the number of good seats and kills. The rider also states that if any counterfeits surface, the agent expects the promoter to pay for them as if they were real tickets. This requirement is included to ensure that the promoter will aggressively pursue scalpers and counterfeiters in his market.

If the actual gross revenues presented at the accounting differ from the gross that was reported on the face of the contract, the agent expects the act to be paid the higher of the two. As you now know, there are a number of formulas for paying the artist based on the percentage of the gross potential, but the net result is that the agent always insists that the artist be paid on the highest figure. And in many cases, the contract states that if there is a discrepancy between the two numbers (the reported gross potential and the actual gross revenues), the act must be paid the difference in cash on the night of the show before they go onstage. Although disputes arise, the act generally is paid before they perform, and the accounting is sorted out later. There's something about an arena full of fans who are ready to tear the place apart that motivates promoters to pay, regardless of their opinion about who is right or wrong.

Most artists include a restriction on discount tickets or series tickets. The contract states that the full ticket price, and only one ticket price, must be printed on each ticket. An agent will not allow two different prices, for example, the full price and a student discount, to appear on the ticket because there is no way of knowing which price was paid and therefore how much money the promoter should be presenting as the gross potential.

As a backup, the promoter must have on hand, on the night of the show, all the unsold tickets, which are called the *deadwood*. The concept, although it seldom is actually put into practice, is to count all the money that the promoter has put on the table and to figure out how many tickets it represents. Then the deadwood is counted and the two figures are totaled and compared to the gross potential. If they match, there's no problem. If they don't, then something's wrong, and the accounting is reviewed. Before ticketing was computerized, tickets were just pieces of cardboard with information printed on them. They were easy to counterfeit and were called *hard tickets* (you may sometimes also hear this term used to describe any full-price ticket for an event).

If there are any discrepancies about the number of tickets that may have been sold or the attendance at the event, the agent or road manager may ask for what is called the *drop*, or all the torn ticket stubs collected by the ticket takers at the turnstiles. The box-office personnel will then go thorough the arduous process of counting the ticket stubs and then comparing the total to the money collected by the promoter, what the promoter says that he has sold, and the remaining deadwood. This is all done to get an accurate accounting of how much the act should be paid for the number of tickets that have been sold.

The rider also restricts the number of complimentary tickets that the promoter can distribute without the artist's approval. Only a small number of these tickets are distributed, usually to the media, a list of whom must generally be presented to the act for approval. And finally, the artist's agent always insists that his representative be allowed in the box office on the night of the show to monitor activities and watch out for his client's interests.

Settlement

Next comes the *settlement* section. So far, I've referred to the meeting that takes place after the show to divide up the money as the financial accounting. In the business it is referred to as the settlement. The settlement section of the rider addresses what kinds of expenses will be allowed, in what form they must be presented for payment, and how the artist expects to be paid what he or she is owed.

Allowable expenses means that the agent will allow a promoter to bill back only those costs that the promoter had to pay out money for. If, for example, the promoter obtained one thousand dollars worth of stereos to be used as prizes for a radio contest in exchange for mentions of the name of the stereo store on the air (this is called a *trade out* or *contra*), he is not allowed to deduct this amount from the box office receipts because he didn't actually pay for the stereos. The promoter also does not get to charge the act a fee for his involvement in the show. Speculating on the success of an event and taking the risk to make a profit is the promoter's job, and the profit is the only compensation to which he is entitled.

All other receipted expenses for the show are allowed, and they are presented on a cost or expense sheet. To avoid problems at the settlement, the agent and the promoter agree on the costs of the show before the date is even booked; these costs include rent for the building, advertising, catering, salaries for local stagehands, and the like. In some cases, the expenses are qualified. For example, all expenses for radio, television, and print ads are billed at net rather than gross. That is, the agent agrees to pay only the actual cost of the media (net), rather than the media plus ad agency commissions (gross), especially since many promoters own the agencies that book the ads. And finally, unless he is well known by the agent, the promoter must pay the artist in cash or certified check, not a personal check.

Settlements are an important and serious part of the experience of live performances, but many amusing stories are associated with them. Some promoters will take off all their jewelry, including their Rolex watches, before they go into a settlement, so the road manager or tour accountant doesn't get the impression that they are well off financially. One promoter had what he called his "show night" car, a beat-up old Pontiac Bonneville that he drove to his events, instead of the new Mercedes that he drove to work every day. And one road manager had a six-gun he called his "calculator," which he placed on the table at each settlement to, as he said, "make sure all the figures added up right."

Production

Next come the technical aspects of the show, namely, the stage, power, sound and lights, stagehands, and special accommodations for outdoor shows. Since every show is different, your own included, it is kind of pointless for me to walk through a specific technical, or "tech," rider. Instead, let's talk about how the tech rider fits into an important part of the live event: production.

Every tour has a production manager. It is this person's job to ensure that all the technical aspects of the date go according to plan. On the surface, this may sound pretty easy, but believe me, it isn't. For even a basic tour, you are dealing with a couple of semitrucks full of equipment, plus a minimum crew of ten or twelve, plus local stagehands, riggers, electricians, and the like, and keeping it all sorted out takes a lot of time and logistical coordination. There are probably more horror stories about production than about any other part of the touring business because production is where most of the problems can and do occur. It is the production manager's job to contact every local promoter for upcoming dates and to discuss the details of production long before the act ever gets to town or even sets out to go there. This is called *advancing* the date. Simply to arrive in town with your equipment is asking for trouble. There are so many things to think about in production that the mind virtually boggles.

Things happen in production that the average fan or even musician simply never considers. For example, what fan would ever think that the band would arrive in town and find out that their stage doesn't fit into the building in which they are supposed to play. Or better yet, how about arriving in town and finding out that the trucks that your gear is in won't fit down the tunnel to the loading area of the venue? These things happen if you don't advance the date and, more important, advance the date with all the right questions.

Most bands are content to allow the local promoter to build the stage from specifications supplied in the contract rider. This is much cheaper and easier than carrying their own. The stage requirements take into account things like performing surface, strength, and construction and barricades between the stage and the audience—things that will affect the artist's performance in any way. Stage diagrams, or *plots,* also outline the requirement of the sound wings, that is, the platforms on each side of the stage on which the PA system is placed.

As I said earlier, all these staging requirements will determine the number of kills in the seats and will affect the gross potential. Therefore, the production must be compact and efficient to do the best job while taking up the least amount of space. The stage must provide a secure and safe platform for the band on which they can perform their show, and it is the job of the production manager to advance the date and make sure that this basic element meets the artist's specifications.

Next comes the discussion of power. Most rock tours carry enough electrical equipment to cause a minor brownout in a mid-sized city. This equipment requires a lot of power and specific types of power. Usually, the contract specifies sound power, light power, and a separate power requirement for motors and other electrical gear. Once, while I was on the road with a major act, we appeared in Anchorage on Friday night, Honolulu on Saturday night, and Eugene, Oregon, on holiday Monday afternoon. While we were in Anchorage, there was an earthquake that, aside from scaring the hell out of us, also had an adverse effect on the power generators for the city, and for a while we were concerned that they wouldn't allow us to play the gig that night. When we landed in Hawaii, we found out that the earthquake that had rocked Anchorage had caused an off-shore tidal wave that knocked out power on the island. We spent the rest of the day, jet-lagged out of our faces (see Routing), looking for several giant generators to create the incredible amount of power that we needed for the show.

Sound and lights have become an incredibly important part of live concerts. The sound system for a concert used to be the public address system in the arena and the lights were a couple of spot-lights already in the building. Today, sound and lights are so sophisticated and such an integral part of the promotion that many bands rely on them for entertainment almost as heavily as they do their music. Sound and lights are an essential part of advancing the date. *Flying* the sound and hanging the lights require some-thing called *hanging points.* Flying the sound means that instead of placing the big black speaker boxes on the stage, you put them on platforms that are hoisted to the ceiling with chains and motors where they are suspended for the duration of the show. Flying has two benefits: improved *sound fill* in the hall (that is, more people can hear better, so the sound quality is improved) and fewer kill seats because the sight lines to the stage are improved with the removal of the stacks of speaker boxes.

But flying a PA requires that there are load-bearing points in the ceiling structure that can bear the weight of the platforms and speakers. Lighting systems that are composed of a variety of truss-es require the same hanging points, all of which depend on the structure of the ceiling. On more than one occasion, a poorly advanced date has resulted in the act being unable to fly their equipment and having to scramble to make do on the day of the show. The result is usually more killed seats and a nightmare of relocated seats for ushers, not to mention disappointed fans.

The other sound-and-lights issue is the mixing platform in the middle of the floor, where the consoles, computer, special effects, and groupies are kept. Generally, a lot of kill seats are held for these platforms, but only about two-thirds of the seats need to be killed. So here's a tip for all you concertgoers: If you can't get good seats when the tickets go on sale, don't buy tickets for bad seats. Just wait till about 3 P.M. on the day of the show, when they decide how many seats they have to kill for the mixing console and how many they can release to the box office. The seats they release will go back on sale, and they will be on the floor, about halfway back. Great seats and far below scalpers' prices!

Other items that may make it to the sound-and-lights section of the rider include an intercom system to be provided by the promot-er, so the lighting designer can communicate with the spotlight operators and a notice that *only* the band's sound-and-light specialists are permitted to run sound-and-lights during the show.

Crew

The section on the *crew* includes the *road crew* and the *stagehands*. These are the workers who set up all of the thousands of pounds of sound, lighting, and other equipment that you see at every concert.

Generally, local stagehands are broken up into two groups and four "calls," or shifts. The two groups are tradesmen and laborers. The tradesmen include an electrician to handle the power requirements for the sound and lights and riggers to handle the chores of flying the PA and hanging the lighting trusses. Riggers are the high-wire act of the rock-and-roll business. They are brave men. There isn't enough money in the world to entice me to crawl around on top of a lighting truss that hangs thirty feet above a concrete venue floor. This Bud's for you guys!

The four calls are these:

•*Load-in and rigging call:* usually about 7 or 8 A.M. This is a small crew of 3, 4, or 5 riggers, plus a forklift operator, an electrician, and some loaders and stagehands.

•*Stage call:* when the gear actually gets loaded onto the stage. This call requires about ten to fifteen stagehands and last all day through a lunch break until the sound check at about 4 P.M.

•*Show call:* which requires spotlight operators (about ten to twelve for an arena show), as well as a few stagehands.

•*Load-out call:* which includes riggers, an electrician, a forklift operator, and a lot of stagehands. The idea here is to strike (tear down) the set and get it on the trucks and get the trucks on the road as quickly as possible to save money on overtime bills in the venue.

One thing you should remember about stagehands: These guys are union, serious union, and they "don't take no shit from nobody." There are a lot of things to consider when handling the local crew, including breaks, rules and overtime, and protocols, and the production manager for the band relies heavily on the local promoter's production people to walk him through all the local union politics on site. Simply put, production is the most important part of touring. Without a good production team, there is no show. Things that can go wrong are so myriad and strange that you can never take anything for granted, and that's why the rider is such an important part of the contract, especially when it comes to the technical aspects of a gig.

Outdoor shows present a whole new set of production challenges to the production team. When you move outdoors, there must be more and bigger everything, and everybody is going to work harder. One thing that matters more than just about anything else outdoors is inclement weather. If it rains, the act wants to be sure that it stays dry and doesn't get electrocuted and if the promoter doesn't see to it, the band won't play but gets paid anyway. So promoters and production managers go through a lot to ensure that if there's any chance of bad weather on the day of an outdoor show, all the necessary adjustments are made. If you've ever seen a band in an ill-equipped venue doing a rain dance, now you know why.

Hospitality

Touring is a rigorous exercise. Therefore, the rider contains some specific requests for dressing and hospitality rooms. Most promoters supply these rooms as a matter of course, although some do it better than others. In most cases, you'll find one dressing room for the "star" of the band (if there is one) and one for the band members; a band lounge; a tuning room for the guitars; a crew room, where the band's road crew can take a shower and hang out; and a hospitality room, where the band can meet with their label, guests, and others after the show. Since this is the area that actually touches the artist, most promoters are careful to make the dressing rooms as nice as possible. Of course, this only goes for the big-time acts. Most low-budget gigs for up-and-comers have crummy concrete rooms that the band has to share with the roaches, but that's called "paying your dues," and, of course, it sucks. On the topic of dressing rooms, by the way, one band I know considers it imperative to scrawl their name on the walls of every dressing room in all the dumps they play. It's kind of like marking their territory. Your rider should include certain demands for at least a warm-cool, comfortable, and private place for you to be before, after, and between sets. Otherwise, after a few months on the road you, will go insane. I guarantee it.

Catering

The next part of the rider is one that everyone, particularly the press, seems to like the best: the *food rider*.

A food rider usually lists soft drinks, beer, and wine to be placed in dressing rooms and meal requests ranging from "vegetarian" to "Indian curry, if available." When you're a star you can demand mango juice and cases of Jack Daniel's, but on your first tour your rider will probably specify less exotic refreshments. The reality is, of course, that when you tour, you should eat right, whether you are the Rolling Stones or the Screaming Meemies. If you don't, you will die from what we, on the road, call "deli-tray toxicity," which comes of eating nothing but warm pastrami and potato salad for months on end.

Twelve-page-long food riders are for bands that have made it, so why shouldn't they get whatever they want? After all, when *you* make it, you'll want what you want, and you deserve to get it. By the way, in case you are wondering where all the food goes after the band leaves the dressing room, the answer is that the crew eats it, all of it, even though they get their own meals. But usually these guys are so big that nobody dares to stop them.

Security

This is an important part of any contract rider, especially for the artist and the manager. The security section discusses security not only for the concert, but for the instruments, the dressing rooms, and the equipment.

The security section dictates how many security staff there should be, where they should be stationed, and, in some cases, how they should behave. Usually, the head of security for the building works out a strategy with the band's road manager or head of security that will make the band and crew most comfortable at the event. Security is something that new bands take rather lightly, but it is an important part of ensuring that your act, gear, and teeth stay together on the road.

Other Considerations

These are a few other general considerations that you will find in a rider:

Production office: The rider usually requests one or two offices with phones, photocopiers, desks or tables, and the like, where the band's road manager and production manager can do their business. While the show is playing in one city, for example, the production manager may be on the phone advancing the next few dates. Or the road manager may need an office to take care of the myriad business details that pop up during a tour. In addition, the tour accountant will need somewhere to work on the settlement accounting before going to the settlement. Again, regardless of your level of sophistication, if you are away from home on the road, you should try to have at least a section of your dressing room dedicated to business.

Passes: The artist's road manager controls the backstage and guest passes to the event. He decides who gets to go where, so a good level of security is maintained and a minimal number of people get in for free.

The rider also addresses things like cleanup, the arena's scoreboard (should it be raised or lowered for the show?), laundry and cleaning facilities, matting requirements for cables that run along the floor (covering them with gaffer tape, so no one trips in the dark), lights to be turned off in private boxes and exits during the show, on-site promotional activities on the day of the show, recording devices and cameras at the event, merchandise sales, parking for the band's vehicles, legal and insurance requirements, and any diagrams or drawings that are relevant to the event.

As you can see, the contract rider is a thorough document, designed specifically to ensure that the event comes off with the least amount of grief and aggravation. Even early in your career, a reasonable and well-thought-out rider will make your gigs better and your employers certain that they are dealing with a thorough and professional outfit.

ROUTING

When an agent plans and books a tour, he must string together a series of dates so they make the most sense geographically. This process is called *routing* a tour. Ideally, the route should cover the least amount of distance for the highest number of shows, in the most reasonable amount of time. No band in its right mind (although I can't be quite as definite about booking agents) would accept an engagement in Boston on Monday, Los Angeles on Tuesday, and Miami on Wednesday, but if you don't pay attention to your schedule, a plan close to this can easily be made.

On their Thunder Seven Tour, Triumph's road crew christened the band's agent The Dart because they were certain that he chose the dates not by advance planning, but by throwing darts at a map on the wall. However, when I worked on the Rolling Stones Steel Wheels and Urban Jungle tours, the routing was as well planned as Operation Desert Storm.

Whether you are playing a series of bars in your home state or a regional or national concert tour, you must be aware that travel takes a lot out of you, and you have to ensure that your moves from one city to the next are as painless as possible. Allow yourself and your equipment enough time to arrive in the new city and to be set up, so the afternoon before the opening night of your engagement can be used to check the for a sound and equipment.

On a tour consisting of one-nighters, if you go to bed at three in the morning and attempt to get up at six to catch an eight o'clock plane, your performances after three or four days of this routine will be disasters from sheer fatigue.

Routing relies heavily on the availability of venues in which the event is to take place. Although the agent may want to book the act in Chicago on the fifteenth so it "routes" between Detroit on the thirteenth and Indianapolis on the sixteenth, the building in Chicago may be available only on the fourteenth, which means that the artist would have to play four days in a row, something that he may have already made clear that he will not do. If another event is booked for the building, in the building the agent will sometimes ask the promoter to try to get it moved. In some cases, the building is not actually booked on the fifteenth, but is merely being held by another producer for an event that he hopes to put in there on that day. In this case, the promoter would "challenge the hold," and the other promoter would either have to commit to renting the building on the fifteenth or release it. This is just one of many scenarios that can take place in the routing of a tour, but each one is targeted at making the transition from city to city and concert to concert as easy as possible for the artist and the production crew.

Routing is important to a variety of players in the touring business. The record-company personnel have a vested interest in seeing the band appear in markets where there is airplay, where the record sales are strong, or where they think they may have a chance of getting the act on the radio if some demand is created by the artist's appearance. In this instance, the agent usually talks with the record label to get a sense of where the band is doing well with airplay because this is an obvious benefit to the agent in doing the deal. He may also advise the label of the markets where the tour is going, so the label can gear up marketing efforts in them, especially for the opening act. Although the headliner may be strong in one market, the opening act may never have been there. Generally, the opening act doesn't matter much, but on occasion it makes a difference, particularly if the label supports the tour with advertising, promotions, press, and in-store displays. Meanwhile the label gets what it wants by having the band play live where they are needed.

The promoters have a stake in routing as well. If you are a promoter who has just bought a date on the tour for a lot of money in what you consider a tight financial deal, you want to ensure that your radius of potential ticket sales is as wide as possible. If you believe that the agent has booked another concert date too close to your city, you will be very upset.

Let's say, for example, that you bought a stadium show for Buffalo, New York, and then find out that the agent has booked another stadium show in Rochester, New York. These two markets are literally right down the road from one another, and, although they are two separate cities, a stadium concert by a major act would draw audiences from both cities. No doubt the Buffalo promoter would attempt to have the Rochester show canceled and, if it wasn't, he would either try to renegotiate his deal, now that his potential profit was reduced, or would cancel the Buffalo date. Just to show you how the business works, if the Buffalo promoter canceled the date, the agent would probably first offer it to the Rochester promoter and, if he refused, would look for another promoter for Buffalo. In a case like this, the agent might even try to bring a promoter from another territory into Buffalo. Doing so would serve two purposes: It would save the Buffalo payday for the act and would teach the Buffalo promoter who withdrew his original offer a lesson. Sometimes the music business can get pretty ugly.

Artists and managers are the next ones to have a stake in the routing of a tour. Artists need time off between shows, and they need it in a high-quality atmosphere. Traveling is not a high-quality atmosphere, so to expect an artist to put out night after night while traveling during the day is the fastest way to kill the goose that's laying the golden eggs. No manager in his right mind will allow an agent to book such a nightmare for his act, not if he wants to keep the act as a client. Usually, artists ask to play two or three nights and then to have two or three nights off. In this way, they get to rest their vocal chords, fingers, or whatever and to recharge their emotional batteries, so they can give the best performances. Routing is a key element in allowing this to happen, and the agent needs to be aware of the physical as well as promotional needs of the artist.

Finally, the road crew must also be considered in routing the dates. However, no matter how much time there is between shows, the road crew will always believe it isn't enough. If you give them three days, they'll want four, and if you give them four, they'll ask for five. They aren't lazy, nor are they wasting time, rather, they have to deal with reality. While the agent in his New York office argues with the promoter on the phone from his office in Chicago about something being wrong with the building in Phoenix, it's the road crew who are standing in the building in Phoenix where the ceiling is leaking and there's no place to hang the lighting truss. But the tickets are sold and a lineup is forming in front of the building at 7 A.M. The road crew have to deal with these problems, so they are always looking for extra time for the margin of error to allow them to get the job done.

It's the road crew that have to drive six tractor trailers through a midwestern snowstorm in January at twenty miles an hour for fourteen hours, and it is the road crew that have the most to lose from poor routing. Agents usually listen to road crews about their routing concerns (the average roadie outweighs the average agent by about a hundred pounds) because most road managers have been on the road for a number of years and they can advise an agent of the peculiarities of a specific building or city that may slow things down.

A friend once told me an incredible story about an R & B band who had two shows back to back a mere sixty miles apart. But in planning their route, they neglected to take two things into consideration: how long it would take to set up and tear down the production and how many people it would take to do the setting up and tearing down. The first show on the tour was set up and played and ended about 11 P.M. The crew began tearing down the set and were still at it at 11 A.M. the next day. They finally left the first show at about 11:30 A.M. and arrived at the second show sixty miles away at 1:30 P.M. on the day of the show, with a production that took a minimum of twelve hours to set up. As a result, the second show used only about half the equipment and was four hours late in starting. After that, they had to scrap the production, postpone the tour for three months, and then start again; after three months, their record was off the radio and attendance at their concerts was disastrous. Poor advance planning of the production and routing can end in just this kind of nightmare.

PLANNING A TOUR

As you can see, tours don't just fall together. They are preplanned long in advance and address a number of important needs for the artist. What follows is an outline of the things that you will need to consider when you begin to plan your tour.

The planning process for a tour should begin at least six months before the first date. There is a lot to do, and if it is all left to the last minute, things can, and will, go wrong. Often an artist is so preoccupied with finishing the record, which usually precedes the tour, that he or she has little time to devote to planning the tour. This is where the services of a good manager and road manager are invaluable because these two begin the planning. The details involved in the planning of a tour make up a pretty long list. Here's a look at the important elements:

Timing

The first thing you'll need to consider is when you want to tour. This is a lot more complicated than, "Gee, summer would be nice," for it isn't a vacation that you are planning, but work. Several things go into the timing of a tour. The first is the release of your record. You cannot release an album and set out on your tour the following week. You must allow enough time for the record to have an impact in the marketplace, and if you start your tour too early, it will be over before your record peaks, and you will have lost all the promotional benefit a hit record can provide. If you try to go out too soon, several people will try to stop you, namely, your agent and the concert promoters for whom you will be working. Your agent will probably tell you to wait and if he doesn't, the promoters will, because they are risking their money and they want to be certain that your appearance has the full promotional effect of a successful album behind it.

As a general rule, you should wait about eight weeks after the release of your album to begin your tour dates. This period will give your label enough time to get your product on the radio and into the stores, to get it played and displayed, to get the video made and on MTV, and for the consumer to know it's out. Believe it or not, it takes about three weeks for a new record to catch on with the public, and even longer for a new act, so eight weeks after its release seems to be the standard.

If you are a new act going out on your debut album, the rules are a little different. Basically, your agent and manager will probably take whatever dates they can get, just to get you out in front of people. But even in the early stages, it should be a planned effort. When you begin to plan your tour, you need to tell your label right away, so it can start working on the markets you are going to play.

Timing is everything when it comes to matching the success of the tour with airplay and sales, and you have to ensure that the timing of your dates coincides with airplay and the demand in each city you visit.

Another aspect of timing is the season of the year in which you tour. It is better to tour the South in the winter and the North in the summer, but not just to perfect your tan. It's hard to move trucks, buses, equipment, and people in bad weather and remain on schedule. Planes get delayed and highways get closed, especially in the snow belt. And if the weather is too brutal, concertgoers will stay home, and that's bad news for you and the promoters.

The timing of all your tour-related activities will be vital to your ultimate success on the road.

Advancing the Date (for Promotions)

If you are signed to a record company, you should call the local promotion manager a few weeks before the show to ensure that he or she has contacted the radio stations and newspapers about it and that the sales department has put your album into the front racks in stores, has put up some displays in the stores, and has bought some advertising.

If you are not yet signed to a record deal, you should contact the media yourself and let them know when and where you will be playing and any other pertinent information about the date. You should arrange for them to announce your concert information on their calendar or events programs and ensure that they include it on the "concert information phone line," if they have one. Check with the promoter or club manager to find out if they have purchased advertising on the radio stations or in the newspapers, if that is part of your deal, and make sure that the ads are running. One tip here: Record companies traditionally buy advertising on radio stations after you have played a show, assuming that once people have seen you, they will go out and buy your album. Research has shown, however, that the people who come to see you play already have your record, and after you've played, the radio and press interest in you dies down. Thus, the best time to advertise is three or four weeks before the show, just after the concert is announced. It's at this time that interest in your appearance is highest because the news is fresh. Also, most fans agree that they prefer to buy an artist's album three or four weeks before a concert, so they have time to learn the new songs on the album and can better enjoy them at the show.

You may also want to ensure that the promoters set up contests at radio stations to give away tickets to your show, copies of your album (if you have one), T-shirts, or other promotional items, to promote the date. As well, you should arrange telephone interviews with the local newspapers and radio stations at least one week before the show. For radio, talk with whatever announcer appeals to your particular audience. For example, if you are a rock act, you'll want to talk to the night-shift personality on the local rock station. If you are an easy-listening or country act, you'll want to talk with the adult contemporary or country station in the area, during the day or during afternoon drive. The reason for this difference is that rock fans tend to listen more to the radio at night, while pop and country fans are usually daytime listeners to the radio and television viewers in the evening.

On the day of your performance, you should arrange to drop by the radio station in the late afternoon for an interview, so that people who are making their plans for the evening can include your show in their list of things to do.

Don't forget the newspapers. A few weeks before your show, send them a press kit with details about the concert. Follow up with a telephone call and arrange a phone interview, so a story can appear in the papers before your engagement. This kind of free advertising is invaluable and can substantially increase attendance.

As I've already mentioned, someone from your organization should contact the promoters in advance of the date and discuss what kind of advertising is being done for the show. Since it's your concert, you have the right to know where and how they are advertising and how much they are spending. This will directly affect attendance, and if you are playing for a percentage of the gross ticket sales, it will directly affect how much you will be paid. In general, promoters will provide this information and are willing to discuss any alterations or suggestions that you may have for the ad schedules. Remember that they are the experts in that market, but a new or innovative approach that you may suggest can make a great deal of difference. If the promoter refuses to discuss advertising with you, find out why. There is no reason for him to hide this from you, unless, of course, something is amiss, and if it is, you'd better correct it or risk the possibility that you will be playing to an empty room.

When You Get to Town

The first thing that you should do, if time allows, is to go to your hotel, drop off your baggage, and have your manager, road manager, or label rep make phone calls to the radio stations, newspapers, television stations, and the venue that you are playing to let them know that you have arrived. In the case of the media, try to confirm that they will be at the show.

Your next stop should be the concert hall that you are playing. There you should do a sound check of your gear for sound levels, to make sure everything works and to get used to the room. Play a few songs and get comfortable, but don't do the whole set. It's just a warm-up, not a show. Besides, you've got work to do.

You or your road manager should meet with the promoter and discuss the gig. Talk to him about security, bouncers, and what kind of crowd reaction is normal for the city or town. For example, does security allow the people in the front rows to stand or dance during the show, or do they make them sit down? It can be very distracting for you to be onstage playing, while World War III is raging between the fans and the security staff in front of you.

Discuss how many entrances there are to the venue and if they will all be policed by security to stop people from sneaking in. Remember, if you are playing for a percentage of the gross receipts, this could cost you money. A trick here is to have one of your own people go around and check the door security at the beginning of the evening. On occasion, some enterprising security men have started their own ticket businesses at a side door selling admittance for cash.

Find out about guest lists and complimentary tickets as well. Give the promoter your guest list, including the names of local newspaper reviewers, radio people, record store staff, and friends, and obtain from him any backstage passes that you may need for yourself and your crew. There is nothing more embarrassing than being in the band and not being able to get through the backstage door. Take a look at the promoter's or owner's guest list and ensure that there is a good reason for each person on it to get a free ticket. You don't want the promoter letting in half the city for free. You have the final say here unless the promoter wants to pay you for his guests.

If you are leaving tickets or passes for the media at the box office or the backstage door, be sure that the details are clear to both the people who are picking up the tickets and the people at the venue who will give them out. Many members of the press and radio will go to a show only if they have their tickets in advance. Too many times they've been told that their tickets would be at the box office, but when they arrive at the concert hall or club, they find that nothing has been left for them. These passes are important, so make a list and check it twice. If the media people helped you fill the place, ensure that they are well looked after for their efforts this time, so they'll help you the next time you come to town or put out an album that you want them to review or play.

After your sound check, your next stop should be the radio station to do a live-on-air interview. Then go back to your hotel to take it easy for a while before the show.

Ticket Counts

In the days and weeks leading up to your show, you should keep tabs on the daily ticket count. Your agent or manager should contact the promoter or club owner two or three times per week and find out how many tickets have been sold, that is, of course, if tickets are available in advance. This count will let you know how effective the promoter's advertising schedule has been and if it should be increased.

Also, it will give you a general idea of how your concert dates are going. For example, if you are to play in a five-thousand-seat arena and three days before the show you've sold only four hundred tickets, then you have an important decision to make. Will it be more costly to perform the concert for a small number of people, or should you consider canceling the show to cut your (and the promoter's) losses? Sometimes you'll have no say in the matter; the promoter will simply decide to cancel the show and will advise you of his decision. If you think the date can still be saved, however, you will have to convince the promoter to increase his advertising schedule, change to a different form of advertising (like TV, for example), and convince the radio station that is involved with the show to promote it heavily. If the promoter agrees, he will probably try to renegotiate your deal to pay you less money in the event that the date does not break even. It's a good idea to give him a break if you can. After all, you may want him to book you again in the future, and if you are reasonable to deal with, he'll probably book you again, even if he loses some money this time.

After the Show

After the show, there are two things that you must consider. One of them is the backstage party. In many contract riders, artists include the requirement that extra refreshments are to be placed in the dressing room after the performance for press and guests of the band. Bear in mind that after-the-show parties at the venue should be for promotion, not for hanging out. Local radio and press people, record executives, and retailers should be invited into the dressing room, given a drink, and afforded an opportunity to talk to the band members. Any other parties that take place at the hotel or elsewhere can be for other reasons, but get your business done first.

It's a good idea to check with the club owner or promoter in advance to find out if there is a room or area that you can use for the party after the show. If you are going to have something more formal that just a dressing-room meeting, try to get some kind of invitation out before the show, even if it's just by telephone, so that people will know about the party and not leave right after the show. Playing a great show is only half the battle; you have to let your fans and the industry *tell* you that it was great. Doing so allows them to participate actively in your career and become a part of your team.

Settlement

As I mentioned earlier, the most important thing that must be done after the show is the *settlement*, that is, the final accounting with the promoter or club owner. The settlement, especially for a big concert in a large venue, is usually a complex and difficult. Generally, it is handled by the group's road manager, but early in your career you'll probably be settling your shows yourself. Here are a few things you may want to keep in mind when you do your settlement:

1. Many booking agencies have established elaborate financial formulas for comparing amounts of expenses to gross revenues, venue fees, fees for the band, advertising, and so on. They generally refer to *fixed costs* (rent, security) and *variables* (box-office charges), and a percentage factor that is applied to the final outcome to arrive at the band's fee. Until you are headlining Madison Square Garden, however, a more practical approach to settlements is called for.

2. If your contract stipulates that you are playing for a flat fee, then any expenses that you or the promoter bring to the table are irrelevant. Keep this in mind, and don't assume that your bar tab is on the house unless your contract says it is. If you and your band drink like a school of tuna all week, and if, at the end of the engagement, the club owner presents you with a bar tab that is equivalent to your fee, don't complain. This is the kind of thing that must be worked out in advance so there is no confusion.

3. If, on the other hand, the club owner or promoter attempts to make on-the-spot deductions from your paycheck that were never agreed to, battle it out! If the owner or promoter makes the deductions anyway, take what you can get and have your agent or the union fight about it later. Be careful of one thing though: If the promoter wants you to sign anything that says that you accept what he is giving you as payment in full, then take nothing. Once you accept any money on this basis, a court can say that, by accepting payment, you have agreed to the promoter's terms.

4. If a club or concert hall has promised to provide lights, sound, or anything else at its expense, and upon arriving at the venue you find that they haven't, the charges to supply the missing items should be deducted from its portion of the receipts. If you are playing for a percentage of the gross and the promoter tells you that there isn't enough money from the receipts to pay for the lights or whatever, insist that he give you the money from the bar receipts or from his own pocket. If he refuses, sue him. By signing the contract he has legally obligated himself, and you should have little trouble recovering your money. Rather than take this money out of your own pocket, however, it's always a good policy to avoid the hassle and get the money from him up front or bill the equipment to him directly. A threat that you will refuse to play unless the terms of the contract are met is usually a great motivator, especially if it's just hours before showtime.

5. Remember, what you are talking about here is the money that you are going to be paid, so you will have to be sharp when it comes to your settlement expenses. But the most important rule is to make sure that you and your employer are absolutely clear on your deal before you play.

FITNESS, FOOD, AND FINANCE

> *Our time isn't that much our own anymore. It's*
> *like living in jail, only they take us out to eat lunch*
> *at the Ritz.*

> —*MIKE BORODIN,*
> *DRUMMER FOR FAITH NO MORE*

Artists describe touring as everything from the most fun you can have to a necessary evil. Whatever the case, it is something that every band must do if they are to become successful. Most artists recognize this fact and, as a result, have come up with their own unique ways of dealing with the rigors of the road. Often when bands first set out on their first real tour, they just do what comes naturally; they're being so excited to be touring that they forget that they are human beings. After about week of gigs, parties, all-nighters, and hangovers, they begin to realize that this is an eight-week tour and if they don't want to die somewhere around week three, they had better figure out what's going on.

The first things that artist have to figure out is what they need on the road. Of course, as you become more successful, need and want become interchangeable, but that comes with fame and is the payback for the years of doing without. A musician needs about five things to be successful on the road: ease of movement or transportation, decent accommodations, good food, sufficient time to rest, and some free time just to be themselves. If you don't have those things, then your tour is going to be more of a struggle than an event.

Fitness and Nutrition

Veteran acts like Van Halen, Don Henley, and Rod Stewart know what is expected of them and therefore what they have to expect of themselves and of the need to prepare themselves mentally and physically for a concert. Steve Tyler of Aerosmith, for example, does laps around the mezzanine level of the arenas in which he plays. He runs flat out for about an hour, and it takes three guys from the road crew, running in twenty-minute shifts, to keep up with him (Steve likes to have someone to run with). Other artists do other things, from taking long naps to meditation to sports. For instance, Michael Bolton and his band are great ball players and look for games in every city they play. Whatever you do, it adds up to treating your body well if you expect it to perform for you.

Another important element of your well-being on the road is food. If you live on pizza, beer, and cookies, you'll not only be light in the nutrition department, but you'll probably be nominated for the world's-fattest-rock-star category of the Grammys. Some artists, like Sinéad O'Connor and k.d. lang, have found that a vegetarian diet gives them the stamina they need for good health on the road. In most cities where an act performs the local promoter is expected to provide meals for the band. Earlier in this section, I talked about the catering rider, and as I said before, some people may think that demands for certain kinds of food are just the posturings of spoiled rock stars. But if an act has gotten into a regimen of eating certain kind of food to keep fit, that food is as important to the show and the tour as are the guitars, roadies, or anything else.

Maintaining a Positive Attitude

Even though the rest of your band and crew become your family when you're touring, the reality is that you can get mighty lonely and depressed when you're away from your home, friends, and family, especially if the tour or your new record is not going as well as you had hoped it would. The good bands who have spent many successful years on the road attribute much of their success to maintaining a positive attitude. They claim that if you are up, enthusiastic, and practical and have an intelligent attitude about how you treat yourself physically, you could theoretically tour forever.

Another important part of maintaining a positive attitude is not to cave in under the pressures of the road, especially since you'll be dealing with record-company reps, radio people, and the press. More than one act has self-destructed right in front of a whole roomful of media people because they have done just that. For example, midway through their 1991 summer tour, Axl Rose of Guns 'n' Roses started acting pretty strange. He lectured one audience from the stage about how lame his record label was: showed up hours late for gigs; went berserk in St. Louis, jumping into the crowd when a fan took a picture of him and precipitating a riot at the show; and generally appeared to be suffering from a bad case of tour fatigue. The band played well and the shows sold out, but poor Axl was probably so stressed out that touring became even more of a chore than it normally is. Handling the stresses of the road in the right way will allow you to remain focused, so you can be your best on stage and, most important, deliver your best to your fans.

In most cities, the record-company people will want to bring radio people, especially the ones who are playing your record, backstage to meet you before or after the show. Along with the radio people will come contest winners, girlfriends, and other sundry pals. You'll have to greet everyone cordially, make small talk, and appear to give a damn about who they are and what they have to say if you want to keep getting your record promoted and played. You can't do so, however, if you're in a perpetual funk. You also can't give a good interview if you're not in good shape. For example, if you do an interview midway through the tour on a bad day when you are tired and have a cold, you may tell the reporter that everything sucks—the road, the band, the record, the record label, and the press. Now guess which interview, out of all the interviews that you do on the tour, will get picked up by the national wire services and be distributed around the world. Good guess. So again, a positive attitude will keep your foot out of your mouth and will keep you out of trouble.

Money

Let's talk about everyone's favorite topic: cash. I know that you play music for art's sake and that money has nothing to do with it. However, you're going to have to pay for certain things like touring, your manager, equipment, and such, so you're going to have to concern yourself with money. Here's how money works in the touring business.

Every band has someone who performs the money function. For the big acts, it may be a tour accountant or a road manager, or for a lot of bands starting out, it may be one of the band members. Whoever handles your money needs to be sure of a few things. He or she must know how to handle money on the road. Before the tour begins, your agent, manager, and road manager will have devised a plan as to how the accountings will be done, the shows will be reported, and the like, and the person who handles the money will have to follow it. These days, through the miracle of fax machines, you can send the settlement sheet back to your manager just seconds after the settlement is finished, so he knows right away how much money the band made and can continue his cash-flow projections to keep the tour going. From salaries, to per diems for the band and crew, to watching that the promoters are paying what they owe, and to ensuring that the settlements fall mostly in your favor and that the bank gets the money that you mail, courier, or wire transfer to the tour account—all these things are important components of your road-accounting program that must be covered.

A new act can reasonably expect that there will be times when they run out of money on the road and will have to scramble to meet payrolls and expenses. Since promoters are slow in paying deposits to new acts, your cash on hand may be tight. You'll need to consider this problem before you hit the road. There are several ways to improve your financial position in this regard, from making a deal with your bank to making a deal with your record label. Whatever the case, be aware that touring costs money and that in the early days, you'll probably spend a lot more than you make.

After you spend some time in the business, you'll discover that, as in life, everything you do is connected to something or someone else. As in any other business, there is a domino effect in the music business and, as the artist, you are always the first domino in line. As long as you maintain your focus and determination, all the elements of your career—recording, publishing, touring, merchandising, publicity, and more—will remain on track. Make no mistake, it is a difficult and time-consuming task. But the rewards that can be had from hard work and good sense are considerable, and artists like Rod Stewart, the Rolling Stones, and others show that the rewards can last for years or even decades if you have the right attitude. Nothing worth having comes easy, but if you are willing to work for it, you can be successful and make a good living doing what you most like to do: make music.

Touring is an important part of the music marketing process, especially when it comes to promoting records. Whether you tour as a headliner or as an opening act, it is important that you know all the details of your appearance and that you and the people involved with your group promote, market, and police each performance to the maximum. Live concerts are an important part of your image and exposure to the audience. More important, they can be a considerable source of revenue for your career, and one that increases in value as your popularity grows. In the section on recording contracts, I discussed the fact that recording costs, videos, and tour support are recoupable from royalties. Well, nothing is recoupable from live-concert receipts, so while you are waiting for that big hit that will pay off the record company (and will start putting money in your pocket), your tour dates will be all that you have to pay the bills.

THREE

The Next Level

MERCHANDISING

*There's going to be a Maurice Starr doll. But it's
going to be five times bigger than ours.*

—DONNIE WAHLBERG,
NEW KIDS ON THE BLOCK
(AT THE LAUNCHING OF THEIR DOLLS)

The story goes that after each of Elvis Presley's early performances, his manager, Colonel Tom Parker, sold photos to adoring
fans so they would have something to have autographed. He insist-
ed that Elvis sign autographs after each show, not because he
cared about the fans, but because it did wonders for his picture-
selling business.

Autographs and pictures of stars have been hot items since the
heyday of Hollywood and, in fact, souvenirs of stars have been
around for many, many years. I'm sure that young cavegirls fought
to get souvenirs of their favorite rock singers (get it, *cave*girls ...
rock singers? OK, forget it). Not until recently, however, has the
marketing of a star's image become such an enormous business. T-
shirts, sweatshirts, headbands, tour jackets, and even shoes, socks,
and sweaters are sold at concert venues, clubs, and retail stores
around the world.

The undisputed champions for merchandise sales are heavy-
metal bands, which account for an enormous share of the merchandise pie and probably singlehandedly maintain the black T-shirt
manufacturing industry throughout the world. Although superstar
acts like the Rolling Stones, New Kids on the Block, and the
Grateful Dead hold the individual records for the highest per capi-

ta merchandise sales at concerts, bands like Mötley Crue, Cinderella, and Poison sell vast quantities of merchandise, with income from sales often surpassing their record royalties. In the mid-eighties, Blackie Lawless of the heavy-metal band WASP even stated publicly that he was primarily a T-shirt salesman—that the band made albums and toured to promote their merchandise sales.

Sarcasm aside, the fact remains that the sale of clothing that features a famous face can be worth a great deal of money, and you must be prepared to participate in this aspect of your music-business career. In the merchandise business there are four areas that you must deal with: tour sales, licensing, mail order, and retail.

TOUR SALES

Every time a major artist appears at a concert venue, the right to sell merchandise is part of the contract. This right to sell, however, is far more complicated than you may think. It isn't a matter of an artist simply showing up at the hall with a truckload of shirts, loading them into the building, setting up a stand, and selling away. Several negotiations take place before you get to that point.

First, the merchandise has to be made. There are two ways for an artist to have this done. One way is to make a deal with a merchandising company to manufacture, market, and sell your merchandise and to pay you a percentage of the net proceeds. This is much like a recording deal, when a record company pays all the up-front costs, in some cases including an advance on royalties; it minimizes your risk, but reduces your profit.

The other way (and probably the method that 99 percent of new bands use) is to handle your own design, manufacture, and sale of goods. Granted, this way increases the risk that you may be stuck with a truckload of unsold T-shirts, but it maximizes your profit if you do sell them. In the early stages of your music career, Brockum or Winterland (the two merchandise-industry heavies) will probably not beat down your door to make a deal, so no doubt, you'll have to handle it yourself.

Why do it at all? Why risk the money? There is a simple two-word answer: *profit margin.* The profit margin (or *markup*) on music merchandise is considerable. I'm sure that the only twenty-dollar T-shirt you own has someone else's name or face on it, whereas your blank ones cost about six bucks apiece. That's a fourteen dollar spread, and guess where a good part of that money goes? Right into your pocket.

In the early stages of your career, it's a good idea to sell merchandise, even if it's just T-shirts. The reasons are obvious. If your fans like your band enough to pay to come and see you play, then some of them will most probably buy shirts. This is a good way for you to make some extra money and to create walking billboards for your band.

So, now I've convinced you, and you're going out to print up five thousand black T-shirts, right? Wrong! If you decide to go this route, here's a list of simple rules to follow to ensure that you make the right moves and don't lose money.

Research the Market

Figure out about how many people you play to each month and then estimate how many of them you think are big enough fans to part with fifteen or twenty dollars to buy a shirt. As a rule of thumb, major acts sell some item of merchandise to about 15 to 20 percent of their audience at each show. Early on, you will probably sell about 5 to 10 percent. Therefore, if you play to 2,400 people per month, you will sell about 240 shirts. At $10 profit per shirt, that comes to $2,400 or about $28,800 a year!

Create Good Artwork

Nothing is uglier than an ugly T-shirt. Remember, you are selling a piece of clothing, and it has to be attractive so people will want to wear it. Make the graphics interesting and exciting, geared to appeal to your audience. (One suggestion here: limit your colors to one or two because four-color print jobs are expensive and will eat a huge hole in your profits.)

Print Limited Runs

As I said before, running out to print five thousand shirts can be a huge mistake. It will cost you a fortune to print that many, and you run the risk of being stuck with a truckload of outdated shirts if your band decides to change its logo six months later. Find a manufacturer who is willing to print up ten, fifteen, or twenty dozen a month on a yearly contract. The yearly contract here is important; one run of twenty dozen shirts is expensive because the up-front preparation charges are the same whether you print five dozen or a hundred dozen. This cost must be taken into account when you work out the price to charge per shirt.

Make Good-Quality Items

If a fan buys your shirt for fifteen bucks, washes it once, and it falls apart, how long do you think he or she will remain a fan? If the difference between fair and good quality is only a few dollars per shirt, then spend the extra money. Remember, the shirt is also a part of your image.

Watch Your Inventory

It's easy to start giving out freebies to girlfriends, boyfriends, relatives, and friends, but then, when it comes time to go on the road, you suddenly realize that your inventory is gone. Institute an inventory-control system that requires anyone in your organization who takes a shirt (including any shirts you may give to club owners, agents, or radio stations for contests) to sign an invoice of some kind and keep those invoices on file. One trick here: Write the words "for promotional use" on as many of these invoices as possible, so that at the end of the year, when the tax man comes around to get his share of your merchandise money, you can write off all the promotional giveaways.

Set Reasonable Prices

Remember, not everyone makes the same kind of big money that rock stars do, so you can't charge twenty-dollars a shirt everywhere you go. There's no rule that says what a shirt should cost. You can set whatever price you think the fans in your area can afford. Don't get greedy. Remember, this is basically found money in the early stages of your career and you're doing it partly as an image builder. Shirts that nobody buys are worthless, so be realistic and your sales will be brisk.

Advertise

I don't mean that you have to start running commercials on the Home Shopping Network every fifteen minutes. Just be sure that your road crew wears the shirts, that you wear them when you're offstage and, most important, that someone in the band wears one onstage (I don't recommend this for solo artists; it looks kind of goofy), and ensure that the shirts are displayed and on sale at whatever venues you play.

Negotiate

Even in the early stages of your merchandising career you'll probably encounter a club owner or two who will want a percentage of your merchandising profits. Don't panic. You'll find out later in this section that this is a standard practice in the merchandising industry. Don't, however, let the club owner fix the price. There's no set fee in this area, and it's up to you to negotiate. Remember, it's the owner's club, and he probably thinks he is entitled to a piece of this money. There are two ways to avoid this situation. One, when your agent makes the deal, have him put it right into the contract that you have the right to sell merchandise (a good idea in any event) and that the club will not charge a commission. While he's making the deal for your services, the agent is in a much better position to do this than you are standing in the lobby of the club on the night of the gig.

Two, if the club owner is being a jerk, don't sell at the club. Leave your shirts in the truck and be sure that the next time you play his place, your agent sets up the deal in advance.

MERCHANDISING CONTRACTS

Let's assume that your career is rolling along and your fledgling merchandise business attracts the attention of one of the big guys.

He offers to make a deal to take over this aspect of your career. Here's a rough sketch of the kind of things that you can expect to see in the deal.

Cost of Goods

The merchandiser will pay to manufacture all the items that he will sell for you. He will no doubt also expand the list of articles that he will sell, from T-shirts to bandanas, to sweatshirts, to key chains, or to whatever else has proved to be successful for other artists on his roster. The cost of making these goods will be factored into the profits and will affect what you will be paid. Since you already know how much it costs to make T-shirts, don't take the merchandisers numbers for granted. Realize that since he is doing big volume with his manufacturer, he is probably getting an excellent deal. So negotiate these costs and make sure that your profit stays as high as possible.

Sales Crew

The merchandiser will put a salesperson or a sales crew on the road with you to sell your merchandise. It may be one guy in a van or maybe a crew of two or three, and they may even rent space on your equipment truck to carry the merchandise from show to show. In any event, you will have to negotiate with the merchandiser as to whether he will be allowed to charge the expenses of this crew and its transportation (hotels, gas, meals, and so on) against your profits. Most contracts make you absorb at least a portion of these charges.

Artwork

Remember, it is *your* image that is going on the merchandise, so insist that all artwork that is used is subject to your final approval. You won't find a lot of resistance from the merchandiser, in that he is used to the band having the last word. In the past, only one design appeared on all T-shirts and sweatshirts for sale at a particular concert, and it was generally the artwork from the album cover. Today, there are often several different designs on different items, with the aim of selling more than one shirt to the fans. You and your manager will be consulted on the designs and will have approval of the final art, not only the design but the way it actually prints on the shirt. Take the time to make changes and to approve the final product. This is an important part of the communication of your image to your fans.

Percentages

Generally, a sliding scale of percentages is included in a contract, and it works as follows: You will be paid X percent on the first $250,000 worth of goods, $X + 1$ percent on the next $250,000, and $X + 2$ percent on everything over $500,000 in sales, or some formula like this. This formula is an incentive for you to make the deal with the merchandising company, and it can be done because the company's costs go down as the quantities go up. Also, when you begin to sell $500,000 worth of merchandise, you are starting to become a good profit center for the company.

Advances

The merchandising business is very competitive, so to sign new artists, some companies offer advances, just like the record companies do. In the early stages of your career, these advances may be nominal, but you should insist on them just the same. As a guide, take about 30 percent of your sales for the previous year and ask for that. You'll probably get around 20 percent.

Venue Commissions

Remember when I said earlier that the sale of merchandise in a large venue can be difficult? The reason is an individual called the *concession manager.* Since most major concert venues are arenas of some kind that are the homes of basketball or hockey teams who also sell souvenirs, each venue has a concession manager who is responsible for all sales in the building. This person regulates what percentages the hotdog, popcorn, and beer vendors will pay to the building and what percentage of the sales of your merchandise will be deducted. These percentages are usually high—30 to 40 percent of the gross—and unfortunately there is no way to get around them.

When your merchandise people arrive, they *count-in* the merchandise under the concession manager's watchful eye, so the

manager knows exactly how many shirts and other types of merchandise are available for sale in his building. At the end of the
night, your merchandiser will meet with this manager, and while
your road manager is settling with the concert promoter, the merchandiser will be dealing with the concession manager. A portion
of the percentage goes to pay the sellers that the building employs,
but the rest is just a tariff imposed by the building. You and your
merchandiser will find it necessary to take this percentage into
account when making your deal. Sometimes a good merchandising
deal can affect which building in a market a band will choose to
play, for merchandise has become a major profit center for the contemporary touring attraction.

LICENSING

Another part of merchandising that can make money for you is
licensing. Licensing, in its general sense, is the leasing of rights
from one party to another for some property. In the merchandise
business, it is a deal that you make with a company that allows it to
put your face, logo, or name on products that it sells to the public.
I'm sure that you've seen ads in magazines for rock-star mirrors,
keychains, bumper stickers, and the like. These are all manufactured under license by companies that specialize in a specific area.
Most of the large merchandising companies aren't interested in
manufacturing the "small ticket" items like buttons or key chains
because these items sell for such a low price and the profit margin
is so small.

There are still profits to be made on these items, however, and
many companies have sprung up that specialize in one or more of
them. They will approach your merchandiser and make a deal with
him for the use of your name and face on these items. The percentage or royalty that they pay to your merchandiser will then be split
with you according to the terms of your contract. In many cases,
your merchandiser will even agree to purchase a quantity of the
items from the other companies to sell on the road as part of your
merchandise. Since much of the business for these items is done
through magazine advertising and in retail stores, it is imperative

that your merchandiser make as many of these deals as possible, for two key reasons: The first, of course, is money. The second is image. If you are in a hard-rock band and there is an ad in a rock magazine that includes the merchandise of Mötley Crue, Guns N' Roses, and others, you want your name to be in it. Otherwise fans will not associate you with other big-time groups, and you will fall into the dreaded "B" band category, a place that you do not want to be. Stay on your merchandiser's case about these licenses. In some instances, these companies will even pay a small advance, although your merchandiser will probably apply the advance to your unrecouped balance.

MAIL ORDER

Mail-order sales also account for a fair share of the merchandise business. There are three basic ways that mail-order business is generated. The first is through advertising, primarily in magazines, but occasionally on radio and TV. Advertising can be done directly by your merchandiser, or, as in the case of licensing, be contracted to a third party.

The second way is through the fan club. Fan clubs are strange things. They work best for teen-idol types and country artists, but they can also be a good source of revenue and support for rock artists and bands. True fans are the hard-core people who haunt the record stores waiting for your new record, write nasty letters to any newspaper or magazine that dares to publish unflattering remarks about you, and call radio and TV stations requesting your new record or video until their fingers fall off. The majority of your fans won't be quite so fervent, but in general, they, as a group, will purchase just about anything that you advertise. The best way to reach them is through a monthly newsletter, preferably containing a personal message from the group or artist, with pictures, gossip and, of course, an order form for merchandise. The financial return will be directly proportionate to the size of your fan club, so you will have to decide how much you want to push this aspect of your career. Most of the major merchandisers, by the way, will offer to handle your fan club as part of their service to you.

The third way to sell merchandise via mail order is through inserts in your albums and cassettes. Some bands do not even consider this route, believing that a flyer selling T-shirts cheapens their artistic musical effort. This is a judgment call that you will have to make on your own. Here's a bit of advice that you may want to keep in mind when making this decision. The amount of money that is generated by these sales is generally not very much. Therefore, if you have any reservations about this aspect of merchandise sales, then pass. You won't be losing much money and the peace of mind that you get from keeping your image intact will more than compensate for any lost revenue.

RETAIL SALES

There are two ways to look at retail sales. In most cases, your merchandiser will *wholesale* items, that is, will sell quantities of goods to clothing stores, department stores, music stores, and specialty stores, which will mark them up and sell them to the public. These goods include the shirts, bandanas, and such that feature the name or photo of bands or solo artists. They are usually made available through what is called a license to a manufacturer, which basically rents the right to use a band's name, photo, or logo for a specified period, for specific clothing, key chains, hats, or whatever (I talked about licenses earlier). Usually, one of the big merchandise or management companies that has the band or artist under contract rents out the name to the manufacturer.

Legitimate retail merchandise sales can account for a substantial amount of money for an artist, but only if that artist has become enormously popular like the New Kids on the Block or Michael Jackson or has other specific audience appeal. In most cities there are stores that cater to the hard-rock or heavy-metal fans with such items as studded leather belts, wristbands, and lots of black T-shirts. The clientele of these stores is matched with the kind of stuff that they sell, and it's a pretty safe bet that you won't be finding a lot of Michael Jackson or Hammer merchandise in these locations.

The biggest problem with retail sales of merchandise and, in fact, with the retail business in general, is counterfeiting. Just like people who counterfeit money, there are those who illegally reproduce merchandise, using an artist's name or logo without bothering to acquire a license to do so and without paying any royalties to the artist. This kind of activity is no different from stealing a car or robbing a store; it is simply taking something that doesn't belong to you, namely, the money that is due the artist for the use of his or her name.

The big merchandisers like Brockum or Winterland are the ones who pay the artist in advance for the rights to his or her name, and it is they who suffer most because of the counterfeiters. These companies are always on the lookout for what is referred to as "bootleg merchandise." In fact, in 1990, a major joint effort between these rival companies (on behalf of a long list of artists) and local and federal law-enforcement authorities, raided the manufacturing and storage facilities of the bootleggers, netting millions of dollars worth of counterfeit goods. A warehouse full of phony merchandise was displayed to the media as part of the effort to bring the criminals to justice and to alert people to the seriousness of the counterfeiting problem.

As a consumer, the best way for you to fight counterfeiting is to be sure that you buy your merchandise from reputable stores or vendors and that you look for the label that says something like *sold under license from.* Without this label, the merchandise could be fake, and you should steer clear of it. "Why shouldn't I buy this stuff?" you may ask. The main reason is your own value. Bootleggers use inferior-quality goods (and cheap ink and artwork). Unlike the goods sold under license, the counterfeits tend to fall apart, the colors run, or the shirts shrink several sizes when you wash them, so you get ripped off along with the artist. Don't buy counterfeits; everybody loses when you do.

Retail sales can be a large piece of the merchandise pie, but usually only after you've hit the big time. Don't look for retail sales too early in your career. Rather, when you've gained enough popularity, the retailers will come looking for you.

Merchandising is a big deal. It promotes your act, makes a statement, and can earn you money. However, it's another of those details that you need to watch constantly and vigilantly. From busting counterfeiters to ensuring that you are getting a fair count on your royalty statements, merchandising is a job, but one with a big potential for profit.

SPONSORSHIPS AND ENDORSEMENTS

It kind of makes me mad that corporate America is taking the songs of my generation and turning them into rotten TV commercials. I'm not for hire. There's something about rock and roll that has a certain type of freedom to it. When you tie it up in corporate business, you take the freedom and the spirit away.

—JOHN MELLENCAMP

Sponsorships and endorsements are the use of a celebrity's or event's popularity to sell a product. I'll discuss these two areas separately, and give you little background on each. As we all know, a few years ago, some advertising executives got the bright idea that if sports stars could be used to sell products, then why not rock stars? Initially, they tried to treat musicians the same way they did sports figures, but they found that the musicians' "art" sometimes got in the way of the marketing effort. For example, Pepsi Cola paid Michael Jackson $8 million to appear in a commercial, but he refused to be shown singing the word "Pepsi" or drinking the product. They got around the problem, of course, but this kind of situation creates nightmares for the advertisers and their agencies.

As a result of these problems, a number of companies, which are essentially hybrid advertising agencies, have sprung up. These companies specialize in entertainment sponsorships and endorsements and claim to be able to handle the artistic temperament of the stars in this new and sensitive area of advertising. They began to pick up where the more traditional ad agencies left off and began to get better results. The situation wasn't perfect, however, so artist managers themselves became involved. These days it's kind of an open season for managers, promoters, or record labels— whoever thinks they can make the best deal.

Generally, the practice is to find someone at an ad agency who knows someone who can introduce them to someone else at a company who might become a sponsor. The best way, of course, is for the artist's manager to approach the company himself to get one of the music-marketing specialists at the advertising agency to do so. This approach helps to establish a direct dialogue from the very outset of the relationship.

The mechanics of the actual approach are simple: put together a press kit, cassette, and tour schedule and send it to the marketing department of the companies that you would like to have as a sponsor, follow up with a phone call and a meeting, and get the negotiations under way. Or you can find out which advertising agency the company uses and send it off to the agency. The point is to get the information into the hands of the decision maker. More important than the approach, however, is what the sponsorship business calls *fit*. The fit refers to an appropriate match between the product and the act, and it's very important if the sponsorship is going to be believable to the consumer.

Advertisers have their own business interests at heart in doing sponsorship and endorsement deals, and they have their own language to help express these interests. *Demographics, target group,* and *cost per thousand* are just some of the terms you will hear in your sponsorship talks. I don't suggest that you go should try to learn the advertising business, but if you can't figure out what the admen are talking about, you'll have a tough time making the sale, so take some time to learn the language, hire a music-marketing specialist to help you, and, as always, be sure you ask for an explanation if you don't understand something. Poor communication is one of the biggest problems in the area of sponsorship.

Keep one thing in mind. When you are talking to a potential sponsor, whether it is for a tour, a commercial, or a product endorsement, remember that the sponsor wants to know what an association with you will do for him. Too many bands spend all their time telling a potential sponsor all the good that the sponsor's ad money and promotion is going to do for them. The sponsor already knows that. What sponsors wants to hear is that the association with you is going to do good things for their products.

Sponsors do deals for two reasons: *image* and *sales.* If you are a well-known artist and have a large following and good reputation, an association with you will be good for the product's image. Sponsors figure that if people like you and you like the sponsor's product, then some of your fame may rub off on the product, and more people will feel good about it and maybe even buy it. For example, when Budweiser did a deal with the Rolling Stones in 1989 and 1990, the company knew the deal would probably help sell more beer. But Budweiser is number one in sales, and the deal wasn't made for sales. What Budweiser really wanted was the right to use performance footage of the Rolling Stones in its beer commercials. And the only way that it could get this right was to sponsor the tour because the Rolling Stones weren't interested in appearing in Budweiser's TV ads for any amount of money. As the sponsor of the tour, however, Budweiser got the rights to use the band and spent millions of dollars running these ads on everything from MTV to "Monday Night Football." It was an almost totally image-driven sponsorship.

The other type of sponsorship is sales driven, and it is one that younger bands can get involved with more easily. Companies are in business to sell products. Beer companies, soft-drink companies, and snack-food companies, in particular, and others depend on high volume for their profits. Many of these companies recognize that in addition to their normal retail sales, they can sell additional products at special events like fairs, sporting events, and concerts. Most of the major breweries, for example, have some kind of local music program that focuses on clubs and small concerts where beer is served. These local sponsorships are generally organized by the local distributors and are funded by the head offices.

Budweiser Light's and Budweiser Dry's New Talent Programs and the Miller Rock Network, the most successful programs of this type, have helped a great number of up-and-coming acts. It's easy for young bands to become involved with these programs, which usually provide advertising and promotional support in the way of posters, table cards in clubs, and even radio contests and promotional merchandise for giveaways. In return the beer companies ask the bands to wear beer-brand merchandise onstage and to put up beer signs on or near the stage. These programs have worked well for many new acts and for the breweries as well, so both directly benefit from the sponsorship. Investigate them through the local distributors of the beer or soft-drink companies that you are interested in or by talking to local booking agents, who generally keep up to date on these types of programs.

One thing to keep in mind when dealing with beer companies. Remember what I said earlier about "fit"? Well, fit is very important for beer companies in that the government takes a dim view of them sponsoring artists who appeal to teenagers or those below the legal drinking age. If your fans are generally young teenagers, avoid the beer companies and concentrate your efforts on soft drinks and other uncontroversial products. Just remember, whichever company sponsors you, be sure that your presentation is professional and that the company takes into consideration the fit between your music and its consumers.

A third kind of sponsorship is *venue* or *promoter* sponsorship, through which for an annual payment to the venue or the promoter, the advertiser gets to sponsor all the shows that take place in the venue or are promoted by the promoter year around. Almost all the major concert promoters in North America now have corporate sponsorship deals. These sponsors will pay the venue or promoter for the right to be associated with all the events in the following ways:

1. The sponsor's logo is featured in all the print, radio, and TV advertising for the shows.
2. The sponsor receives a number of free tickets for each show.

3. A sign advertising the sponsor's products appears some-where in the concert venue.

4. The sponsor has the right to do contests and other promo-tions in association with the concerts.

These arrangements work well for both the promoter and the sponsor. The promoter or venue gets money that can be spent on the promotion of events; the bands benefit from the increased promotion; and the sponsor aligns itself with all the big concert events that come to town for one payment, instead of making separate deals with each group—a much costlier prospect. Problems some-times arise in these relationships when a act refuses to be spon-sored, but most of the contracts between the venue, the promoter, and the sponsor provide for such refusals and allow a certain num-ber of shows to go unsponsored without penalty.

Sponsorship and endorsement can be sources of considerable financial remuneration for a well-known performer or group. But as you can see from the quote that begins this chapter, it is also a high-ly controversial area. You'll have to make your own decisions about corporate America and realize that a sponsor can be of big financial and promotional help to you, but sponsorship does bring with it a substantial amount of public relations risk if not handled correctly.

THE SPONSORSHIP PLAYERS

We're all familiar with the news reports of the megabucks paid to Michael Jackson and Hammer by Pepsi Cola, and outside the entertainment world, to football, basketball, and baseball stars, for the right to use their name on T-shirts or shoes or for appearances in TV or print commercials. Sure, not everybody gets the kind of money that Michael Jackson or Michael Jordan gets, but, then, not everybody sells 40 million records either. And the deals made with performers differ considerably from those made with sports figures. But the basic concept is the same: find a famous face and use it to sell a product. Before we actually look into the "whys and hows" of sponsorship, let's talk a little about what sponsorship means to each of the important players in the sponsorship loop.

Artists

> *If it didn't compromise my art, and I didn't think I*
> *was telling kids to drink something that was going to*
> *rot their teeth out or drive something that was going*
> *to get them killed on the highway, I might do it.*
> *You're damned straight I might. The catch-22 is, not*
> *doing it has increased my value.*

> **—BILLY JOEL**

The obvious thing that a sponsorship means to an act is money. If an artist is well known or even just has had a few hits but is hot, a sponsor may be willing not only to give the artist a substantial *rights* fee, or payment for the right to be associated with the act or tour, but to put up considerable marketing-support money for the tour. And that's an important thing for the artist. If the sponsor is willing to spend marketing money to get the artist's name out there and to promote the tour and release of the new album, the result may be the increased sales of albums and tickets. This kind of support advertising is, in reality, much more important to the artist's career than are any lump sums of money that the sponsor pays the act.

Manager

The manager is interested in sponsorship for the money and promotion that it brings to the act. But he is also interested for the leverage that it gives him with the promoters and the record label. In some cases, if the sponsor is going to spend a lot of money advertising the tour dates, the local promoter won't have to spend as much on advertising, and a high percentage of the savings, depending on the deal between the agent and the promoter, goes directly to the artist. In addition, the manager can take the sponsorship deal to the record label and insist that the label get involved with the sponsor and back its involvement with advertising dollars and promotional spending in support of the sponsorship and the tour. Labels generally cooperate with these deals because they know that the sponsorship deal can boost record sales.

Local Promoters

Sponsored tours are a two-edged sword for promoters. On the one hand, promoters don't like them for a number of reasons. First, local promoters usually have their own sponsors and when the act shows up with their sponsors, the local sponsors have to be pushed aside, which creates problems between the promoter and his sponsors. Second, the local promoter has to make free tickets, special seats, hospitality rooms, and the like available; must help remove competitor's signs, and must try to convince the local venue that it should put up a lot of the sponsor's signs. On the plus side, the local promoters gain increased advertising and promotion for the act, which reduces their need to spend advertising money and therefore reduces their risk. In general, local promoters like sponsorship, and it's only the execution that they sometimes find troublesome.

Advertising Agencies

Ad agencies are usually frustrated by sponsorship deals with musicians. In sports deals, bike races, car and boat races, and the like, the sponsor gets the right to put its logo all over everything, to use the name of the event everywhere, and to get the participants to promote its product. In a music sponsorship, the sponsor usually gets none of the above, and the ad agency has to work under a lot of restrictions regarding use of the artist's name, photos, and the like. Invariably the agency will come up with something that its admen think is very clever, and it will present the idea to the client. But when the client takes it to the band, the band refuses to do it. Usually, the band refuses because the admen understand promotion but not the artist's image. The admen fail to understand that an artist cannot do certain things at the risk of damaging his or her career.

I've had this conversation dozens of times with sponsors and ad agencies, and I call it the "don't fix it if it ain't broke" rule. Ad agencies and sponsors get together with specific artists because of their appeal to a specific age group, their image, and their "coolness." Then they proceed to try to change the act to fit the mold of some promotional campaign they have designed that will make the band look silly and will take away all the band's attributes. Such a campaign will make the band's fans turn away from them and will render them useless as a promotional vehicle. The smart sponsors leave well enough alone and capitalize on the strengths of the act that attracted them and made them feel like the band and the product had a good fit in the first place.

Another rule of thumb for sponsors is "less is more." Too often an ad agency for the sponsor wants to have the biggest sign in the world hanging behind the band when they play or before they go on. I once had an argument with a beer company about the size of the sign that was hanging over the stage and that had to be removed before the artist went on. I happened to be with the sponsor when the stage crew began to roll up the sign at the appropriate time. The removal of the sign got a standing ovation from the audience. I turned to the sponsor and said, "See, I told ya." The next day smaller signs were used and were more tastefully placed. Ad agencies have little understanding of the music industry, so you and your manager will need to have clear communication with the sponsor to ensure that your image is not compromised by the sponsorship deal.

THE MEGAEVENTS

What about the megaevents like Amnesty International, Live Aid, and the Rolling Stones' Steel Wheels tour? What do the sponsors get out of them that justifies the large sums of money they put up to be associated with them? Generally, sponsors become involved for two reasons. The first is the *cachet* of the event—the qualities of the event that make it so special and so interesting that people everywhere want to be involved with it, to see it, or somehow to participate in it. Cachet is something special that makes the experience larger than life. It is important for sponsors to associate themselves with these events. In the case of the Rolling Stones, it was especially important for Budweiser to sponsor their tour because it was to be the biggest tour ever and Budweiser promotes itself as the biggest beer company in the world, so the fit for Budweiser was obvious and necessary.

The second reason is to block competitors. Often a company will buy into a sponsorship or promotion just so its competitors cannot get it. But more important, the megaevents create a lot of promotional opportunities, outside the actual events, for radio and TV broadcasts and promotions, as well as other types of contests, displays, and sweepstakes that can be run at the retail stores. All these promotional strategies increase the products profile and sales in the marketplace and therefore help justify the expense of sponsor's involvement.

HOW FAR IS TOO FAR?

Sometimes an artist is asked to go too far. An athletic shoe company once wanted to make a giant, motorized replica of one of their shoes and wanted the band members to come out onstage in it. The company was astonished when the band refused, and simply couldn't understand why it was a problem. The band explained the "don't fix it if it ain't broke" rule to the company reps, who began to understand. Finally, the band proposed a compromise: the sponsor could shoot a poster with the act wearing the shoes.

Consumers have to believe that a celebrity's use of a product somehow enhances the celebrity's performance. It is easy for them to believe this with athletes and with instrument manufacturers and musicians, but it's tough with shoes and rock stars. You have to be clever to make this strategy work, but there are good ways to do so. Rather than a posed band picture, a shot of the lead guitarist leaping into the air wearing the shoes would have made more sense. It would show the shoes enhancing the performance of the rock star in the only way they can, by making him more mobile on stage. If that image was combined with "cool," it probably would have sold shoes to fans of the group.

The bottom line on "how far is too far" is this: If you're not comfortable doing something for the sponsor, don't do it. If you're not comfortable, it means that what you've been asked to do goes against who you are and, as I said earlier, who you are is your image and you need to be true to it. But don't agree to do something and then later refuse (only a jerk would do that) and make it clear to your manager that you want to know everything that the sponsor will require of you before you'll sign. Explain to your manager what you feel, and if he's a good one, he'll agree. If he offers alternatives, listen, don't be pigheaded, because there is usually a way to make the sponsor happy and still get the money and promotion that comes along with the sponsorship. All you have to do is work out the compromise, and the deal can get made.

Now you're an expert. Sponsorships can be tricky, but they can also be rewarding. The increased revenue and promotion that they can bring to your project are welcome additions in your attempt to try to sell your music in a very crowded marketplace. Sponsorships can help you cut through the clutter and make a statement that will be heard by a much larger audience.

ENDORSEMENTS

Endorsements are relevant here. Certainly, in any of your sponsorship deals, the manufacturers will want to imply that you are not only promoting their products, but that you use them as well. Product endorsements are harder for musicians to communicate to the public than they are for sports figures because nobody in his right mind would believe, for example, that Eddie Van Halen will play guitar better if he wears Nikes. But people may believe that he'll play better of he uses a Kramer guitar. When it comes to credibility, musicians are much more believable when they endorse musical instruments or electronics than when they endorse consumer products like shoes or soft drinks. Just as Nikes or Reeboks are tools of the athlete's trade, guitars, keyboards, and drums are those of the musician.

Instrument manufacturers seek out the best players and offer them free instruments on the understanding that they will be able to advertise the fact that these artists use their gear. Some companies even ask artists to do clinics and seminars, sponsored by them, as a part of the endorsement package. Associating an artist with the right company can be of great mutual benefit because it allows the manufacturer to increase its sales through the credibility of the artist and allows the artist to stay at the forefront of instrument technology through a close association with the research-and-development arm of the manufacturer.

If you are interested in product endorsements, I suggest that you look around at the various companies and see how they promote. If a company uses a lot of advertising geared to artists' endorsements, then it's a safe bet that it will be interested in talking with you. If its ads don't follow this approach, however, you could be wasting your time.

And the good news is that you don't have to be a superstar to make some of these deals. Granted, a company isn't going to give you thousands of dollars worth of gear based on a demo tape and a few club gigs, but you may be able to start with a drumstick or string deal, which has the dual benefit of saving you some money and getting your name around. Here's what I mean: Endorsement ads for drumsticks generally use several drummers. Now, you may not be the subject of a full-page ad, but if you are a drummer and your picture appears on the same page as Neil Peart of Rush or Alex Van Halen, then your image is improved by the association.

All manufacturers of guitars, cymbals, amplifiers, keyboards, electronics, drums, and road cases are potential endorsement contacts, especially if you or your band is on the way up, because they like to be associated with discovering tomorrow's stars. Write some letters and make a few phone calls to the Marketing or Artist Relations Directors, or even to the owner if it's a small company. This is not a call for a manager to make, by the way, since these people want to talk music and instruments, and you are the most qualified person to do so. You may not only get a chance to play on instruments that you otherwise could not to afford, but you'll have someone else paying to advertise your music and your career.

A smaller version of this same deal may sometimes be struck with a local music store. Perhaps you won't get the gear for free, but you may get a discount in exchange for some free performances in the store or a few clinics or seminars if you are a particularly hot player.

These kinds of opportunities help you grow and keep the cost of your act within reason. But the only way to find out about them is to investigate and pursue them. They can be a great help in establishing a powerful and positive image.

OTHER PROMOTIONS

Aside from sponsorship, endorsements, and the use of your music, other promotional opportunities in conjunction with companies can result in payments to you. What you need to remember is that every time you do a concert, have a hit, or get a video on MTV, you're adding to the equity in your name. That is, as more and more people get to know you and develop a positive feeling about you, the more value there is to your name in the marketplace.

A sponsorship capitalizes on this equity in something we in the business refer to as *borrowed equity*. This means that the sponsor borrows the equity you have built in your name and applies it to its product in the hopes that the consumers will transfer their positive feelings about you to the product. So, in all your dealings with sponsors, you have to remember that this equity has cost you and your manager, agent, and record label a lot of time and money. Imagine what kind of financial investment the Who, Rod Stewart, and Ray Charles have in their names after twenty-five years. And that's why every time someone wants to use the equity in your name, face, and music, he or she should pay you for the privilege. With that in mind, here are a few ways you can rent your equity, in a tasteful and select fashion, to companies who are willing to pay you for the privilege.

SALES PROMOTIONS

Sales promotions are contests, sweepstakes, or other gimmicks that help a company increase its sales to consumers. Some sales promotions that you may have seen are as follows:

Flyaways

A flyaway promotion provides a chance for consumers to win a trip for two or four to some exotic location or event that is tied in the with the promotion of a band, tour, movie, sporting event, or product. It works like this: The company makes arrangements with an artist to use the artist's name, photograph, and perhaps even video and music in advertising to promote its sales. The winner of the contest receives a trip to an exotic location where the artist is performing or recording. The artist agrees to meet the contest winner backstage before or after the show, and his management ensures that the winner and his or her guests have front row seats to the concert. The company may also arrange limousine transportation, a hotel suite, and so forth. The company then creates displays in stores to promote the contest. It may also buy radio and TV ads or may tie in with a radio station that will promote the event. If the artist is touring, he or she may insist that all the advertising in each city carries information about the upcoming concert dates in each city. In this scenario, the artist may also be paid a fee for the use of his or her name, likeness, and video. Also the artist's publishing company should be paid via a synchronization license for the use of his or her music in making the TV commercial. The upshot is that the artist gets incremental promotion and the company gets the use of the artist for the promotion of its brand.

Premiums

On occasion, a company will make up a promotional item that features the name of its product to be distributed for free or at a nominal cost to the public. You've all seen these kinds of items at places like McDonald's, for example. Premiums are generally designed to get people to come to a store or restaurant, to get existing customers to buy more of the product, or to encourage people who have never used the product to try it. A popular premium is a cassette tape of music. On the tape you may find a few songs from one artist or an entire collection of songs by different artists about a specific theme like summer or Christmas. These deals provide the artist with a royalty for every song used multiplied by the number of cassettes that are manufactured. If the company wants only the music, it usually gets the music from the record company. If however, the company wishes to do a bigger promotion, it may make the premium a part of a larger promotion, in which case the company would go directly to the artist's management. Other premium items are T-shirts, posters, and the like, all featuring an artist's picture or name.

Sampling

Sometimes companies ask an artist to allow them to distribute sample sizes of their product free to people who come to concerts. This strategy is called *sampling*. Chewing gum, mints, cigarettes, shampoo, or anything that can be handed out in small sizes may be distributed. In this instance, the company may approach the manager and ask for permission. The manager would then demand a fee for this right, which the company would pay to the artist.

In some cases, venues have decided that this right belongs to them and have authorized a company to distribute the item. You have to make it clear to the venue managers that the distribution of the product creates a link between the artist and the product. These managers may claim that it is their building and they have the right to allow samples to be distributed, but you should explain to them that they are welcome to distribute the product on a night when no one is playing in the building, but, when you are there, the people are there only because of your appearance, not because of the building. Since you are the drawing card, you have the right to get some of the money from the sponsor. Many venues have this attitude, and you have to take a hard line. Even if only two people come to see you, they are not there because of the sponsor or the building or anything else. They are there to see *you;* you are the center of attraction and should enjoy every benefit that derives from that situation.

THE FUTURE OF SPONSORSHIP

The future of sponsorship is extremely interesting, especially in light of the current state of traditional advertising. More and more experts in the advertising business are stating publicly that the effectiveness of advertising on network TV and radio has hit an all-time low. And the same goes for local or "spot" ads on radio and television. It appears that with the fragmentation of the audience, that is, so many different people with so many different tastes and life-styles, combined with the increasing number of television networks, cable stations, pay-per-view outlets, and other entertainment alternatives, no single advertising vehicle is capable of hitting the number of people needed to justify the cost. And with the incredible number of commercial messages on radio, TV, billboards, magazines, subways, buses, and just about everywhere else, with which the average consumer is bombarded every day, the future of traditional advertising is very bleak.

The experts also say that promotions will be the next big thing in the advertising world. It seems that the media moguls believe that if advertising is coupled with a giveaway, contest, endorsement, or sponsorship, it will have the impact that traditional advertising lacks. And it makes sense, especially if you go back to my earlier discussion of borrowed equity. Consumers want to feel that they are getting their money's worth and more. They want to feel that if they are going to pay attention to a commercial and go out and spend their hard-earned money on a product, it needs to have that little something extra that will make it worthwhile. If the product or commercial gives them a chance to win tickets to a concert, a trip to some exotic location, or even just a tape or a compact disk of their favorite star, they will pay attention, and the product's advertising message may get through to them. This situation is especially true for the youth marketplace; advertisers not only cannot figure out what advertising mediums to use, they don't even know where to find these young consumers. But we in the music business know where they are—in the concert venues and record stores, exactly the same places that we are—and since we found them, we own them. So if advertisers want to get to them, they have to do it through us, that is, through music. That's the future of sponsorship, and it looks like a healthy one for the music industry.

FOUR

Life After Death

THE ZOMBIE SYNDROME

Our story is basically that we had it all and then we pissed it all away.

**—JOE PERRY,
AEROSMITH**

Edgar Allan Poe once wrote a short story called "The Premature Burial." (There was also, of course, a movie version that starred, of course, Vincent Price.) In the story, the main character was terrified that he would be buried alive as his father had been. He worked out an elaborate system of bells and air hoses for his coffin, so if he was buried alive, he could reach out and touch someone and have himself dug up.

Well, at a certain point in their careers, several bands have felt that they have been buried alive. But some of those bands had their own bells and air hoses and wouldn't stay buried. Let's keep this horror movie theme going for a while. The music industry can be a lot like a thirsty vampire. If you aren't careful, it can suck the blood out of you over the years. When it does, you become a kind of zombie, the living dead, walking the halls of the record label or agent's office with people either running away in terror or simply looking at you with a blank stare as if you aren't even there. (Scary, eh, kids?)

You can become a zombie for a number of reasons. If musical styles change drastically, if you've been around a long time, if your label gets new management or heads in a new direction, if radio formats shift from your style of music, if you become dated or difficult to deal with, or if the public simply passes you by. Whatever the case, it's a frightening prospect. Years of work, hit records, tours and, in many cases, stardom just stop, and then all of a sudden, you can't get a call returned or a table at the Hard Rock Cafe. If you saw the movie *This Is Spinal Tap*, then you know exactly what I'm talking about.

ONE-HIT WONDERS

Now I want to point out the difference between the zombie syndrome and a one-hit wonder. With the zombie syndrome a group that has had a credible, successful act simply falls out of favor. However, a lot of acts, and I mean a lot of acts, have had one hit record and then faded into oblivion. These are one-hit wonders, not zombies, but they're more like Frankenstein. You know, a mad producer pieces together something that sort of looks and sounds like a hit record and act, attaches wires to the bolts in its neck, and at midnight on a stormy night, flips a switch that sends thousands of DBs through the body while the thunder roars and the lightning crashes. The problem is that like Frankenstein, the creation lives only for a short while and then dies. *The Milli Vanilli Monster, Bride of the 1910 Fruitgum Company,* and *Taco Meets Abbott and Costello* are just a few of the classic music-horror films that could have come from one-hit wonders. Although some of the records are great, have been covered by other acts, and became hits again, the bands are nowhere to be found. Some of the classic one-hit wonders have included "Fire" (The Crazy World of Arthur Brown), "Israelites" (Desmond Dekker and the Aces), "Hold Your Head Up" (Argent), and my favorite, "Sally Go Round the Roses" (The Jaynettes), which is probably the weirdest girl-group record ever made. These were all Top Ten songs, and all these groups are gone forever after just one look (which, by the way, was another Top Ten one-hitter by Doris Troy in 1963.)

THE COMEBACK KIDS

It will never happen to you, right? I mean if you're successful, you'll stay that way forever. Well, not always. Take Aerosmith, for example. In the seventies, the Toxic Twins Steve Tyler and Joe Perry set a standard for excess, audacity, and flat-out, brain-burning rock and roll. *Toys in the Attic* was a landmark album, and "Walk This Way" became the Saturday-night anthem for a generation of teenage rockers. Then, things started to go wrong.

The debilitating effects of a decade of excess started to take their toll, both creatively and physically. Meanwhile music itself was changing direction. Acts like Elvis Costello and Nick Lowe were challenging the dinosaur rockers with a new stripped-down brand of rock.

Aerosmith's label, Columbia Records, knew that it had a problem. Tyler and Perry were out of control. They missed recording sessions, their concert performances were sometimes horrible, and they generally were becoming impossible to deal with. A prime revenue producer was slipping, and there didn't seem to be anything that anyone could do about it. It looked like Aerosmith was heading for the "what ever happened to" file. Perry left the band, and Columbia essentially wrote them off, figuring as labels do, that a good thing had come to an end.

But then, fate intervened. In this case it was a new record label headed by David Geffen. By this time, Tyler and Perry had cleaned up both their individual and professional acts. The band released its first single for Geffen and it skyrocketed up the charts. Aerosmith was back, and it was a new lean-and-mean band, shed of the excesses that had contributed to its fall from grace. Since that first Geffen release, the band has enjoyed a string of hit singles and albums, and in fall 1991, in what was rumored to be a $40 million deal, Aerosmith returned home to its original label Columbia Records with a five-album deal. This has to be, without a doubt, the rock-and-roll comeback story of the decade, and maybe of all time. But the Aerosmith story, even with its happy ending, is just one of a variety of bad situations in which a band can find itself.

Way back in 1964 in Birmingham, England, a band called the Moody Blues was formed. In 1965 they had their first international hit with a song called "Go Now." Then, they had no hit for three years. The label didn't know what to do, so it did nothing. Then in 1968, the band released an album entitled *Days of*

Future Passed, which became a huge hit and established the band as one of the most popular groups of the late sixties and seventies. But music began to change. Punk rock and new wave came on the scene, and the orchestral sound of the Moody Blues was old hat. The band released a few average albums to little public and industry reaction. Then, in what seemed to be a death blow to the band, two key members, Denny Laine (Wings) and Clint Warwick, left the band. The label and, in fact, the industry pretty much wrote the band off. But Laine and Warwick were replaced by Justin Heyward and John Lodge. Rejuvenated, the band began recording and touring once again. Now, in the nineties, the Moody Blues are one of the more successful bands still remaining from the sixties. They are enjoying good sales and radio airplay and are still drawing crowds on the summer-amphitheater circuit.

In the mid-seventies, Genesis was the number-one art-rock band of the day. Then (gasp!) Peter Gabriel announced his departure from the band. And of all people to replace him on lead vocals they band picked the drummer, some guy named Phil Collins, who, to tell the truth, didn't look a whole lot like a rock star. Well, folks, we all know what happened. Just how big are Phil Collins and Genesis? Well, pretty darn big, and they are making, have made, and are sure to make some of the best rock and roll out there.

A concert promoter, who had booked one of the dates on the first tour after Gabriel's departure, was nervous about ticket sales and was relieved when the show sold out the eight thousand or so seats that had been put on sale. He was so pleased that the new lineup had sold out that he had some T-shirts made up for the band that said "Peter Who?" As he was on the way to the dressing room to distribute the shirts, he was stopped by the record-label rep, who took one look at the shirts, turned white, and yelled at him to get rid of them immediately. Apparently, the rep just left the band's manager, who had told him that the band members and Gabriel were still good friends and that they had grown tired of listening to people tell them how lucky they were to be rid of the "prima donna" Gabriel. Sometimes ideas look a lot better on paper than they do in real life. Meanwhile Peter

Gabriel has not done too badly on his own. We all like happy endings, when everybody wins, but that's not always the case. Read on.

THE KEY-MAN CLAUSE

The loss of a key band member can send a band into the dead zone faster than just about any other situation, although sometimes the situation can also work in reverse. In 1977, just as they were about to break big, Steve Gaines and Ronnie Van Zant, of Lynyrd Skynyrd, died, tragically, in a plane crash while on tour. Although it was considered to be one of the best of the southern rock genre of bands, the group was never able to recover from the loss.

In the mideighties, Lou Gramm, then possibly the best lead vocalist in rock, fell out with the other members of Foreigner over the direction the band was taking musically. With the group's enormous popularity and string of platinum records and Gramm's impressive talent, most in the industry thought that both could continue to have successful careers. But the whole turned out to be much greater than the sum of the parts or, at least, that's what the public said, and neither Foreigner nor Gramm have enjoyed anything close to the success they enjoyed as a unit.

And then, there's Van Halen. No one could argue that the most audacious front man of the eighties was David Lee Roth. It was only Eddie Van Halen's extraordinary guitar talent that kept the rest of the band from becoming nothing more than backup musicians for Roth. But apparently, a backup band is just what David was looking for, and in an incredibly bitter split, David and Van Halen went their separate ways. At first, the smart money was on Roth, but the addition of rocker Sammy Hagar to the Van Halen lineup turned things around. And remember what I said about things working in reverse; it has been Roth, not Van Halen, whose popularity has waned since the parting.

Even superstars Guns N' Roses have had to deal with their share of personnel shifts. First Slash decided that he wanted off the road, and then Izzy Stradlin left the band. But in the early 1990s, the band was so big that even these changes had little effect. They would probably not be so big, though, if leader-singer Axl Rose decided to leave because he is, undoubtedly, the focal point of the group.

But the list of bands who became defunct after the departure of a key member is a long one, stretching back to Rod Stewart's departure from the Faces, through Sting's exit from the Police, to John Wait's departure from the Babys, and to Glenn Frey's split from the Eagles. In most cases, when a key member goes, so goes the band, and it's a tough recovery, if you can recover at all.

THE PETER PAN PROBLEM

Another weird kind of zombieness is the label's failure to realize your position in the business. I call it the *Peter Pan Problem (P-cubed),* that is, your label refuses to believe that you've grown up. I guess the best analogy is the way your mom treats you, no matter how old you are. You know, when you're out with your folks and you run into some of their friends whom you've never met, and and your mother introduces you by saying, "Oh yes, this is my baby." Baby! Usually, you're so embarrassed that you wish you could disappear on the spot.

Well, some record labels have much the same problem. They sign a new act and begin the development process, both at the head office and in the field. Hit singles and gold albums follow over a couple of years and throughout the business—on radio, at retail stores, on video channels, and especially at other labels, the band is perceived as major stars. Everywhere, that is, except at their own label. At their label, they have to listen constantly to stories about the old days when they were just starting out. And worse, people at their label don't see them as the stars they are; they still see them as the baby band that they were. Now when your mom does it, it's cute. But when your label does it, it's deadly. Here's why.

Star acts get special treatment. They get big budgets for promotion, advertising, and marketing. They have a special relationship with the key executives at the label, especially the president. They get what they want. But if your label looks at you as the young band they signed years ago, you will never get the respect you need to get the marketing push you deserve. And while other acts on the label are making progress, you will be stuck in the same place, going nowhere.

PREMATURE BURIAL

Whether it is because of musical styles, changes in personnel, or new directions by the label bands can fade in popularity at their labels and in the business. There are definite signals that it is happening. There are also definite remedies to repair the damage.

THE CLUES (LABEL)

So what do you look for at the label when you suspect that premature burial is beginning to set in? Here's a list that definitely indicates that something is going wrong. If some or all these things begin to happen in your career, there's trouble ahead:

1. The label reduced the marketing budgets for your records.

2. The label provides cut-rate packaging, for example, no extra folds in cassette and CD packaging for album credits.

3. The label cuts off tour-support funds.

4. The label's staff stop showing up at your live shows.

5. The label makes cutbacks in other areas like independent publicity budgets.

6. The label is reluctant to release follow-up singles or tracks if the first track from the album is not a success.

7. The label is reluctant to release any singles to CHR if you are a rock act.

8. Your manager can't get meetings with key people at the label.

9. Your photo disappears from the walls and offices at the label.

10. The label reduces or heavily monitors your recording budgets to avoid overages.

11. The label is reluctant to produce videos.

12. You are not invited to represent the label at industry functions.

13. The label refuses to manufacture catalogue items that are out of stock or deletes some titles from your catalogue.

14. The label sells off most of your catalogue to cutout dealers.

Now these are just some of the label-oriented clues, but as you can see, they paint a pretty grim picture. As far as the overall business is concerned, the signals that you get are just as grim.

THE CLUES (THE INDUSTRY)

1. Radio stations take your music out of recurrent or gold rotation.

2. Classic-rock stations drop your catalogue from their playlist.

3. Cutout dealers sell off your catalogue to retailers who sell them for $1.99.

4. The press starts to refer to you in the past tense.

5. Promoters stop offering headline gigs and suggest opening slots for other acts instead.

6. Concert attendance falls off drastically.

7. MTV and other video channels drop your catalogue of videos.

8. Retailers delete your section in the store and put your records into the "Miscellaneous Rock" section.

9. Radio stations decline offers to interview you.

10. Your catalogue material disappears from all industry charts.

THE REMEDIES

Once you've identified the signals, what do you do? In the case of
the label, there are only two remedies: you renegotiate or leave. In
either case, if you don't have a high-powered music-industry
lawyer, you'll need one. Allen Grubman, Paul Shindler, and Don
Passman: It's a short list, but not so short that you won't be able to
find one to handle you. The best strategy is to find a lawyer who
has leverage with your record label, either because of his relationship with the key executives or the president or because he represents an act or acts that are important to your label.

The lawyer will then set up a meeting with the president of the
label, your manager, maybe you, and himself. He will present your
case to the president without emotion or anger (something you and
probably your manager couldn't do). During the lawyer's talk, you
need to remember the golden rule: "Keep your mouth closed and
your ears open." The president will listen and may take notes. He
may have some of his key people there to dispute some of your
lawyer's claims. Whatever happens, understand this: By taking this
route, you have set something in motion that can have only one of
two outcomes: you will have a successful record or you will leave
the label. The people your lawyer or manager criticizes in the
meeting will no longer be your friends at the label (not that they
were anyway). What they do for you from then on will be because
they have to, not because they want to. Attitudes at the label will
vary from disinterest in you to outright hostility. Some of the people
at the label will openly challenge you to see if you are prepared to
push the issues. You must be prepared to back up what you say.
And you and your manager must keep your emotions in check. You
are now doing hard business that will have a serious outcome.

If your record hits, all will probably be forgotten, and you can
just get on with your career. If your record fails, the label people
will probably begin to push for you to be dropped from the label if
the contract allows. Make no mistake, this situation is a showdown,
and the consequences are serious.

On another front, rather than criticize the company, your lawyer
may attempt to renegotiate of your deal with the label. You may get

some relief by bargaining either for a longer term (during which the label may think it is in a better position to support you because you will be with the label for a longer period) or by asking for a definite commitment in the areas of concern.

The second solution is to get out of your deal altogether. This is a drastic solution, but it is sometimes the only way for you to get on with you career. In this case, you will really need that high-priced legal talent not only to get you out of your deal, but to be sure that he gets you into a new deal.

FAMILIARITY BREEDS CONTEMPT OR WORSE, APATHY

Now, what I'm about to say may sound stupid, but, believe me, it's the truth. Sometimes a label can just get tired of you. That's right, tired. Maybe you are the signing of a previous regime at the label. Maybe the new promotion department is oriented toward a different kind of music. Maybe you've had a couple of soft albums in a row and the label has moved on to a few new darlings it just signed. Or maybe you've just been around too long.

The only remedy for the label and the band is for the act to go elsewhere. A change in label usually rejuvenates the band; if they have gotten stale at another label, they suddenly get a new lease on life and start making interesting music again. And generally, if you fix your label problems, your industry problems will go away as well.

There is a long list of bands who have changed labels and had reborn careers. After Heart had several big hits with CBS, they lost the edge and spent several years and albums treading water. When they were signed to Capitol and hired a new manager, everything changed. Their first record for the label sold an incredible 5 million copies, and a whole lot of people had a whole lot of explaining to do.

Likewise it took a change in label to breathe life back into the career of Chicago, who had pretty much had it at Columbia Records. The shift to Warner Brothers and the pairing with producer David Foster, plus some well-chosen soundtrack work for the film *The Karate Kid* put the band back on the both the singles and album charts.

Sometimes all it takes is a change of scenery and some new people who believe in you to get your confidence, focus, and hit records back. The business can put you down before your time, but the tough ones fight back and usually come back stronger than ever.

FIVE

The Ten Commandments

The Ten Commandments

Here are the ten steps to success or, as I prefer to call them, the Ten Commandments of Rock and Roll. If you obey these commandments, you have a good chance of making it in to music heaven. If not, you can be in a hell of a mess.

Throughout this book, I've been hammering at the notion that success is 1 percent inspiration and 99 percent perspiration. You have to want success bad enough to be motivated to work for it. If music is just a hobby for you, keep it a hobby. Don't wreck it by making a halfhearted effort and becoming embittered by your lack of success. That will only waste your time and may even spoil your love of music.

There is no time for whining, bitching, moaning, or crying because things aren't going your way. That is a waste of time. Visualize your success; see yourself where you want to be and then work the plan that will get you there. And, of course, follow the Ten Commandments.

First Commandment: Thou Shalt Have an Image

Figure out exactly who you are and who you want to be, what you sound like, and what makes you stand out from the crowd. Make your music and your personality as unique as your fingerprint, your signature, the same time, every time.

Second Commandment: Thou Shalt Be Informed

If you are making music your business, make it your business to learn how the industry works. Subscribe to the trade papers and tip sheets and read them. Talk to people in the industry. Understand the rules before you begin to play the game.

THIRD COMMANDMENT: THOU SHALT NOT BE A JERK

For every act who makes it, there are at least a hundred who don't. And many among that hundred die by their own hand. There is a big difference between a good rock-and-roll attitude and the chip on your shoulder that alienates everybody from the paperboy to the president of the record company. Cultivate all the allies that you can. You'll need every one of them.

FOURTH COMMANDMENT: THOU SHALT TRUST ONLY THOSE WHO EARN IT

This is a tough one. Many times you will be lured into the temptation of signing a contract or making a deal that just doesn't feel right, but the money, fame, or potential for exposure look great. *Think.* If you don't know the person, can't get a recommendation, or just have a lousy feeling in your gut—pass. If someone hasn't earned your trust, it's safer to put things on hold until they do.

FIFTH COMMANDMENT: THOU SHALT ALWAYS DO THE BEST THAT THOU CAN

This means no half measures. No "we'll fix it in the mix." No "It's good enough." Give your best—every time, no matter how long it takes or what it costs. This goes for your music, your business dealings, your image, everything. Always do your absolute best.

SIXTH COMMANDMENT: THOU SHALT SAY "I DON'T KNOW" WHEN THOU DON'T KNOW

Don't pretend to understand things. If you have a question about something, ask. If you need clarification on something, take it to a lawyer, an accountant, or a manager, but find out. It's a lot easier to handle things before they happen than to repair the damage afterwards.

SEVENTH COMMANDMENT: THOU SHALT NOT DISS THY BRETHREN

Don't be a bitch. In the competitive world of music, it's easy to take potshots at your competitors and others in the business. Sometimes it's just a joke. Other times, you may be trying to make points with someone. Don't do it. You never know who you are talking to. If you make an offhand comment about some studio engineer who you think is a jerk, you may be talking to his brother, the president of your new record label. If you crack off loudly in a restaurant about someone, there's a good chance that it will get back to him or her, and after a couple of tellings, your original remark will become magnified quite a bit. Take care of yourself, and the rest of the world will do the same.

EIGHTH COMMANDMENT: THOU SHALT REMAIN TRUE TO THYSELF

Don't compromise. Your original ideas are who you are. They are unique, and in the long run, they will help you to make your own individual mark on the music business. Don't sell out your ideas for short term success. Set a course and stay on it, even if the weather gets rough.

NINTH COMMANDMENT: THOU SHALT REALIZE THAT NOTHING LASTS FOREVER

Enjoy every success and use it as a building block for your next effort. Be consistent with people, your music, your image, and your plans. Be relentless and be prepared to work hard to keep what you have earned. Change is inevitable, and only through constant effort can you make change work as a positive force for you.

TENTH COMMANDMENT: THOU SHALT NOT LOOK BACK

What was, was. What is, will make the difference to what will be. Your attitude can be contagious. If you believe in yourself and your music, really believe, that belief will sustain you in times of doubt and will affect everyone with whom you come in contact, from managers, to agents, to record executives, to fans. Look ahead, there's where you'll find your future.

Well, that's it. There's a lot of information here, and you'll probably want to read through some sections a few times before taking on the business. Don't forget to take a look at the sample contracts and familiarize yourself with the terms in the glossary. And remember, success is mostly hard work and common sense. I've given you some of the language, introduced you to some of the mechanisms and players, and, I hope, provided a few insights that will allow you to go ahead with a higher level of confidence and understanding. So now it's up to you. Be tough when you have to. Be truthful to yourself and to the people you work with, and, above all, trust the music because whatever else happens, your music will always be there.

GLOSSARY OF INDUSTRY TERMS

Every book of this kind has a glossary. I suppose if I were writing about anything other than the music business, I would be comfortable including the one that follows. The problem is that I'm not comfortable. Jargon and industry buzzwords change so quickly that no sooner does one word catch on than another comes along to provide a new or more precise definition. Meanwhile the media, publicists, record labels, and bands themselves are constantly inventing new terms or subgenres of music. I've avoided including a lot of these terms, for, to tell the truth, I'm hard pressed to believe that they will be around for long. Add that to the fact that different words mean different things to different people, and I had a tough assignment. What I've offered here is a collection of terms that have been around for a while, combined with the up-to-date buzzwords as of this edition. The definitions are specific to the recording and music industry. If the word exists outside as well as inside the music business, I have given only its music-related definition; after all, everyone knows what a board is, I think. I'll certainly have to update this section in new editions of this book, but the following list will provide you with enough information to decipher any music-industry conversation.

Adds: Addition of a new single to a radio station's playlist.

Ad mat: A prepared piece of artwork used in print advertising.

Administration agreement: A publishing contract in which one party performs the function of royalty collection and copyright control for the other.

Adult contemporary (AC): A radio format that appeals primarily to the twenty-five to forty-nine-year-old group and plays music by artists like Natalie Cole, Michael Bolton, and Harry Connick, Jr.

Advances: A sum of money paid to an artist representing royalties for a recorded product that has not yet been sold.

Afternoon drive: A radio station daypart. Usually 3 P.M. to 6 P.M.

Airplay: On-air exposure given to a recording by a radio station.

All night: A radio station daypart. Usually midnight to 6 A.M.

Album-oriented rock (AOR): A radio format that appeals primarily to the twelve to twenty-five-year-old group and plays music by such artists as Jon Bon Jovi, Guns N' Roses, and Metallica.

Alternative: Artists whose music is considered to be outside the mainstream. Once difficult to get on the air, alternative music now has its own radio format and charts in *Billboard* and other trade publications.

Arranger: An individual who creates the different musical parts for each instrument in a band, ensemble, or orchestra.

Arrangement: The combination of different parts created to give a composition greater depth and emotion.

Artist development: The department in a recording company that is responsible for career development, live performances, publicity, and the image of its artists.

Artist relations: A part of artist development. It is the department in a recording company that deals with artists and their managers in all areas of live performance and touring.

Artist and repertoire (A & R): The department or individual in a recording company that is responsible for auditioning and signing new talent. It also works with the artist and manager on the budgets, choice of producer, and material for new recordings and schedules the dates of new releases for the company.

Avant-garde: Music that is on the leading edge of the art form. It is often well out of the mainstream and has difficulty obtaining airplay on radio. Some college and alternative radio stations have special programs devoted to avant-garde music.

Beautiful music: A radio format that programs orchestral versions of pop songs and recordings of "crooners" from the forties and fifties like Tony Bennett, Frank Sinatra, and Perry Como. It appeals to a fifty-plus demographic.

Bed tracks: The basic recording of each instrument on its own track or tracks before the overdubbing of other instruments and vocals.

Biography: The personal and career history of a group or solo artist that is distributed to the media for the purpose of obtaining press coverage. It is sometimes abbreviated as *Bio.*

Blanket license: A license granted by an artist, recording company, or publisher for the use of a copyright for a number of months, years, or projects, rather than for just one specific use.

Board: The console found in a recording studio, mobile recording truck, concert venue, or television studio that is used by the recording engineer to "mix" all the different parts or tracks of a recording. The board contains all the electronics that control tape machines, frequencies, special effects, and the volume of each track in the final mix.

Boilerplate: Standard legal language found in every contract.

Booking agent: An individual or company that obtains employment for a group or solo artist in return for a percentage of the fee paid to the performer.

Bootleg: A counterfeit record or tape recorded or manufactured and sold without the knowledge of an artist or the record label and for which no royalties are paid to the artist, publisher, or record label.

Bootlegging: The act of illegally recording, manufacturing, and distributing material without the payment of royalties.

Borrowed equity: The use by a sponsor of the good name and reputation of an artist, athlete, or event in association with the company or product for the purpose of favorably positioning it with the public. Tour sponsorship and the endorsement of products by celebrities are based on *borrowed equity.* Examples include Michael Jackson and Pepsi Cola, the Virginia Slims Tennis Tournament, and the Rolling Stones and Budweiser for their 1989 Steel Wheels tour.

Breaker: Achieved when a new single is added to 60 percent or more of the radio stations that report to the trade publication *Radio and Records.* A *breaker* is a signal that a single is almost certain to become a hit.

Business affairs: The department of a record company that deals primarily with legal and contract matters.

Buy/Sell: A distribution arrangement between an artist or independent label by which a major label or distributor buys a finished product and sells it to record retailers at a marked-up price.

Catalogue: The collection of recordings made by an artist for a particular label or labels or all the product distributed by a specific label.

Chart: (n) A numbered list of songs based on airplay and/or sales that is published by a trade magazine, tip sheet, radio station, or retailer. The best known are *Billboard magazine*'s Top 200 Album Chart and Hot 100 Singles Cha.+. (v) To add a record to a chart when it has obtained sufficient sales or airplay.

Collaboration: The act of two or more songwriters working together on a single composition.

Commercial: Music that a recording company believes will or does have mass appeal; a radio or television ad. ·

Compulsory license: A mechanical license for the use of a copyright on a recording that becomes automatic for any third-party user thirty days after the original controller of the composition licenses it for use on a recording.

Concession manager: A person working for a concert venue who is responsible for the sale of souvenirs, merchandise, and food.

Contemporary hit radio (CHR): The modern equivalent of Top Forty. A radio format that relies on high-rotation play of mass-appeal hit records. Michael Jackson, Gloria Estefan, and Hammer are representative of CHR core artists.

Copyright: A notice or registration that establishes ownership of a particular composition or creative work.

Counterfeit: See Bootleg.

Cross-collateralization: The recovery by a recording company from an artist of advance money for one license from money generated by another license, e.g., recoupment of recording advances from publishing revenues.

Cult following: A small, specialized group of fans for a particular act or type of music.

Current: A recording that has been recently released.

Daypart: One of the units or time devised by radio stations in their programming day.

Dayparted: A recording that has been assigned to airplay during just one time of the programming day on radio.

Dead room: A room whose acoustics make it virtually echo free.

Default: The failure by one party to live up to the terms of a contractual agreement with another.

Delete: (v) To remove a recording that is removed from a company's catalogue and to sell off all existing stock at substantially reduced prices to record dealers. (n) A record that has been removed from a label's active catalogue.

Demo: Short for demonstration tape. A recording made by an artist or band for submission to record labels or publishers to obtain a publishing or recording contract.

Demographics: The age of a radio station's audience. Demographics are usually broken up into five groups, each of which correponds to a specific radio format: 12–17 (CHR), 18–24 (AOR), 25–34 (AC, country), 35–49 (MOR, classical, jazz), 50-plus (classical, beautiful music).

Direct signing: The signing of an artist directly to a record label, rather than through an independent label, production company, or other third party.

Double breaker: A record that attains breaker status on two charts or formats in *Radio and Records,* e.g., CHR and AOR breaker. *See also* Breaker

Engineer: A recording engineer. The person at a recording studio who operates the tape machines and recording console. He or she is responsible for translating the ideas of the artist or producer into technical activities and for commiting them to tape.

Exposure: Press profile, radio and video play, and consumer interest for an artist or band.

Favored nations: A contract point that requires all artists or bands participating in a specific recording or project to receive identical compensation.

Fit: The believable relationship between a product, a company, and a celebrity in a tour sponsorship or endorsement.

Fixed costs: Costs associated with a live performance that do not vary according to attendance. Rent, sound and lights, and cleanup are fixed costs.

Format: The type of music played, demographic appeal, and general programming philosophy of a radio station.

Free goods: Recordings offered to retailers as an incentive discount to stock the recordings of a particular group or artist.

Full-time add: Airplay given to a single by a radio station that is not a test or otherwise qualified.

Gig: A live performance.

Generation: The deterioration of the sound quality of an analog tape that takes place with each successive duplication. Digital recording and digital audio tape (DAT) now allow copies to be made without the loss of a generation.

Gold: Hit records from the past that have become standards for radio airplay.

Hanging points: Reinforced points in the ceiling of a concert venue that can bear heavy loads and from which the sound and lighing trusses and platforms and hung.

Hard tickets: (1) The actual printed piece of cardboard used for admission to an event. (2) A full price-ticket.

Hitbound: A test rotation afforded a record by a radio station. It is one step removed from a chart position.

Hook: The memorable melody, rhythm, or lyric of a hit song.

Image: The public likeness presented by a band or solo artist.

Indie: Records promotion experts contracted by a label to promote a record on a weekly basis for a fee; independent record labels.

International territories: All countries outside the United States.

Jam: An improvisational performance by a group of musicians.

Lead sheet: A written notation of a composition that includes notes of the melody line and chord progression with lyrics.

Licensing: An arrangement whereby the owner and controller of a copyright allows another to represent the copyright in return for a percentage of royalties earned through its exploitation. It refers to recordings, publishing, and clothing or other merchandise bearing the likeness of an artist or band.

Lighting director: The individual who designs and operates the lighting for an artist's performance.

Lip-synch: A public performance in which the artist mouths the words to a prerecorded tape, giving the audience the impression that he or she is actually singing.

Live room: A room or venue, the acoustic properties of which cause sound to echo.

Load-in call: The morning call for road crew and stagehands at a concert hall during which all the artist's equipment is brought into the venue for setup.

Load-out call: The stage call after the completion of a performance, during which all the equipment is packed up and taken out of the venue.

Market: (n) A country, city, or region, as in "the Boston Market." (v) To promote, advertise, and publicize an artist or the artist's product.

Marketing: The department of a record company that is responsible for the promotion, advertising, and publicity of recorded product.

Master lease: A deal in which an artist or production company allows a major label to license a master tape to manufacture and distribute product in exchange for an agreed-upon royalty rate.

Master recording: The contract term used to refer to the original studio tape copy of an album or single.

Master tape: See Master recording.

Mechanical license: A contractual permission granted by the owner or controller of a copyright to allow the recording and use of a composition on a tape or compact disc.

Merchandising: The sale of T-shirts, posters, buttons, and so forth that feature the photo, likeness, or logo of an artist to the public in exchange for a royalty paid to the artist.

Midday: A daypart of a radio station's programming day, usually 10 A.M. to 3 P.M.

Middle of the road (MOR): A radio format that appeals primarily to the thirty-five to forty-nine-year-old demographic group and that features the music of Frank Sinatra and Tony Bennett.

Mixing: The blending of the rhythm, instrumental, and vocal tracks at different levels to produce a balanced sound on the final recorded product.

Morning drive: A daypart of a radio station's programming day, usually 5:30 A.M. to 9:30 A.M.

Multitrack: Recordings that utilize more than one track of a magnetic tape.

National Association of Retail Merchandisers (NARM): An organization of music retail merchants who meet and communicate regularly to discuss the status of the recording and music-retail industries; acts as a lobby group for the music retail industry.

New music: See Alternative.

Night: A daypart of a radio station's programming day, usually 8 P.M. to midnight.

Option years: Any years for which a contract may remain in effect that are beyond the oringinal term of the agreement.

Overdub: A recording technique in which additional vocals or instruments are added to a recording after the original rhythm tracks have been recorded.

Paper add: A radio add that is reported to a trade paper or a record that the station is not playing. It is usually done to help a record label secure a breaker or to make the record appear to be more successful than it actually to entice more radio stations to add it.

Part-time add: *See* Dayparted.

Payola: Money, sex, or drugs given to a radio programmer to entice him or her to play a particular record.

Pirate: *See* Bootleg.

Points: A percentage of royalties paid to producers artists, and record labels from the sale of recorded product; (syn.) percentage.

Postterminaton compensation (PTC): A claim made by managers that they are entitled to compensation for deals made while an artist was under contract to them even after that contract expired.

Power of attorney: A limited right to sign documents on an artist's behalf given by the artist to a third party, usually an attorney, manager, or agent.

Pressing and distribution (P & D): A contract between a production company and a major label through which the major label manufactures and distributes recorded product from a master supplied by the producton company for an agreed-upon royalty or per-unit payment.

Producer: The individual who directs a recording session and who works with the artist, engineer, arranger, and label to create a finished album or single.

Product: The recordings of an artist or group.

Production: Sound-and-light equipment, as well as other gear used in the performance of a live concert.

Production contract: A contract signed by an artist and a record production company through which the company agrees to produce the artist's recordings and to place them with a major label or distributor for promotion and distribution.

Production office: The on-site office at a concert event from which the band's road manager or production director organizes and executes activities connected with the staging of the event.

Profile: The level of popularity of an artist or celebrity in the marketplace.

Profit margin: The difference between the manufactured cost and the sale price to the consumer less any costs incurred in distribution.

Progressive: A term used in the sixties and seventies to describe the FM radio format that played the psychedelic bands of the day like the Jefferson Airplane, Cream, and Jimi Hendrix.

Promotion: The marketing of an album or artist, generally at the radio and video levels.

Promotional copies: Copies of product distributed to radio stations or retail stores for airplay or in-store play to promote the release.

Public domain: If a copyright registration is not renewed, the composition is no longer protected, and the song may be recorded by anyone without payment of royalties to the composer.

Recording Industry Association of America (RIAA): The organization that acts as a lobby for the recording industry; the RIAA certifies all rewards for gold and platinum albums.

Recurrent: A record that is no longer active on the charts, but that has sufficient popularity to warrant continued airplay before going into gold rotation.

Release: Product that has been made available to the public.

Retail: A sales outlet for recorded product; the price paid by the consumer.

Return authorization: A form issued by a record company that, when completed, allows a retail store to return unsold product for credit.

Rhythm tracks: See Bed tracks.

Rigger: The person who is responsible for attaching the lighting and sound trusses to the hanging points in a venue.

Rigging: The system of trusses and cables used to hang the lighting, sound, and special-effects systems from the ceiling of a concert venue.

Road crew: The group of people who travel with an artist or group on a tour and are responsible for the setup and operation of all the equipment used in a performance.

Roster: The listing of artists or groups represented by a particular agency, manager, or label.

Routing: The arrangement of concert or club appearances in an order that allows for the most efficient travel schedule.

Royalties: The percentage of the sale price of recorded product that is paid to an artist under the terms of a recording agreement.

Sampling: (1) The distribution of a sponsor's product at a concert venue as part of a sponsorship arrangement with an artist. (2) The use of different recorded sounds, stored digitally in a synthesizer, either for recording or live performances.

Sequence: (v) To place the cuts appearing on a recording in an order that allows them to flow most smoothly from one to the other. (n) The order in which songs appear on a tape or compact disc.

Service: To mail or deliver recorded product to a radio station or the media.

Settlement: The accounting that takes place after a live concert performance to determine how much the act will be paid after all expenses and other costs are deducted from the gross revenues from the sale of tickets; a mutually agreed-on solution to a lawsuit or other legal action.

Show call: The crew call of technicians and stagehands needed during an artist's actual performance.

Showcase: A performance arranged by an artist, agent, manager, or label to expose an act for business purposes.

Side letter: An agreement on certain terms and conditions between an artist and a booking agent for things not contained in the Standard Booking Agreement.

Single: A recording of one song, usually taken from an album, sent to a radio station for airplay and sometimes made available for sale to the public in cassette or other format.

Songwriters' warranties: Representations made by a songwriter in a publishing contract that the compositions that the songwriter claims to have written are in fact original and not copies or derivative of other songwriters' works.

Sound fill: The amount and quality of sound that reaches all areas of a venue at a live concert performance.

Sound man: The person who is responsible for the technical aspects of the sound system at a concert, including setup, sound fill, and mix.

Spot: A special kind of light that casts a concentrated beam to illuminate an artist on stage; a radio or TV advertisement.

Stage call: The crew call that requires all persons connected with the production of the event to be present for rehearsal on the afternoon of the event.

Stagehands: Local union laborers hired for a concert performance.

Staging: *See* Production.

Statutory copyright notice: The symbol "c" in a circle that, when affixed to a song, manuscript, product label, or artwork, provides protection for the compositions and artwork under the copyright laws of the United States or the artist's home country, provided that the country is one of the participating countries in the variety of international copyright treaties currently in existence.

Stiff: An album, single, or tour that has been a commercial failure.

Subpublish: A situation in which a publisher who controls a copyright transfers some percentage of ownership of that copyright and hence a portion of the revenue to a second publisher.

Suspension clause: A clause in a recording agreement that allows the label arbitrarily to extend the term of the agreeement because of the artist's failure to perform some obligation of the contract, such as the failure to deliver an album by the date required by the contract.

Synchronization license: A license granted by a publisher to any third party wishing to use a particular song in a film, TV show, or commercial. It allows the user to synchronize the music with pictures of some kind.

Syndication: The sale of preproduced radio or TV programs to networks or independent stations.

Sweetening: The addition of strings, horns, or other instruments to a recording. It is generally the final step in the recording portion of the project before the mix.

Target group: A particular age or income group at which a marketing campaign is addressed. For example, the target group for a Guns N' Roses marketing campaign would be males aged eighteen to twenty-five.

Term: The duration of a contract, including all options and renewals.

Termination: The end of a contractual agreement, either by the action of one of the parties or because of the expiration of the term.

Test: A rotation given a record by a radio station to determine if it gets sufficient response to warrant an add.

Ticket count: The report from a ticket agency or promoter that indicates the tickets sold on a daily basis leading up to the date of an event.

Ticket manifest: The document issued by the box office that indicates the total number of seats in the venue less all kills providing the number of tickets available for sale. When multiplied by the ticket price, it yields the gross potential for the event.

Tip sheet: A weekly industry publication that reports on the airplay and sales success of albums and singles currently released in the marketplace. Usually a tip sheet will concentrate on a particular format such as *Album Network* (AOR) and *Hits* (CHR).

Top forty: The AM radio format created by Bill Drake in the fifties that rotated forty of the hottest records on the charts in a twenty-four-hour period. It was designed to increase the frequency of play of listeners' favorites, thereby increasing listenership. It evolved into today's CHR format.

Tour accountant: An individual who travels with an artist on tour and attends to all the accounting-related functions, including the settlement of all shows.

Tour support: Recoupable advances made to an artist to cover any deficits that may be incurred in touring in support of the release of an album or single.

Track: One of the spaces available on a recording tape onto which is encoded the electromagnetic information that reproduces the sound of a particular instrument, e.g. "the guitar track."

Trade magazine: A weekly publication that contains music industry news, sales and airplay information, charts, and advertising for current releases.

Tune-out: When a radio listener hears a record, commercial, or disc jockey that he or she doesn't like and changes to another station, the listener is said to have "tuned out" the station. Radio stations try to avoid tune-out through careful programming and the selection of music, commericals, and on-air talent.

Underground: *See* Progressive.

Unrecouped: The situation that exists when an artist has not earned back advances made to him or her by the label with sales of product.

Urban: A radio format that plays a combination of rhythm and blues, rap, and dance music. It is a format that is endemic to big cities and their ethnic mix and culture.

Variables: Costs, such as ticket commissions, associated with a live event that can vary according to the number of people in attendance.

Venue: The club, arena, concert hall, or stadium where a concert event takes place.

TRADE ASSOCIATIONS
AND UNIONS

American Federation of Musicians (AF of M), 1501 Broadway, Suite 600, New York, NY 10036. Tel: (212) 869-1330.

American Federation of Television and Radio Artists (AFTRA), 260 Madison Avenue, New York, NY 10016. Tel: (212) 532-0800.

American Guild of Musical Artists (AGMA), 1727 Broadway, New York, NY 10019-5284. Tel: (212) 265-3687.

ASCAP, One Lincoln Plaza, New York, NY 10023. Tel.: (212) 595-3050, FAX (212) 724-9064. In Los Angeles: 7920 Sunset Boulevard, Suite 300, Los Angeles, CA 90046. Tel.: (213) 883-1000, FAX (213) 883-1049. In Nashville: 66 Music Square West, Nashville, TN 37203. Tel.: (615) 742-5000, FAX (615) 742-5020

BMI, 320 West 57th Street, New York, NY 10019. Tel.: (800) USA-BMI1, FAX (212) 489-2368. In Los Angeles: 8730 Sunset Boulevard, 3rd Floor West, Hollywood, CA 90069. Tel.: (213) 659-9109, FAX (213) 657-6947. In Nashville: 10 Music Square East, Nashville, TN 37203. Tel.: (615) 291-6700, FAX (615) 256-7502.

Country Music Association (CMA), 17 Music Circle South, Nashville, TN 37203. Tel.: (615) 244-2840.

Gospel Music Association, 7 Music Circle North, Nashville, TN 37203. Tel.: (615) 242-0303.

Library of Congress, Copyright Office, Washington, DC 20559. Information: (202) 479-0700. Forms: (202) 707-9100. FAX (202) 707-8366

National Association of Broadcasters, 1771 N Street NW, Washington, DC 20036. Tel.: (202) 429-5300.

National Association of Music Merchandisers (NARM), 11 Eves Drive, Suite 140, Marlton, NJ 08053. Tel.: (609) 596-2221.

National Music Publishers Association, 205 East 42nd Street, 18th Floor, New York, NY 10017. Tel.: (212) 370-5330.

New Music Seminar, 632 Broadway, 9th floor, New York, NY 10012. Tel.: (212) 473-4343.

Recording Industry Association of America, Inc. (RIAA), 1020 19th Street NW, Suite 3200, Washington, DC 20036. Tel.: (202) 775-0101.

The Songwriters Guild of America, 276 Fifth Avenue, Suite 306, New York, NY 10001. Tel.: (212) 686-6820. In Los Angeles: 6430 Sunset Boulevard, Hollywood, CA 90028. Tel.: (213) 462-1108. In Nashville: 50 Music Square West, Nashville, TN 37203. Tel.: (615) 329-1782.

ADDITIONAL SOURCES

Sponsorship and Advertising

Advertising Age, 740 Rush Street, Chicago, IL 60611-2590. Tel.: (800) 992-9970.

ADWEEK, 49 East 21st Street, New York, NY 10010. Tel.: (212) 529-5500.

Entertainment Marketing Letter, EPM Communications, Inc., 488 East 18th Street, Brooklyn, NY 11226-6702. Tel.: (718) 469-9330.

International Events Group, 312 West Institute Place, Suite 303, Chicago, IL 60610. Tel.: (312) 944-1727.

Suggested Reading

Album Network, *The Yellow Pages of Rock*. 120 N. Victory Blvd., 3rd Floor, Burbank, CA 91502. Tel.: (818) 955-400, FAX (818) 955-8048.

Braheny, John. *The Craft and Business of Songwriting: A Practical Guide to Creating and Marketing Artistically and Commercially Successful Songs*. Cincinnati: Writer's Digest Books, 1988.

Davis, Sheila. *The Craft of Lyric Writing*. Cincinnati: Writer's Digest Books, 1985.

McIan, Peter, and Larry Wichman. *The Musician's Guide to Home Recording*. New York: Fireside Books, 1988.

Passman, Don. *All You Need to Know About the Music Business*. New York: Prentice Hall Press, 1991.

Rushing, Brian, ed. *1992 Songwriter's Market*. Cincinnati: Writer's Digest Books, 1991.

Shemel, Sidney, and M. William Krasilovsky. *This Business of Music*. 6th ed. New York: BPI Communications, 1990.

Trade Magazines and Tip Sheets:
United States

Album Network, 120 N. Victory Blvd., 3rd floor, Burbank, CA 91502. Tel.: (818) 955-4000, FAX: (818) 955-8048.

Amusement Business, 49 Music Square West, Nashville, TN 37203. Tel.: (615) 321-4250, FAX: (615) 327-1575.

Billboard Magazine, 1515 Broadway, 39th floor, New York, NY, 10036. Tel.: (212) 764-7300.

Friday Morning Quarterback, FMTV Executive Mews, 1930 E. Marlton Pike, F-36. Cherry Hill, NJ 08003. Tel.: (609) 424-7066. FAX: (609) 424-3881.

Gavin Report, 140 Second St., San Francisco, CA 94105. Tel.: (415) 495-1990.

Hitmakers, 22222 Sherman Way, Suite 205, Canoga Park, CA 91303. Tel.: (818)-887-3440, FAX: (818) 883-1097.

Hits, 14958 Ventura Blvd., Sherman Oaks, CA 91403. Tel.: (818) 501-7900, FAX:(818) 789-0259.

Hollywood Reporter, 6715 Sunset Blvd., Hollywood, CA 90028. Tel.: (213) 464-7411.

Radio and Records, 1930 Century Park West, 5th floor, Los Angeles, CA 90067. Tel.: (310) 553-4330.

Europe

Music and Media, Rijnsburgstraat 11, 1059AT, Amsterdam, the Netherlands, Tel.: 31-20-669-1961.

Music Week, Spotlight Publications, Ludgate House, 245 Blackfriars Road, London SE1 9UR. Tel.: 071-620-3636.

Canada

The Record, P.O. Box 201, Station M, Toronto, ONT M6S 4T3. Tel.: (416) 533-9417, FAX: (416) 533-0367.

RPM Weekly, 6 Brentcliffe Road, Toronto, ONT M4G 3Y2. Tel.: (416) 425-0257.

INDEX